SUPREME POWER

CONTACT

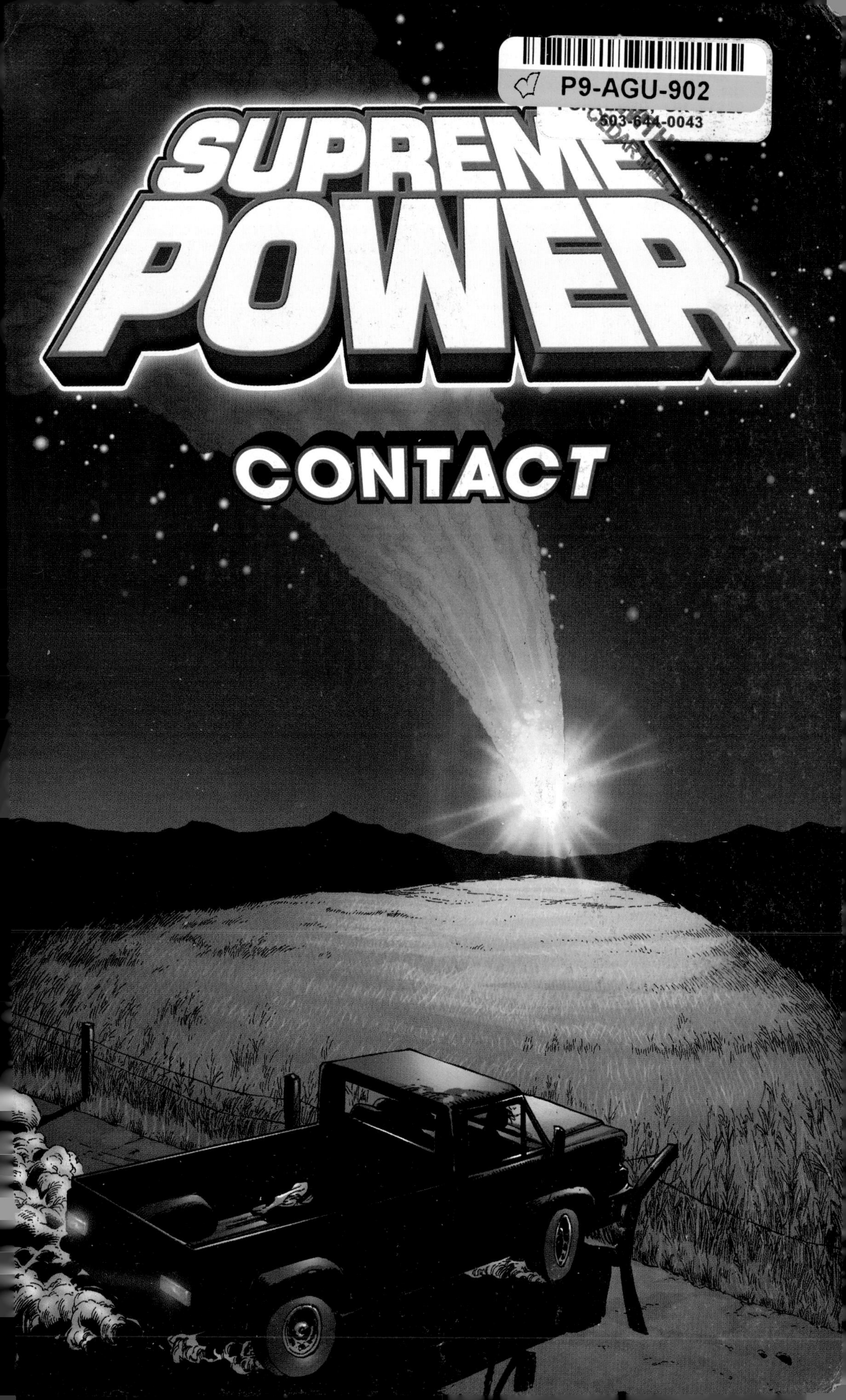

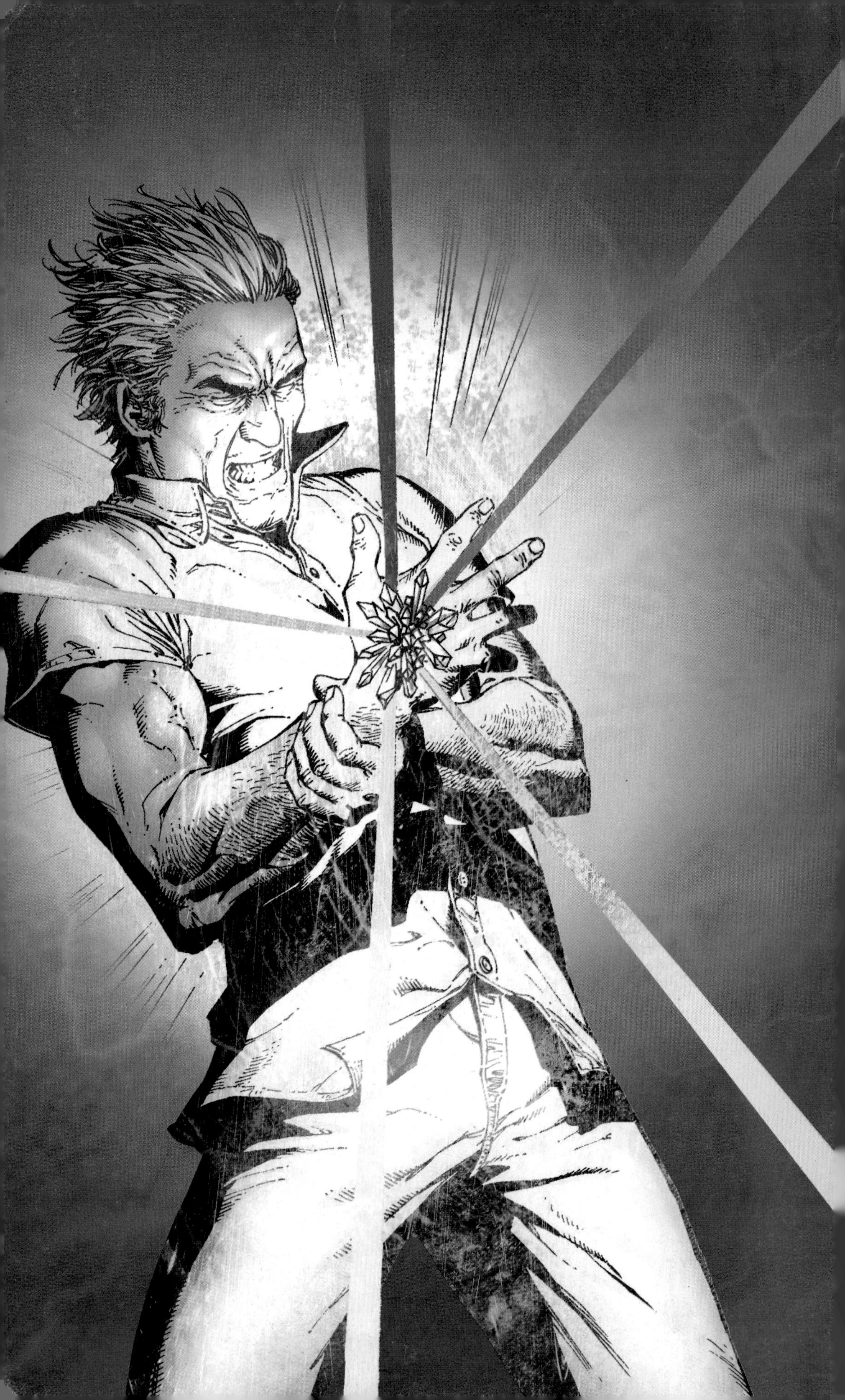

SUPREME POWER

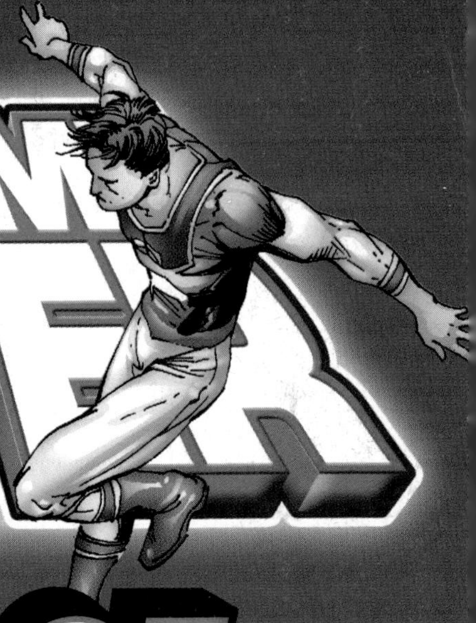

CONTACT

WRITER: J. Michael Straczynski
ARTIST: Gary Frank
INKER: Jon Sibal

COLORS: Chris Sotomayor
LETTERS: Virtual Calligraphy's Rus Wooten & Chris Eliopoulos
COVER ART: Gary Frank & Richard Isanove
EDITOR: Nick Lowe & Mike Raicht
STORY EDITOR: Joe Quesada
Special Thanks to Andrew Lis

COLLECTIONS EDITOR: Jeff Youngquist
ASSISTANT EDITOR: Jennifer Grünwald
BOOK DESIGNER: Patrick McGrath

EDITOR IN CHIEF: Joe Quesada
PUBLISHER: Dan Buckley

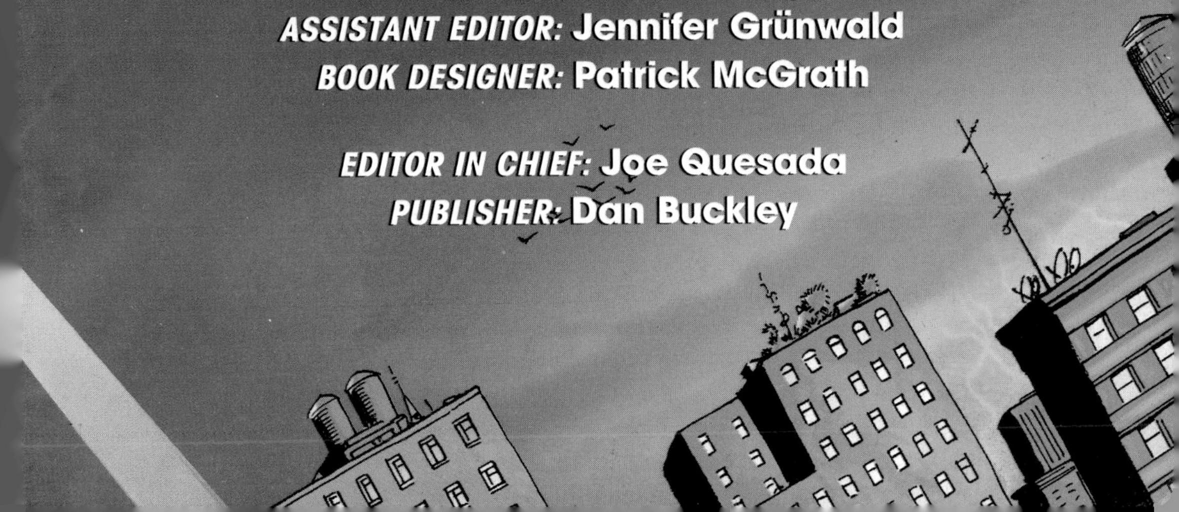

#1

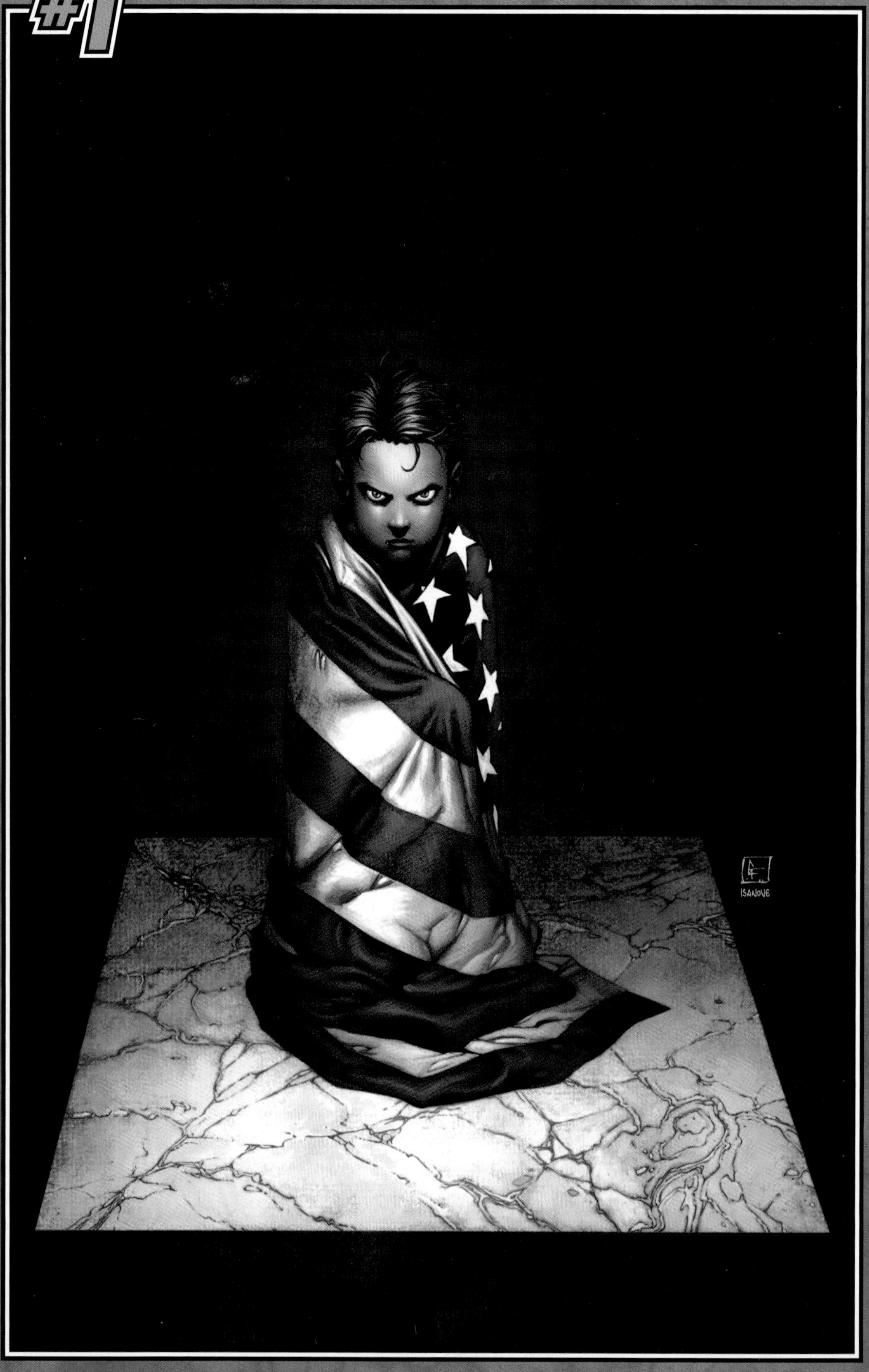
ISANOVE

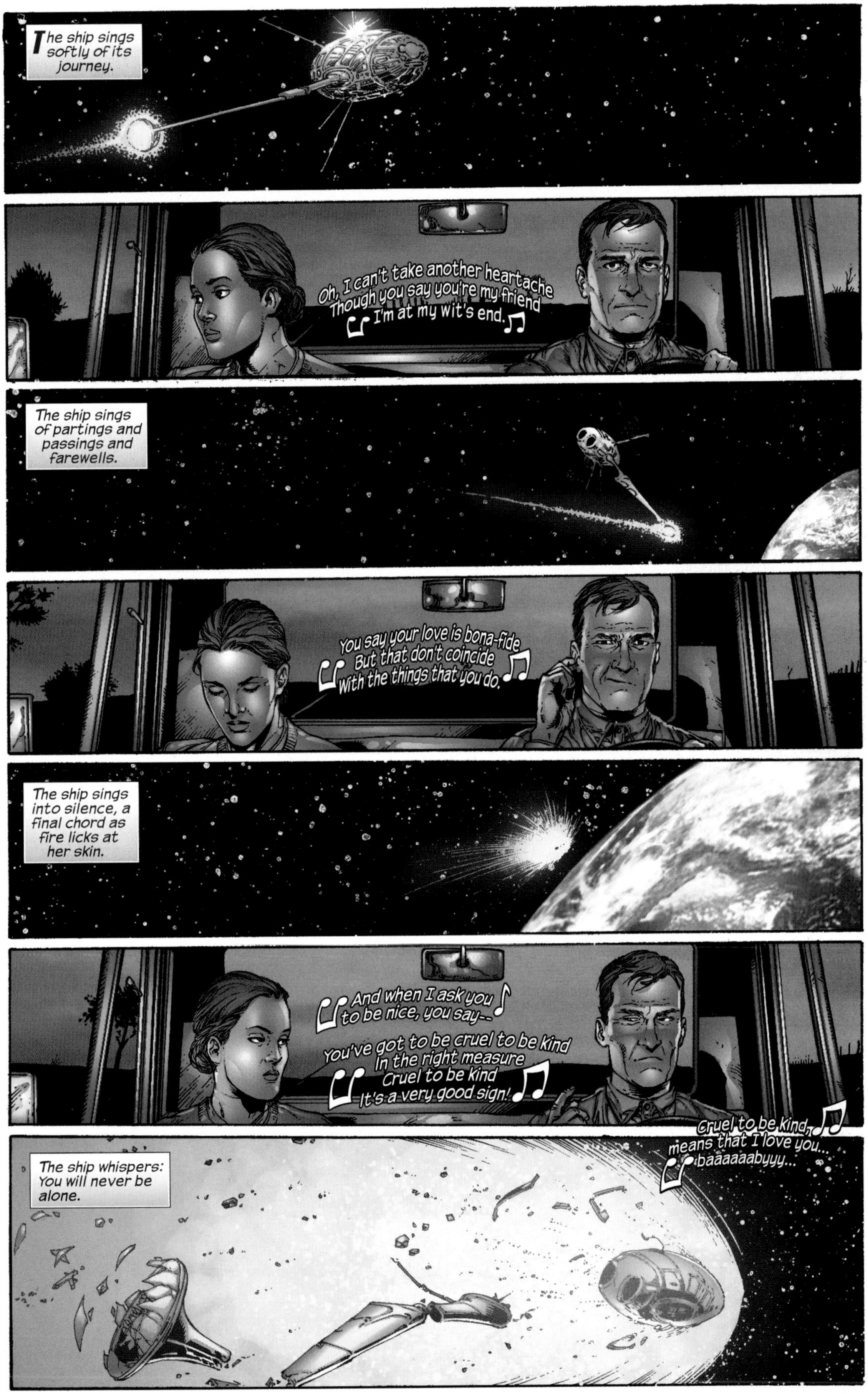
The ship sings softly of its journey.
Oh, I can't take another heartache
Though you say you're my friend
I'm at my wit's end.
The ship sings of partings and passings and farewells.
You say your love is bona-fide
But that don't coincide
With the things that you do.
The ship sings into silence, a final chord as fire licks at her skin.
And when I ask you to be nice, you say--
You've got to be cruel to be kind
In the right measure
Cruel to be kind
It's a very good sign!
Cruel to be kind, means that I love you... baaaaaabyyy...
The ship whispers: You will never be alone.

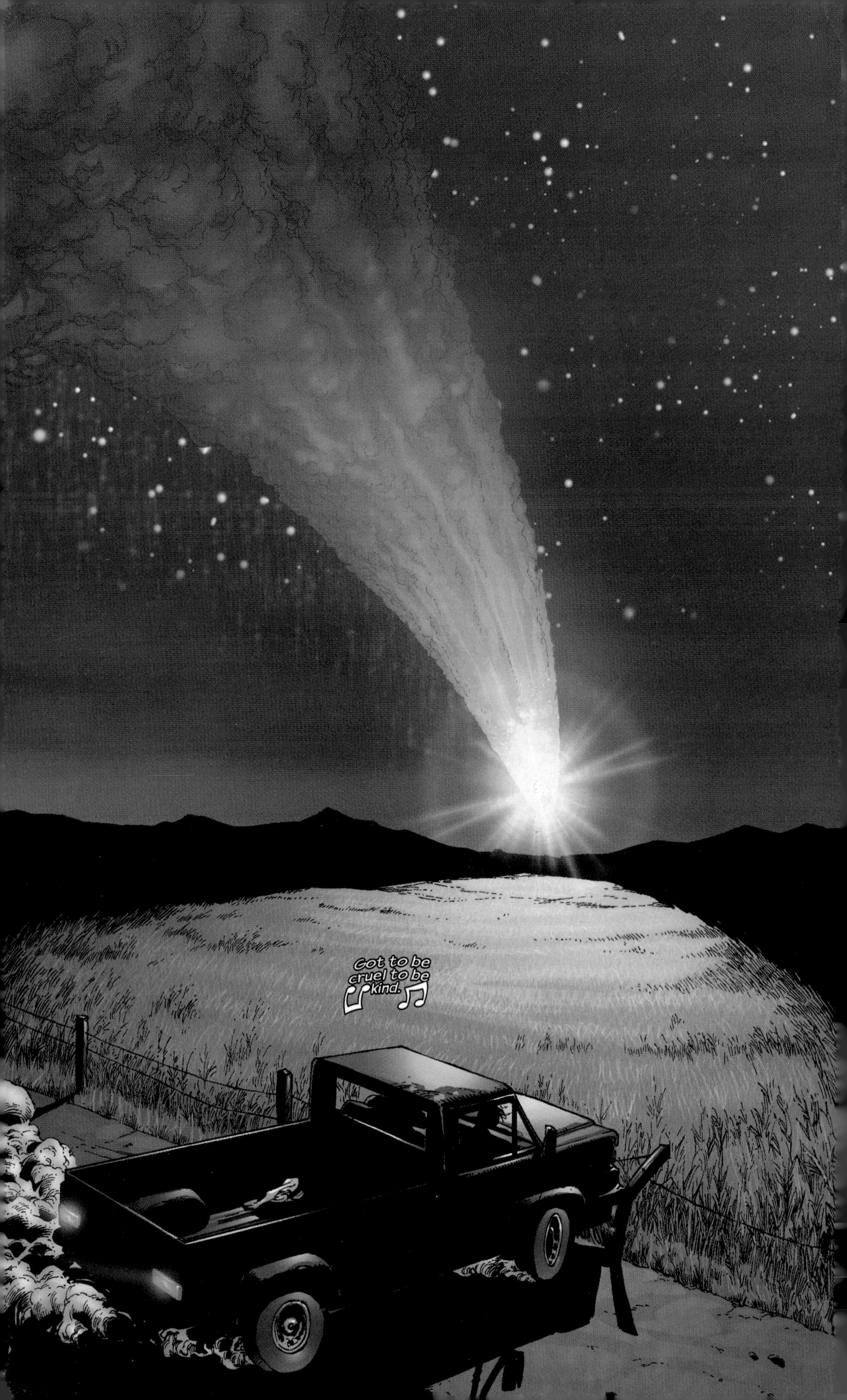
Got to be cruel to be kind.

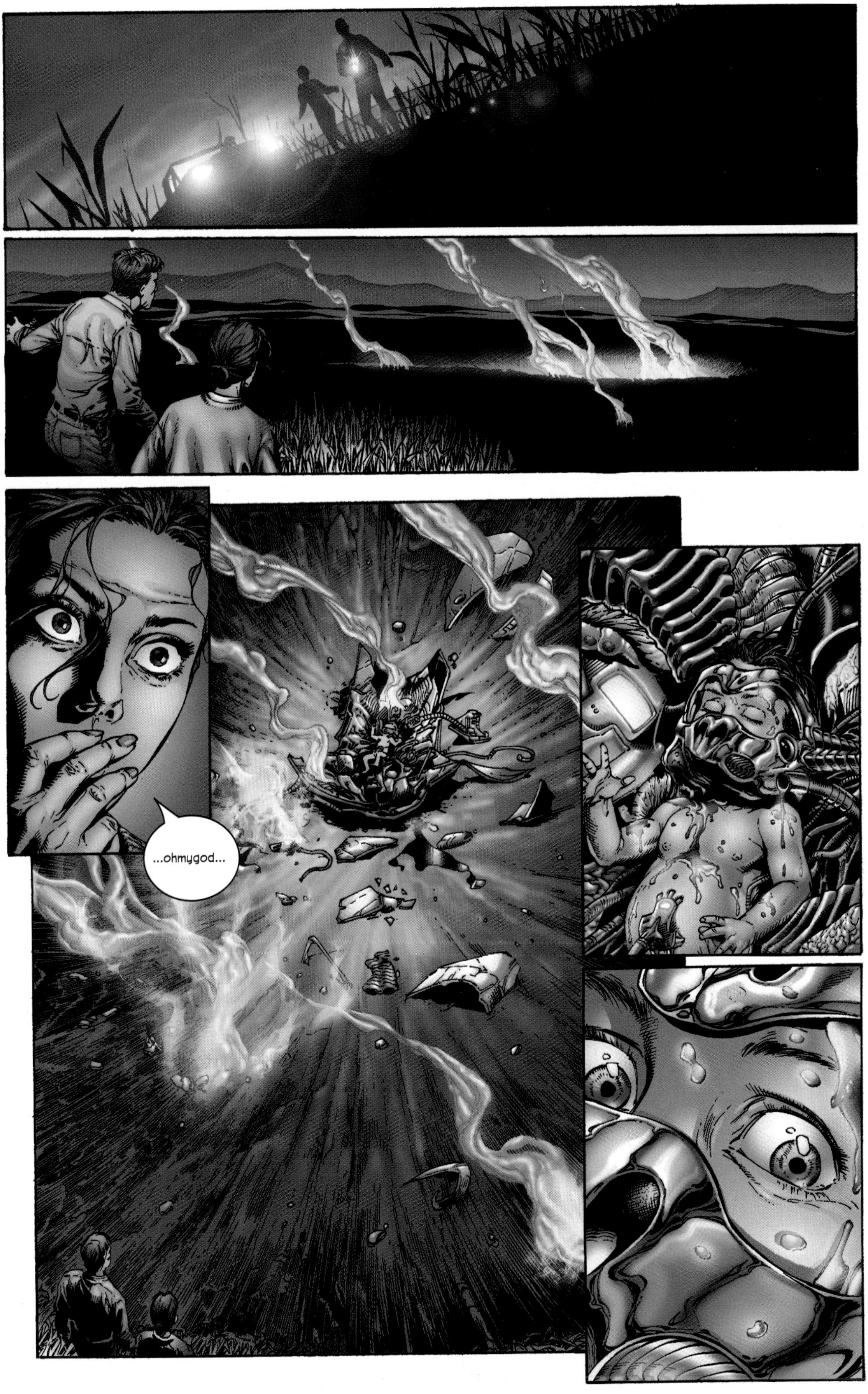
...ohmygod...

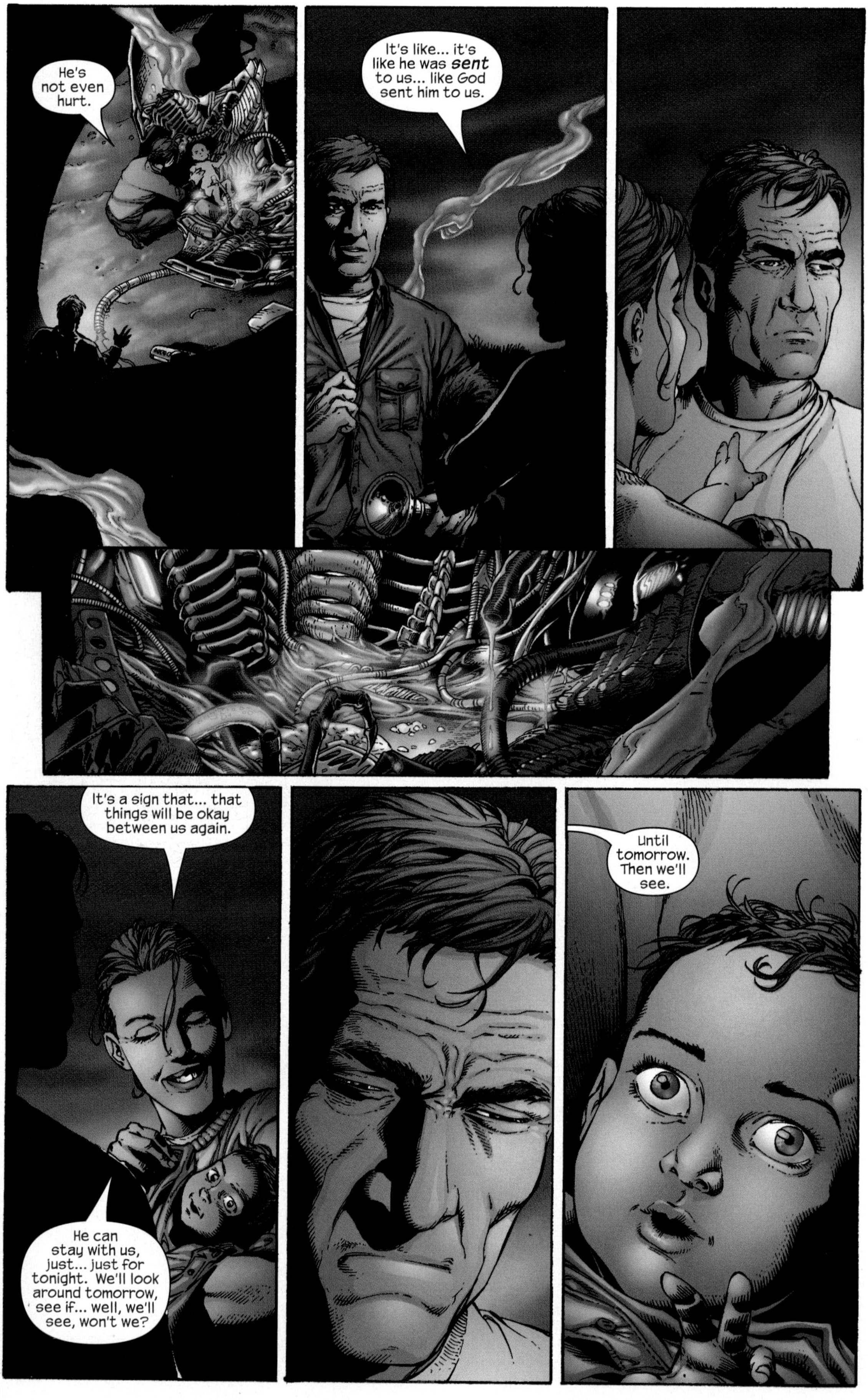
He's not even hurt.
It's like... it's like he was *sent* to us... like God sent him to us.
It's a sign that... that things will be okay between us again.
He can stay with us, just... just for tonight. We'll look around tomorrow, see if... well, we'll see, won't we?
Until tomorrow. Then we'll see.

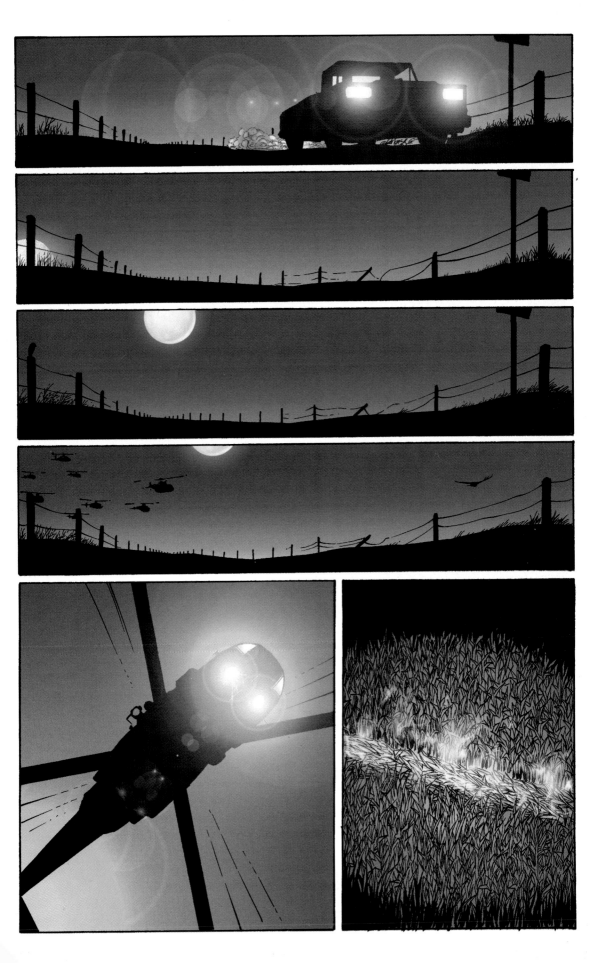

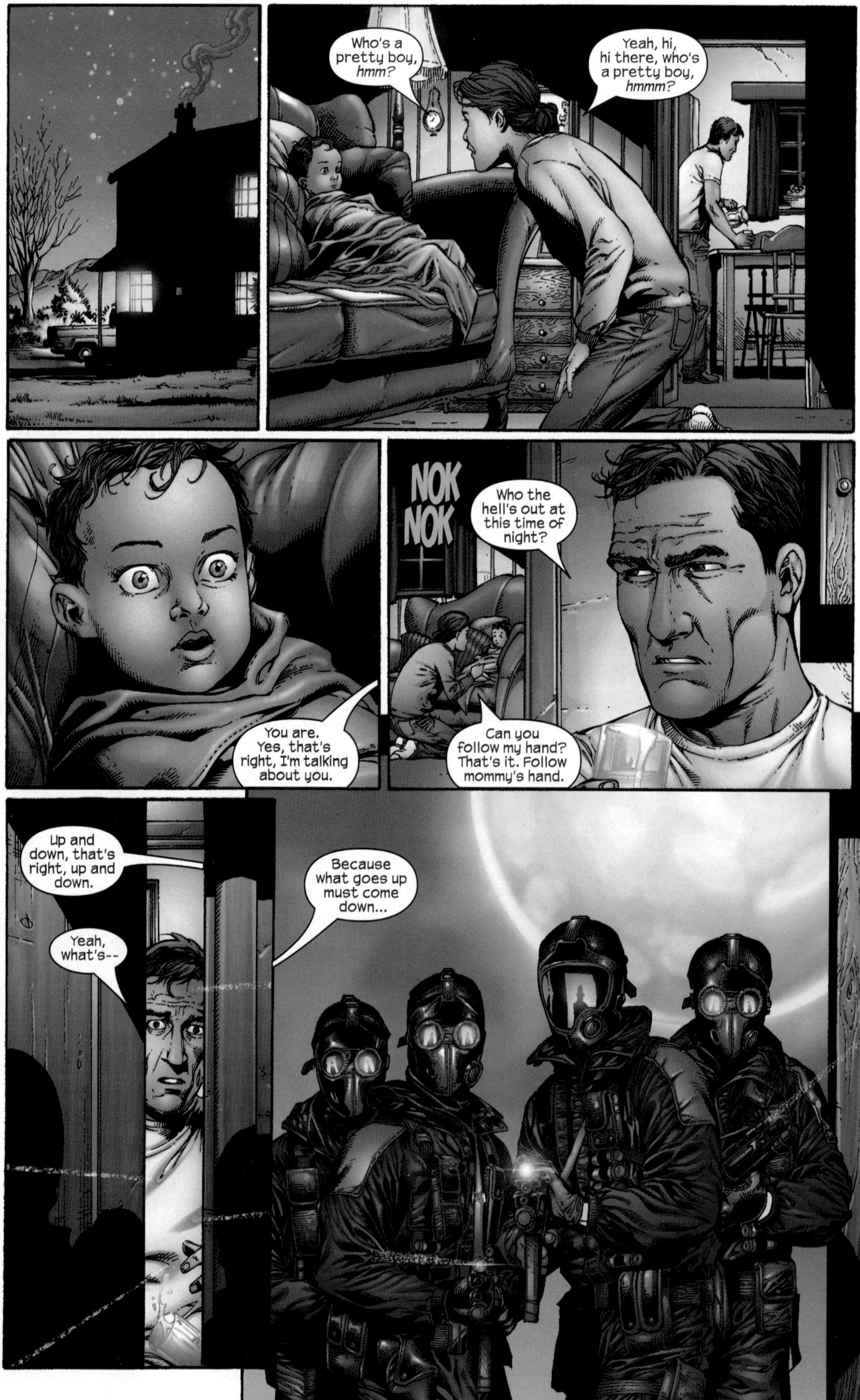
Who's a pretty boy, hmm?
Yeah, hi, hi there, who's a pretty boy, hmmm?
You are. Yes, that's right, I'm talking about you.
NOK NOK
Who the hell's out at this time of night?
Can you follow my hand? That's it. Follow mommy's hand.
Up and down, that's right, up and down.
Yeah, what's--
Because what goes up must come down...

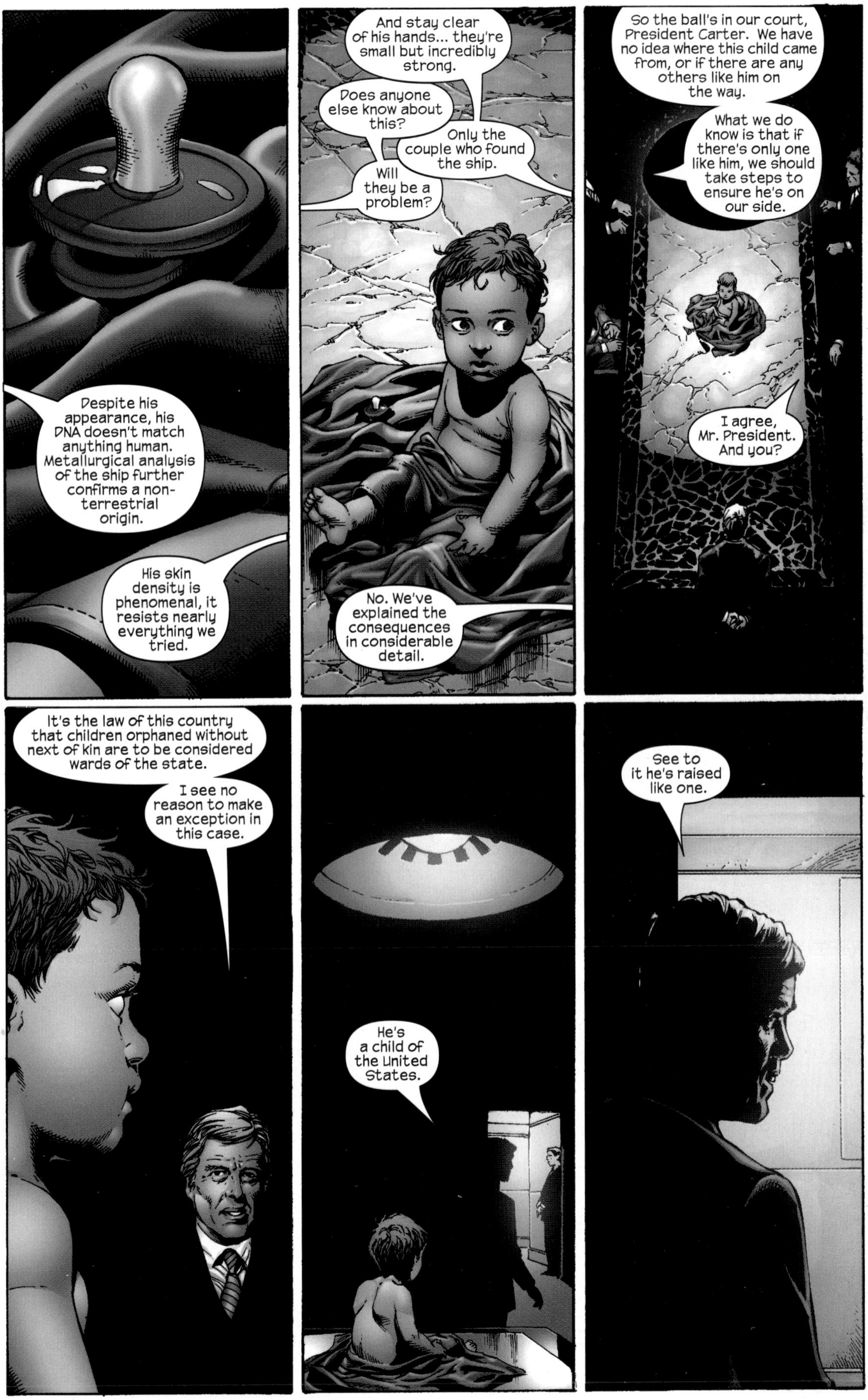
Despite his appearance, his DNA doesn't match anything human. Metallurgical analysis of the ship further confirms a non-terrestrial origin.
His skin density is phenomenal, it resists nearly everything we tried.
And stay clear of his hands... they're small but incredibly strong.
Does anyone else know about this?
Only the couple who found the ship.
Will they be a problem?
No. We've explained the consequences in considerable detail.
So the ball's in our court, President Carter. We have no idea where this child came from, or if there are any others like him on the way.
What we do know is that if there's only one like him, we should take steps to ensure he's on our side.
I agree, Mr. President. And you?
It's the law of this country that children orphaned without next of kin are to be considered wards of the state.
I see no reason to make an exception in this case.
He's a child of the United States.
See to it he's raised like one.

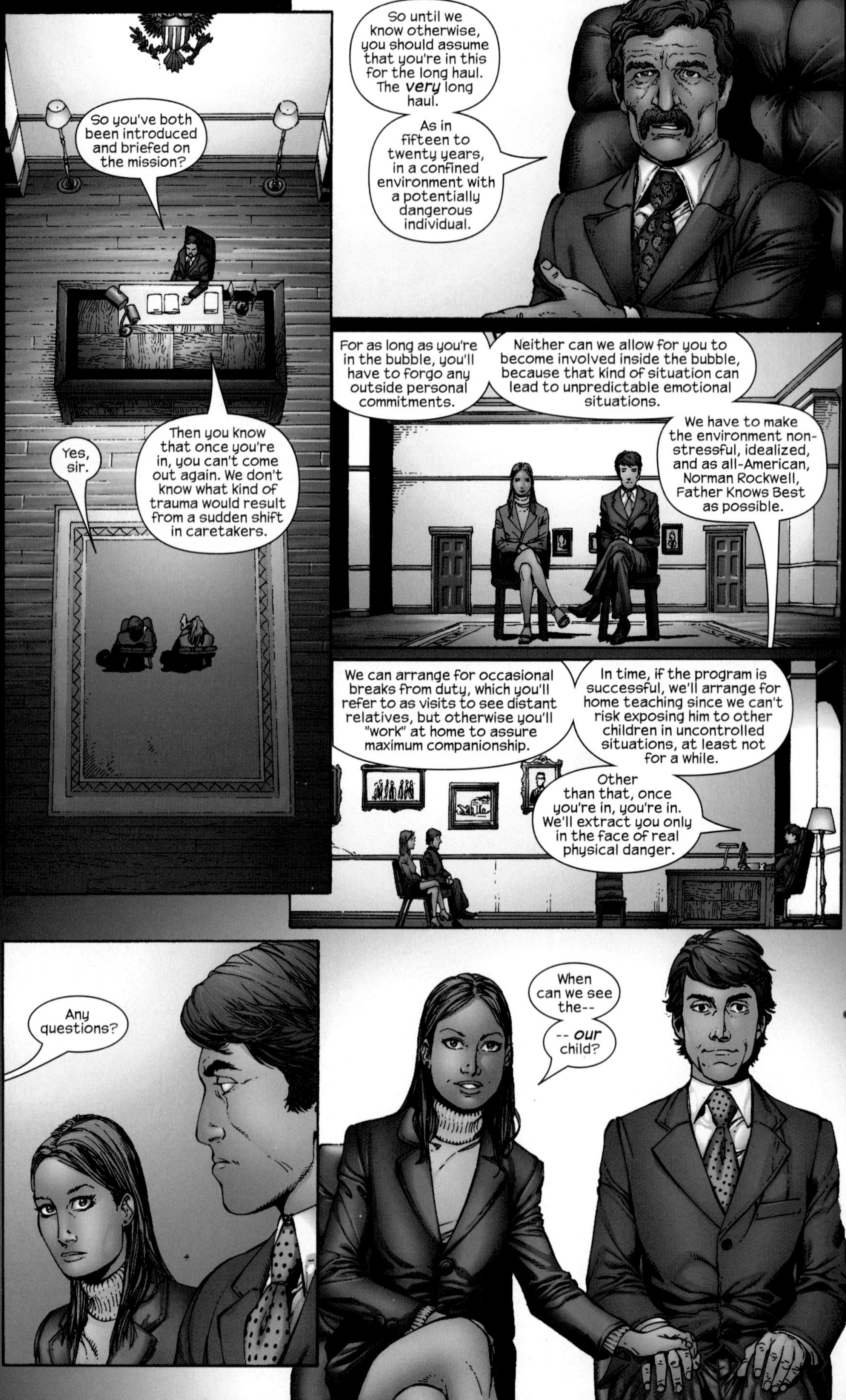
So you've both been introduced and briefed on the mission?
Yes, sir.
Then you know that once you're in, you can't come out again. We don't know what kind of trauma would result from a sudden shift in caretakers.
So until we know otherwise, you should assume that you're in this for the long haul. The *very* long haul.
As in fifteen to twenty years, in a confined environment with a potentially dangerous individual.
For as long as you're in the bubble, you'll have to forgo any outside personal commitments.
Neither can we allow for you to become involved inside the bubble, because that kind of situation can lead to unpredictable emotional situations.
We have to make the environment non-stressful, idealized, and as all-American, Norman Rockwell, Father Knows Best as possible.
We can arrange for occasional breaks from duty, which you'll refer to as visits to see distant relatives, but otherwise you'll "work" at home to assure maximum companionship.
In time, if the program is successful, we'll arrange for home teaching since we can't risk exposing him to other children in uncontrolled situations, at least not for a while.
Other than that, once you're in, you're in. We'll extract you only in the face of real physical danger.
Any questions?
When can we see the--
-- *our* child?

Does he have a name?

The code name, for the child and the project, is Hyperion. It was the name of one of the Greek Titans. R&D thought it was appropriate.

His day-to-day name is Mark. Mark Milton.

Normally I don't approve of alliteration but it tested well with all the appropriate focus groups. Mark for the Apostle, Milton not for the poet, but because they say it resonates with Middle-town America. Milton. Middle-town, Mill Town.

Whatever. It's a name.

Hello, Mark. It's Mommy and Daddy.

That's right, baby, it's Mommy and Daddy.

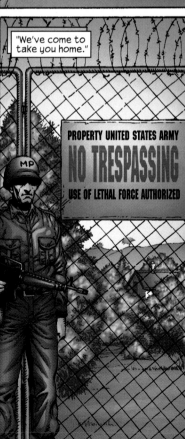

"We've come to take you home."

PROPERTY UNITED STATES ARMY
NO TRESPASSING
USE OF LETHAL FORCE AUTHORIZED

MP

Happy birthday to you...happy birthday to you....

Happy birthday dear Maaaaaaaark. Happy birthday to youuuuuuu!

Ga-da! Ook!

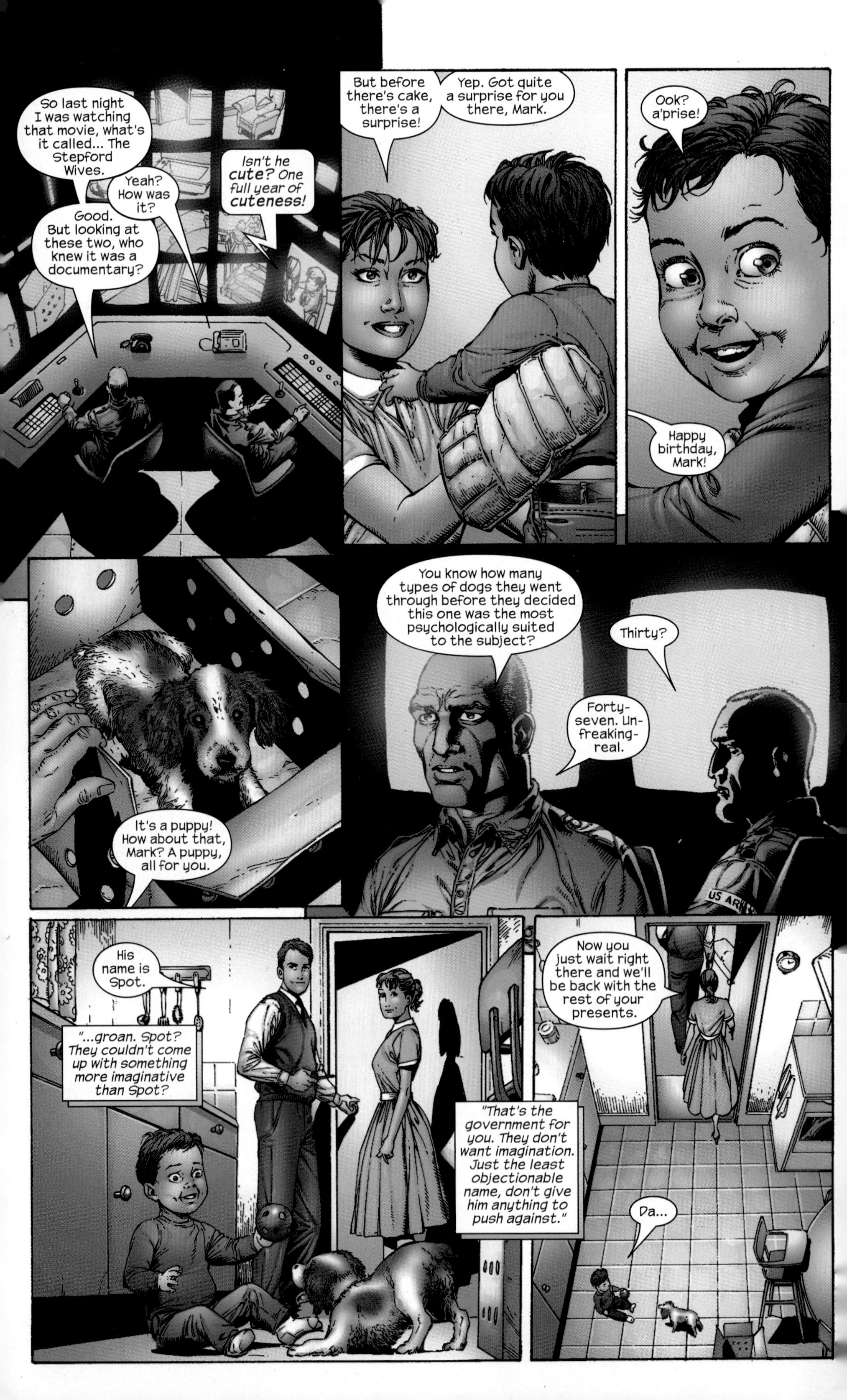

So last night I was watching that movie, what's it called... The Stepford Wives.
Yeah? How was it?
Good. But looking at these two, who knew it was a documentary?
Isn't he *cute?* One full year of *cuteness!*
But before there's cake, there's a surprise!
Yep. Got quite a surprise for you there, Mark.
Ook? a'prise!
Happy birthday, Mark!
It's a puppy! How about that, Mark? A puppy, all for you.
You know how many types of dogs they went through before they decided this one was the most psychologically suited to the subject?
Thirty?
Forty-seven. Un-freaking-real.
US AR
His name is Spot.
"...groan. Spot? They couldn't come up with something more imaginative than Spot?
"That's the government for you. They don't want imagination. Just the least objectionable name, don't give him anything to push against."
Now you just wait right there and we'll be back with the rest of your presents.
Da...

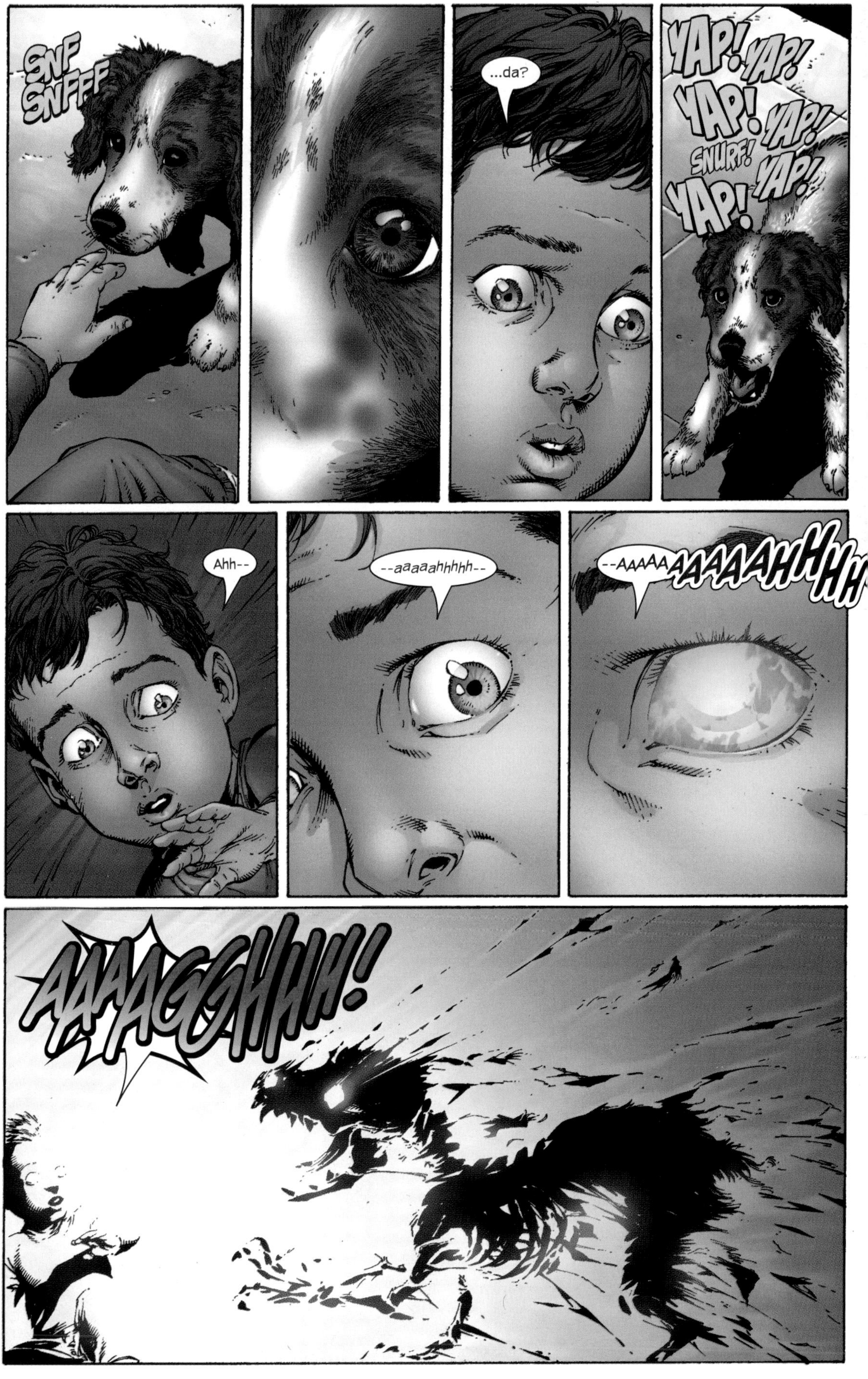
SNF
SNFFF
...da?
YAP! YAP!
YAP! YAP!
SNURF!
YAP!
YAP!
Ahh--
--aaaaahhhhh--
--AAAAAAAAAAHHHH
AAAAGGHHH!

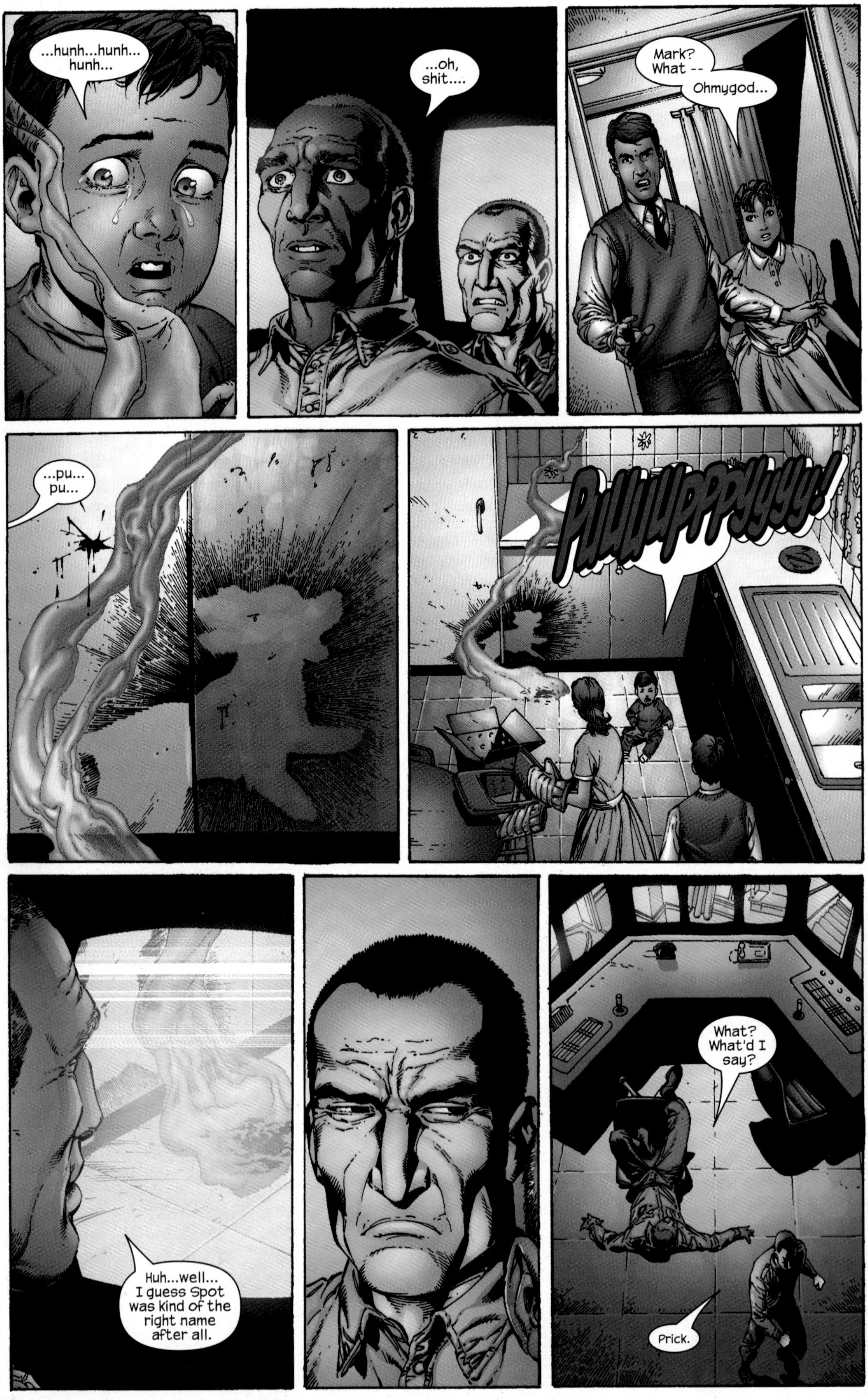
...hunh...hunh... hunh...
...oh, shit....
Mark? What --
Ohmygod...
...pu... pu...
PULLUPPPYYYY!
Huh...well... I guess Spot was kind of the right name after all.
What? What'd I say?
Prick.

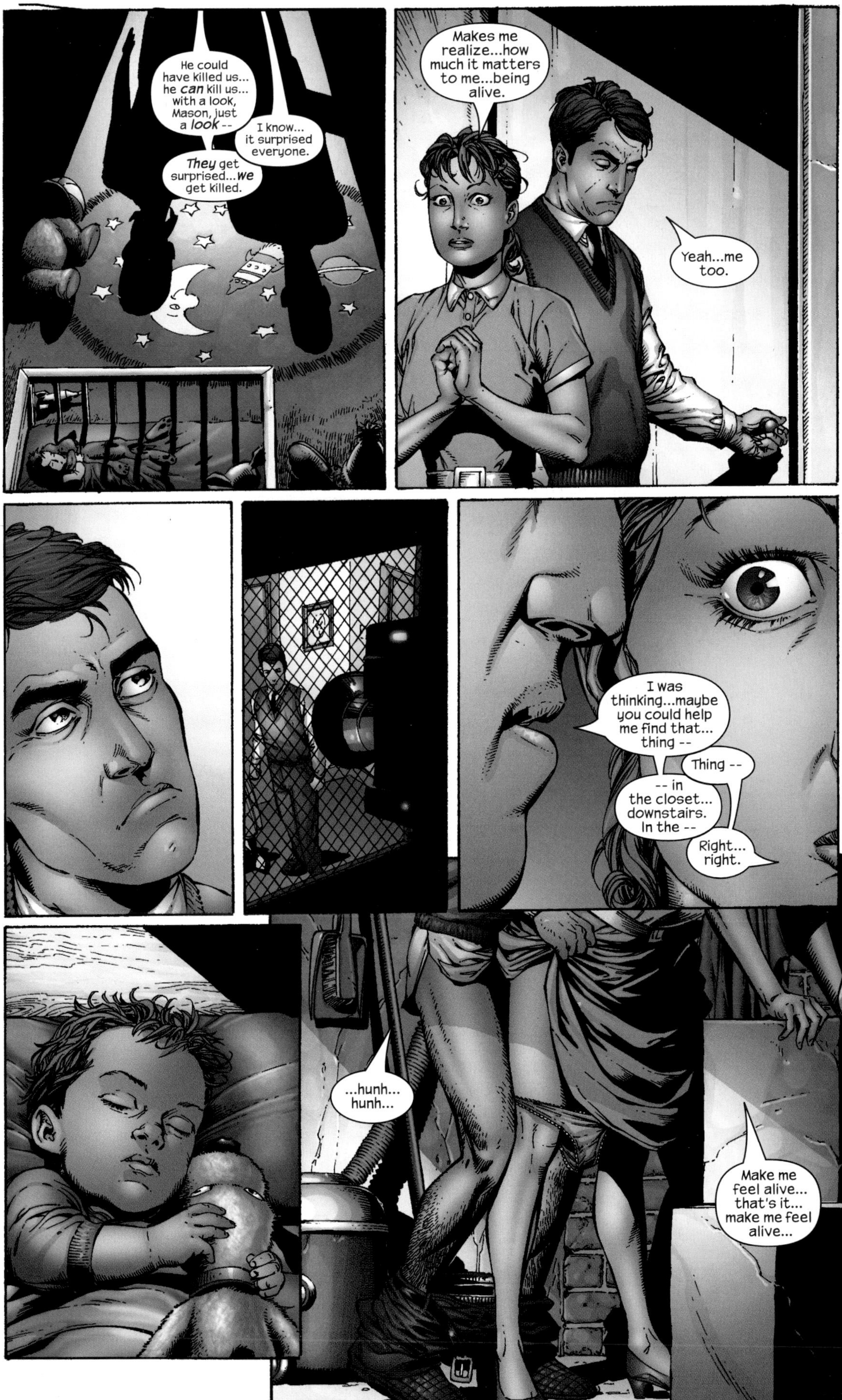

He could have killed us... he *can* kill us... with a look, Mason, just a *look* --
I know... it surprised everyone.
They get surprised...*we* get killed.
Makes me realize...how much it matters to me...being alive.
Yeah...me too.
I was thinking...maybe you could help me find that... thing --
Thing --
-- in the closet... downstairs. In the --
Right... right.
...hunh... hunh...
Make me feel alive... that's it... make me feel alive...

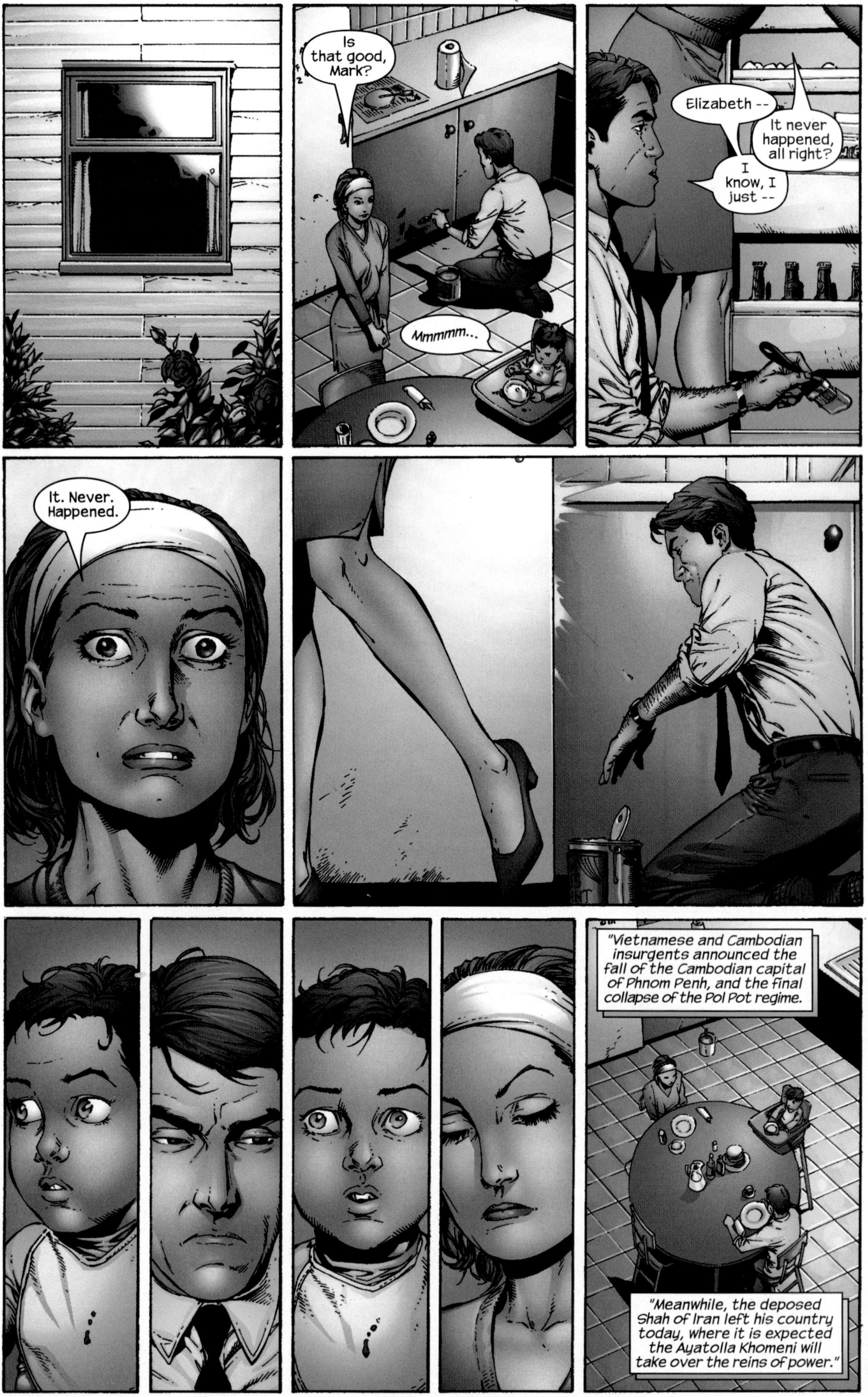
Is that good, Mark?
Mmmmm...
Elizabeth --
It never happened, all right?
I know, I just --
It. Never. Happened.
"Vietnamese and Cambodian insurgents announced the fall of the Cambodian capital of Phnom Penh, and the final collapse of the Pol Pot regime.
"Meanwhile, the deposed Shah of Iran left his country today, where it is expected the Ayatolla Khomeni will take over the reins of power."

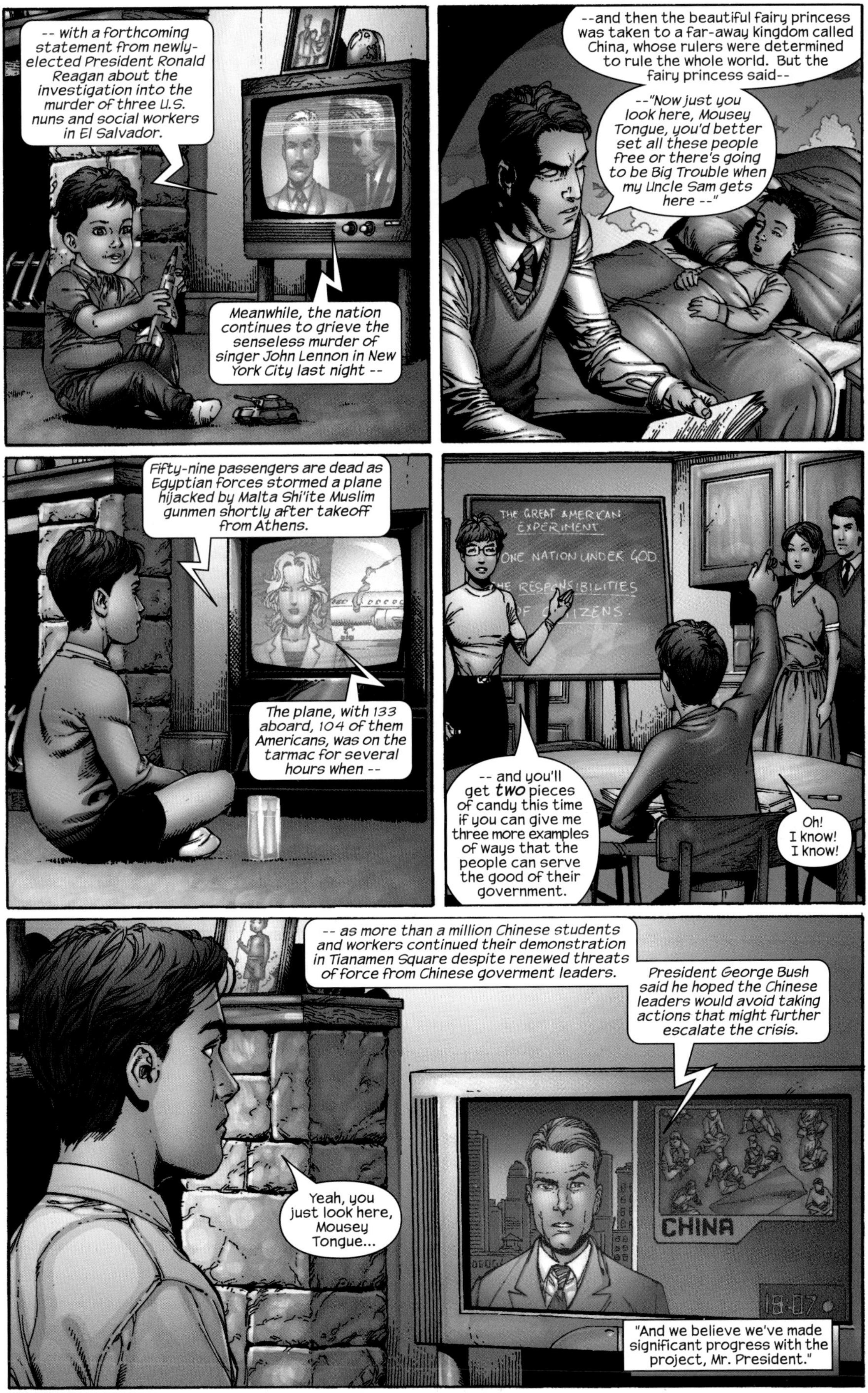
-- with a forthcoming statement from newly-elected President Ronald Reagan about the investigation into the murder of three U.S. nuns and social workers in El Salvador.
Meanwhile, the nation continues to grieve the senseless murder of singer John Lennon in New York City last night --
--and then the beautiful fairy princess was taken to a far-away kingdom called China, whose rulers were determined to rule the whole world. But the fairy princess said--
--"Now just you look here, Mousey Tongue, you'd better set all these people free or there's going to be Big Trouble when my Uncle Sam gets here --"
Fifty-nine passengers are dead as Egyptian forces stormed a plane hijacked by Malta Shi'ite Muslim gunmen shortly after takeoff from Athens.
The plane, with 133 aboard, 104 of them Americans, was on the tarmac for several hours when --
THE GREAT AMERICAN EXPERIMENT
ONE NATION UNDER GOD.
-- and you'll get *two* pieces of candy this time if you can give me three more examples of ways that the people can serve the good of their government.
Oh! I know! I know!
-- as more than a million Chinese students and workers continued their demonstration in Tianamen Square despite renewed threats of force from Chinese goverment leaders.
President George Bush said he hoped the Chinese leaders would avoid taking actions that might further escalate the crisis.
CHINA
Yeah, you just look here, Mousey Tongue...
"And we believe we've made significant progress with the project, Mr. President."

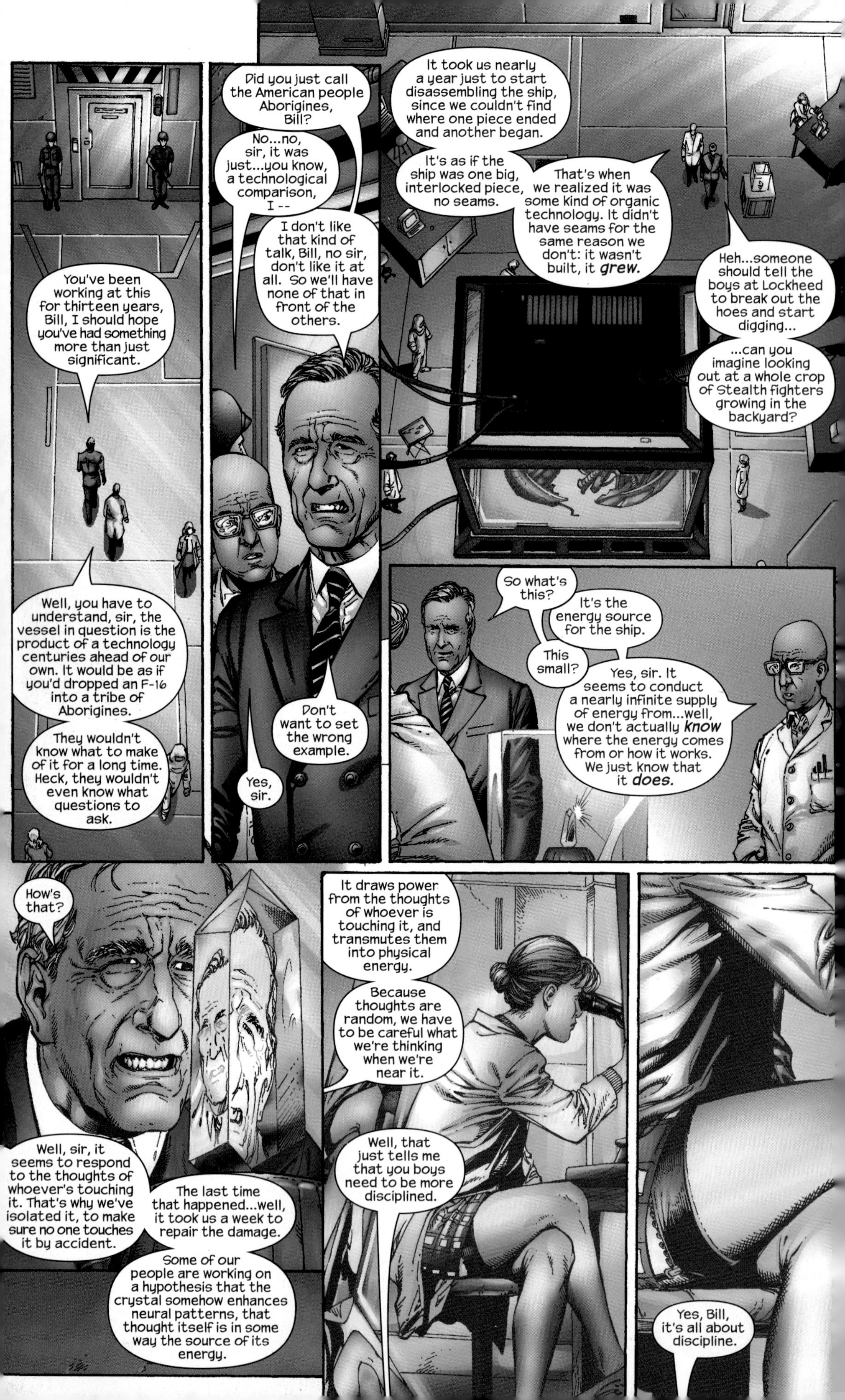

You've been working at this for thirteen years, Bill, I should hope you've had something more than just significant.
Well, you have to understand, sir, the vessel in question is the product of a technology centuries ahead of our own. It would be as if you'd dropped an F-16 into a tribe of Aborigines.
They wouldn't know what to make of it for a long time. Heck, they wouldn't even know what questions to ask.
Did you just call the American people Aborigines, Bill?
No...no, sir, it was just...you know, a technological comparison, I --
I don't like that kind of talk, Bill, no sir, don't like it at all. So we'll have none of that in front of the others.
Don't want to set the wrong example.
Yes, sir.
It took us nearly a year just to start disassembling the ship, since we couldn't find where one piece ended and another began.
It's as if the ship was one big, interlocked piece, no seams.
That's when we realized it was some kind of organic technology. It didn't have seams for the same reason we don't: it wasn't built, it grew.
Heh...someone should tell the boys at Lockheed to break out the hoes and start digging...
...can you imagine looking out at a whole crop of Stealth fighters growing in the backyard?
So what's this?
It's the energy source for the ship.
This small?
Yes, sir. It seems to conduct a nearly infinite supply of energy from...well, we don't actually know where the energy comes from or how it works. We just know that it does.
How's that?
Well, sir, it seems to respond to the thoughts of whoever's touching it. That's why we've isolated it, to make sure no one touches it by accident.
The last time that happened...well, it took us a week to repair the damage.
Some of our people are working on a hypothesis that the crystal somehow enhances neural patterns, that thought itself is in some way the source of its energy.
It draws power from the thoughts of whoever is touching it, and transmutes them into physical energy.
Because thoughts are random, we have to be careful what we're thinking when we're near it.
Well, that just tells me that you boys need to be more disciplined.
Yes, Bill, it's all about discipline.

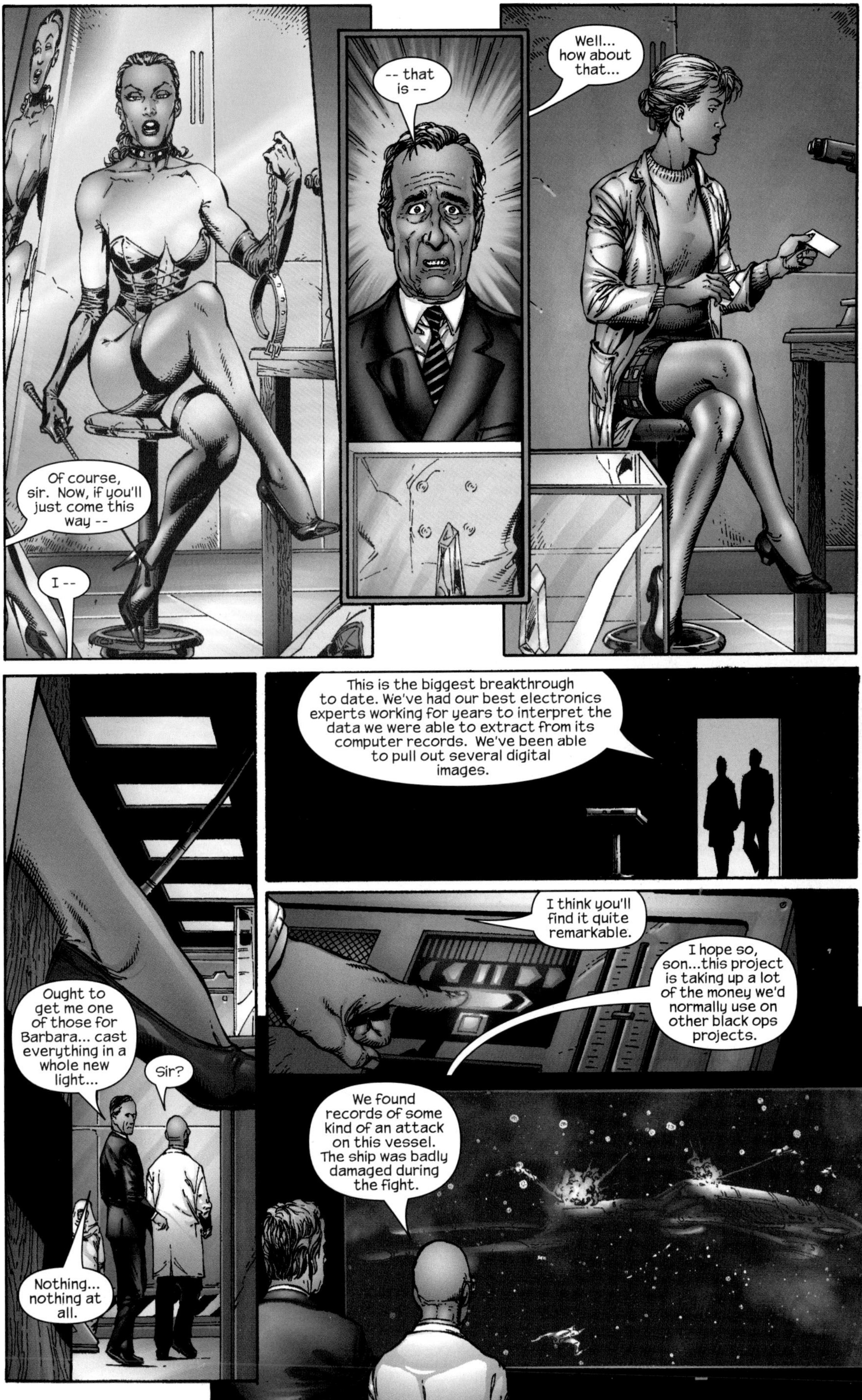
Of course, sir. Now, if you'll just come this way --
I --
-- that is --
Well... how about that...
Ought to get me one of those for Barbara... cast everything in a whole new light...
Sir?
Nothing... nothing at all.
This is the biggest breakthrough to date. We've had our best electronics experts working for years to interpret the data we were able to extract from its computer records. We've been able to pull out several digital images.
I think you'll find it quite remarkable.
I hope so, son...this project is taking up a lot of the money we'd normally use on other black ops projects.
We found records of some kind of an attack on this vessel. The ship was badly damaged during the fight.

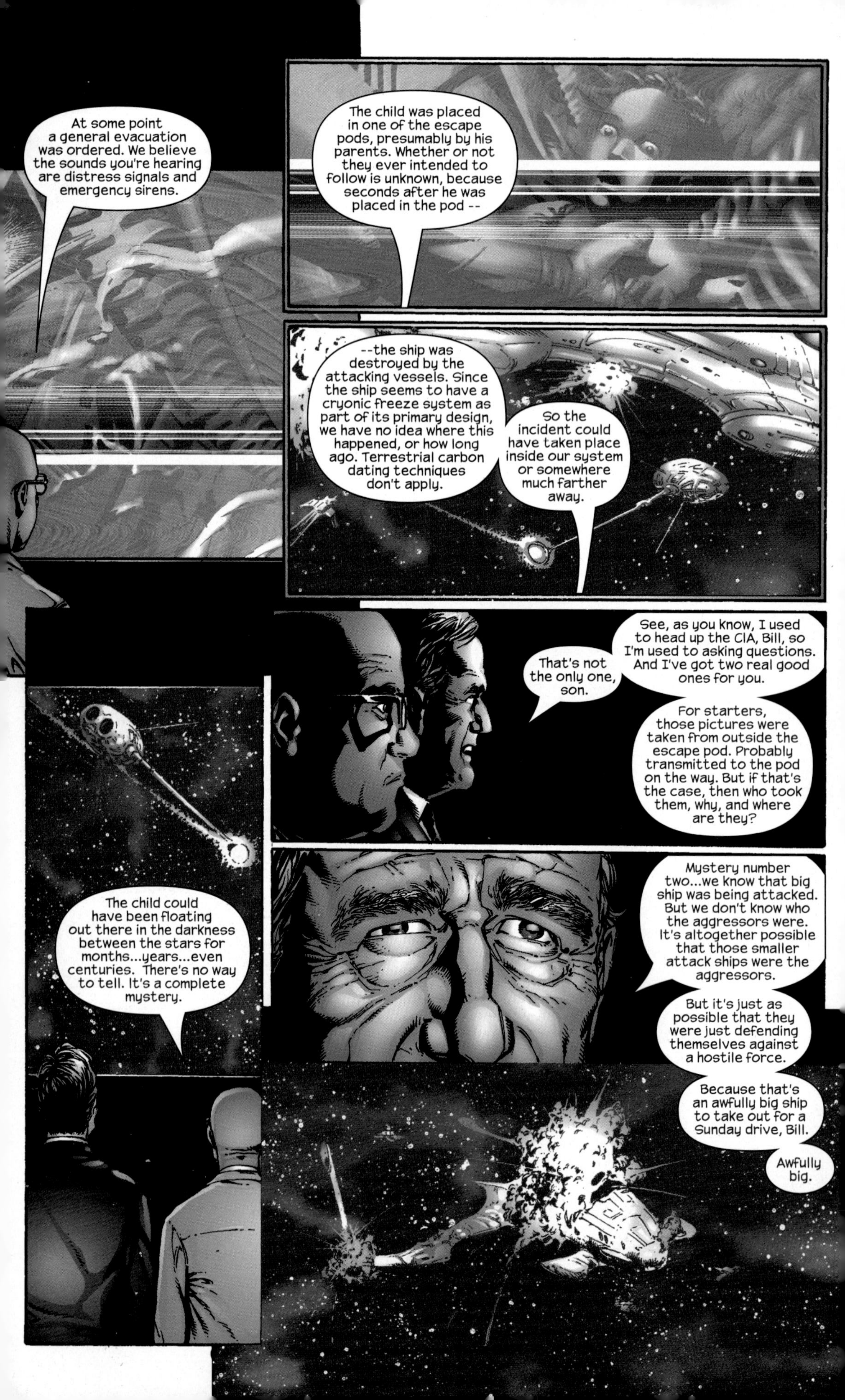
At some point a general evacuation was ordered. We believe the sounds you're hearing are distress signals and emergency sirens.
The child was placed in one of the escape pods, presumably by his parents. Whether or not they ever intended to follow is unknown, because seconds after he was placed in the pod --
--the ship was destroyed by the attacking vessels. Since the ship seems to have a cryonic freeze system as part of its primary design, we have no idea where this happened, or how long ago. Terrestrial carbon dating techniques don't apply.
So the incident could have taken place inside our system or somewhere much farther away.
The child could have been floating out there in the darkness between the stars for months...years...even centuries. There's no way to tell. It's a complete mystery.
That's not the only one, son.
See, as you know, I used to head up the CIA, Bill, so I'm used to asking questions. And I've got two real good ones for you.
For starters, those pictures were taken from outside the escape pod. Probably transmitted to the pod on the way. But if that's the case, then who took them, why, and where are they?
Mystery number two...we know that big ship was being attacked. But we don't know who the aggressors were. It's altogether possible that those smaller attack ships were the aggressors.
But it's just as possible that they were just defending themselves against a hostile force.
Because that's an awfully big ship to take out for a Sunday drive, Bill.
Awfully big.

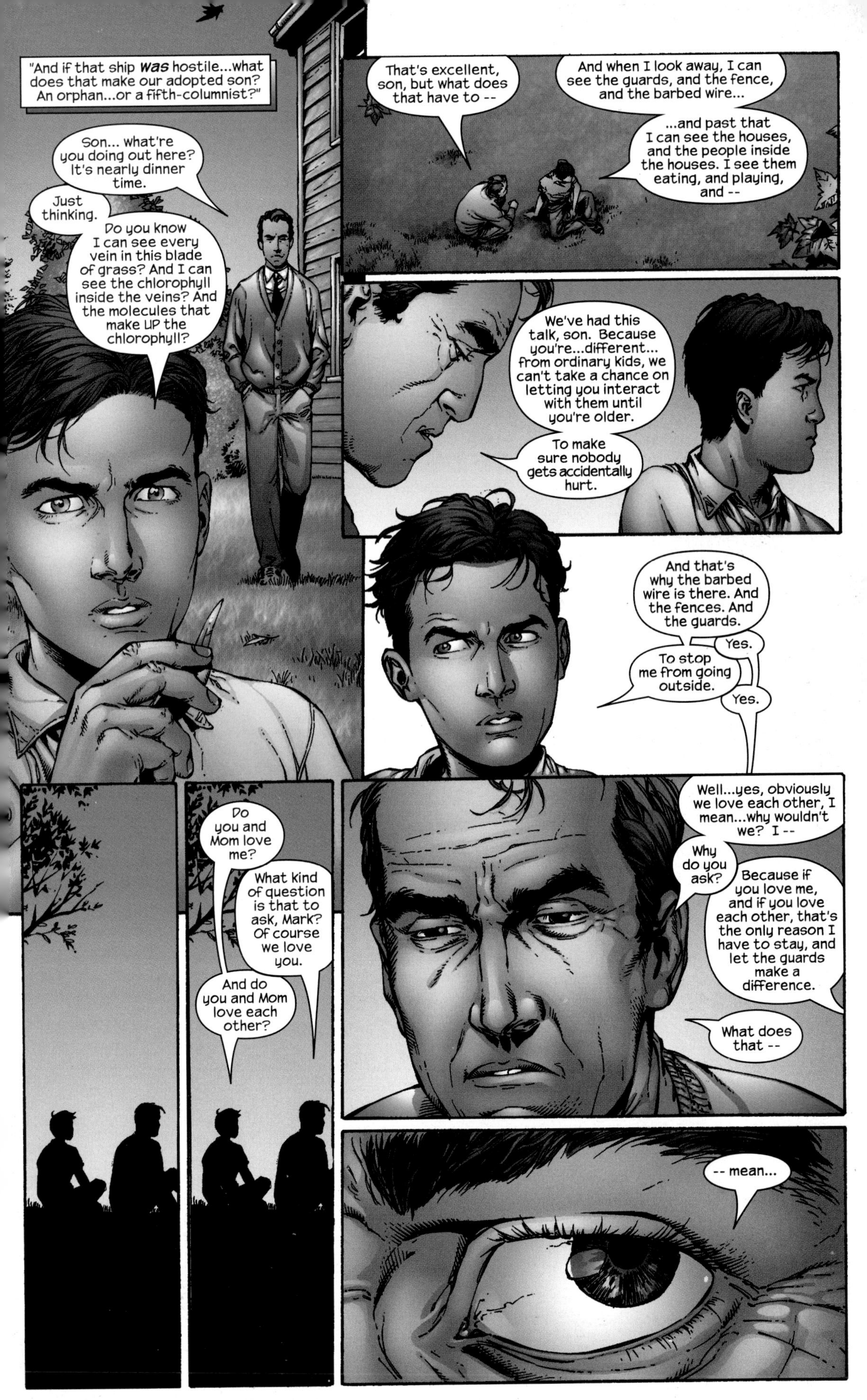
"And if that ship *was* hostile...what does that make our adopted son? An orphan...or a fifth-columnist?"
Son... what're you doing out here? It's nearly dinner time.
Just thinking.
Do you know I can see every vein in this blade of grass? And I can see the chlorophyll inside the veins? And the molecules that make UP the chlorophyll?
That's excellent, son, but what does that have to --
And when I look away, I can see the guards, and the fence, and the barbed wire...
...and past that I can see the houses, and the people inside the houses. I see them eating, and playing, and --
We've had this talk, son. Because you're...different... from ordinary kids, we can't take a chance on letting you interact with them until you're older.
To make sure nobody gets accidentally hurt.
And that's why the barbed wire is there. And the fences. And the guards.
Yes.
To stop me from going outside.
Yes.
Do you and Mom love me?
What kind of question is that to ask, Mark? Of course we love you.
And do you and Mom love each other?
Well...yes, obviously we love each other, I mean...why wouldn't we? I --
Why do you ask?
Because if you love me, and if you love each other, that's the only reason I have to stay, and let the guards make a difference.
What does that --
-- mean...

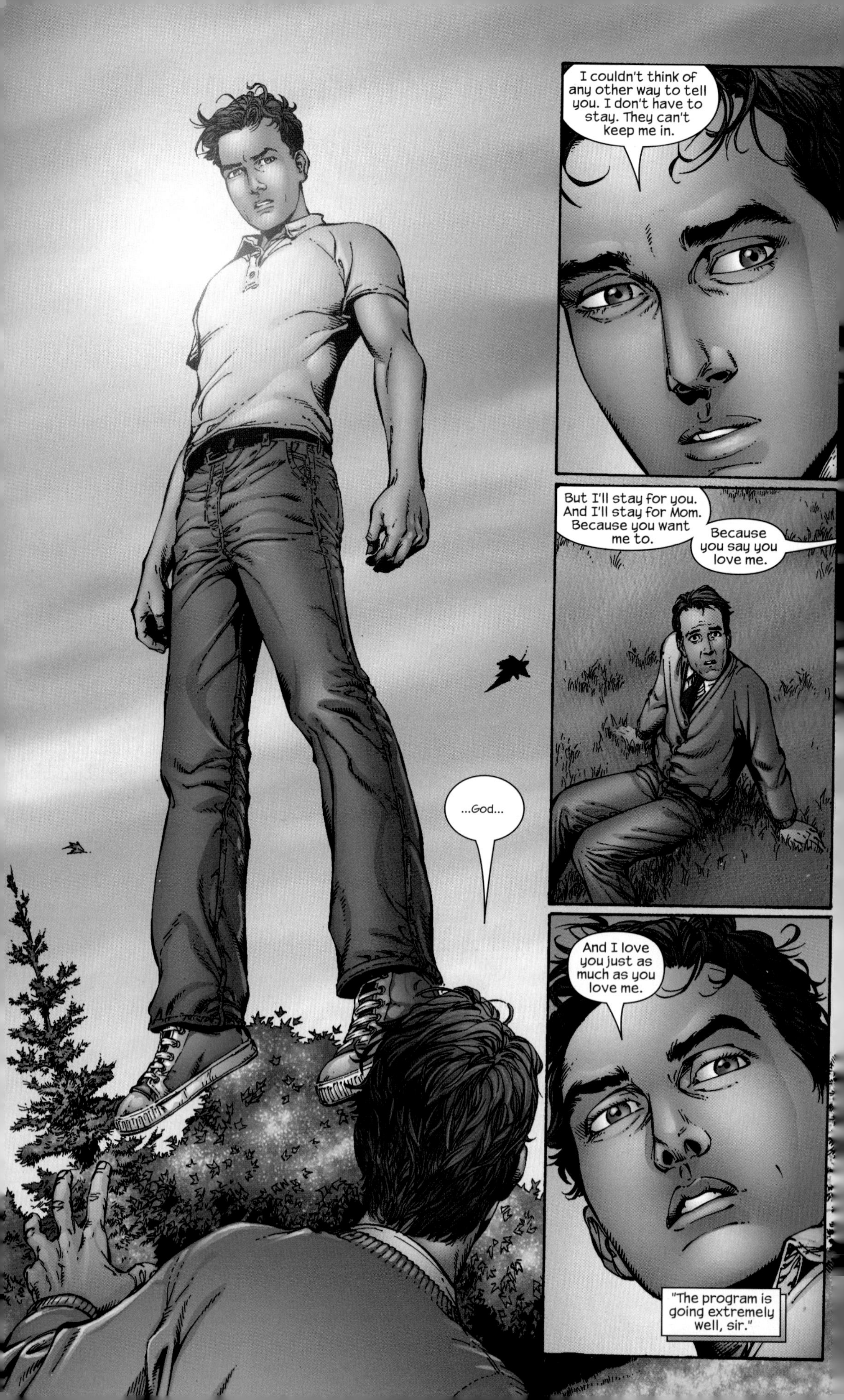
...God...
I couldn't think of any other way to tell you. I don't have to stay. They can't keep me in.
But I'll stay for you. And I'll stay for Mom. Because you want me to.
Because you say you love me.
And I love you just as much as you love me.
"The program is going extremely well, sir."

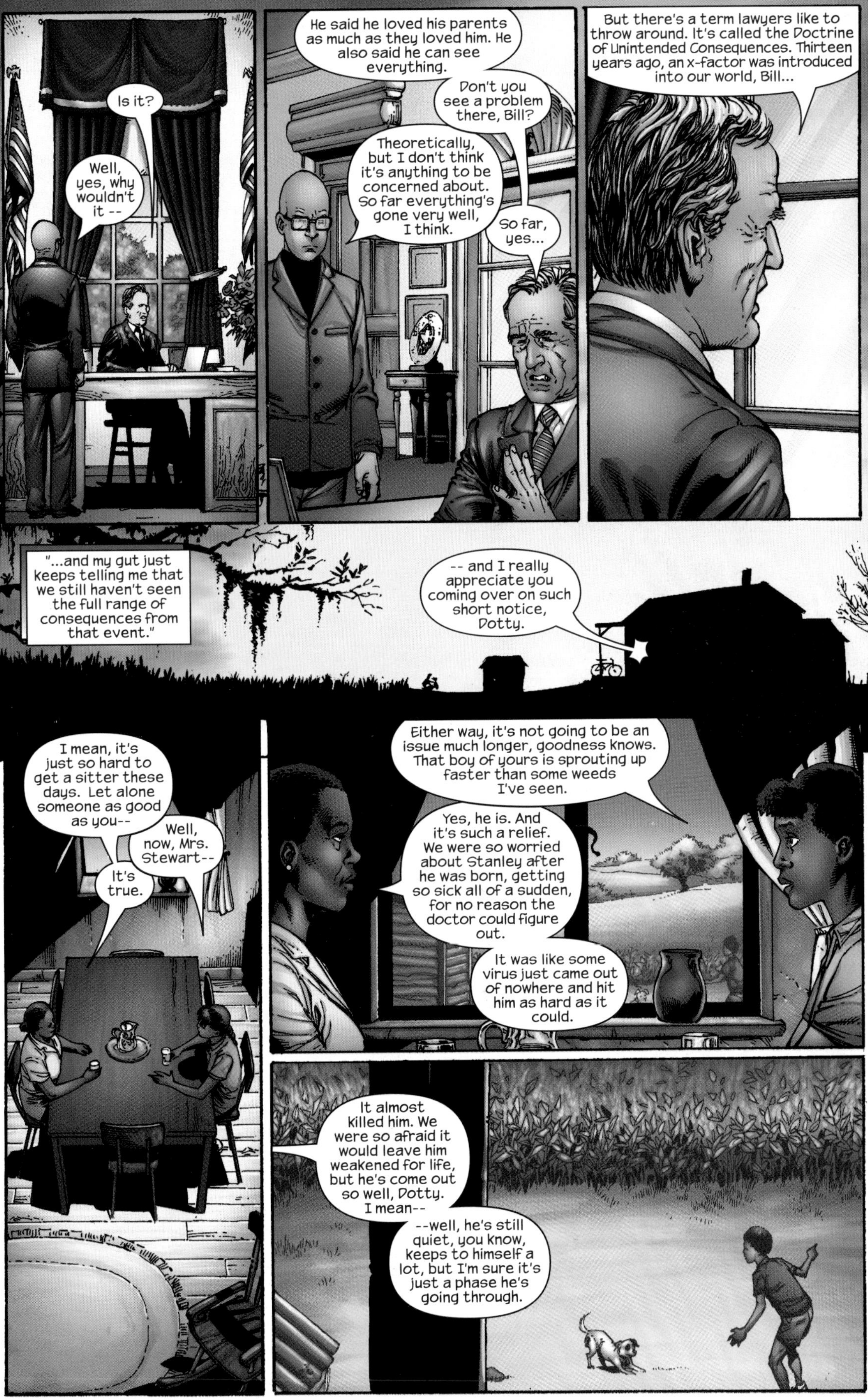
Is it?
Well, yes, why wouldn't it --
He said he loved his parents as much as they loved him. He also said he can see everything.
Don't you see a problem there, Bill?
Theoretically, but I don't think it's anything to be concerned about. So far everything's gone very well, I think.
So far, yes...
But there's a term lawyers like to throw around. It's called the Doctrine of Unintended Consequences. Thirteen years ago, an x-factor was introduced into our world, Bill...
"...and my gut just keeps telling me that we still haven't seen the full range of consequences from that event."
-- and I really appreciate you coming over on such short notice, Dotty.
I mean, it's just so hard to get a sitter these days. Let alone someone as good as you--
Well, now, Mrs. Stewart--
It's true.
Either way, it's not going to be an issue much longer, goodness knows. That boy of yours is sprouting up faster than some weeds I've seen.
Yes, he is. And it's such a relief. We were so worried about Stanley after he was born, getting so sick all of a sudden, for no reason the doctor could figure out.
It was like some virus just came out of nowhere and hit him as hard as it could.
It almost killed him. We were so afraid it would leave him weakened for life, but he's come out so well, Dotty. I mean--
--well, he's still quiet, you know, keeps to himself a lot, but I'm sure it's just a phase he's going through.

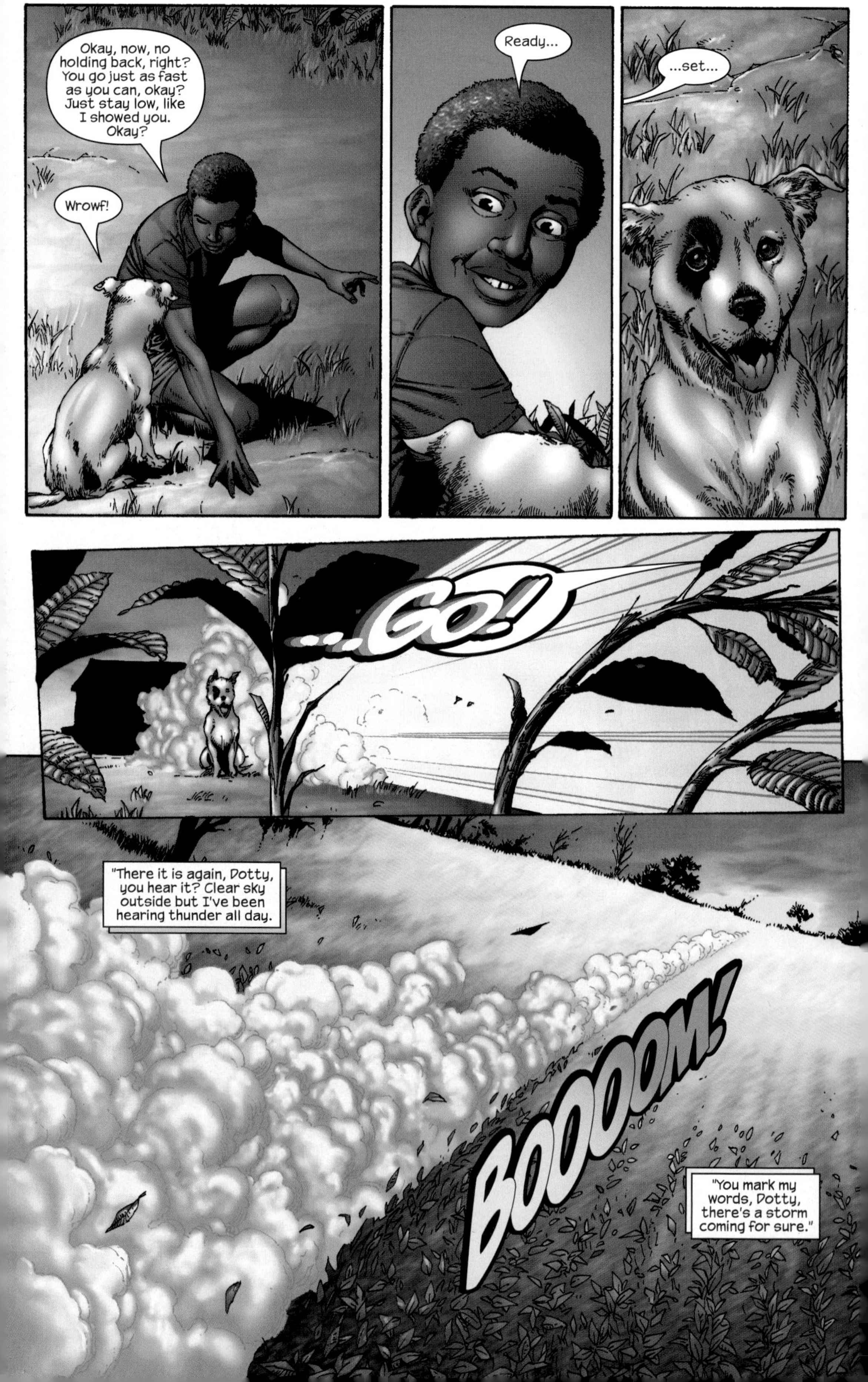
Okay, now, no holding back, right? You go just as fast as you can, okay? Just stay low, like I showed you. Okay?
Wrowf!
Ready...
...set...
...GO!
"There it is again, Dotty, you hear it? Clear sky outside but I've been hearing thunder all day.
BOOOOM!
"You mark my words, Dotty, there's a storm coming for sure."

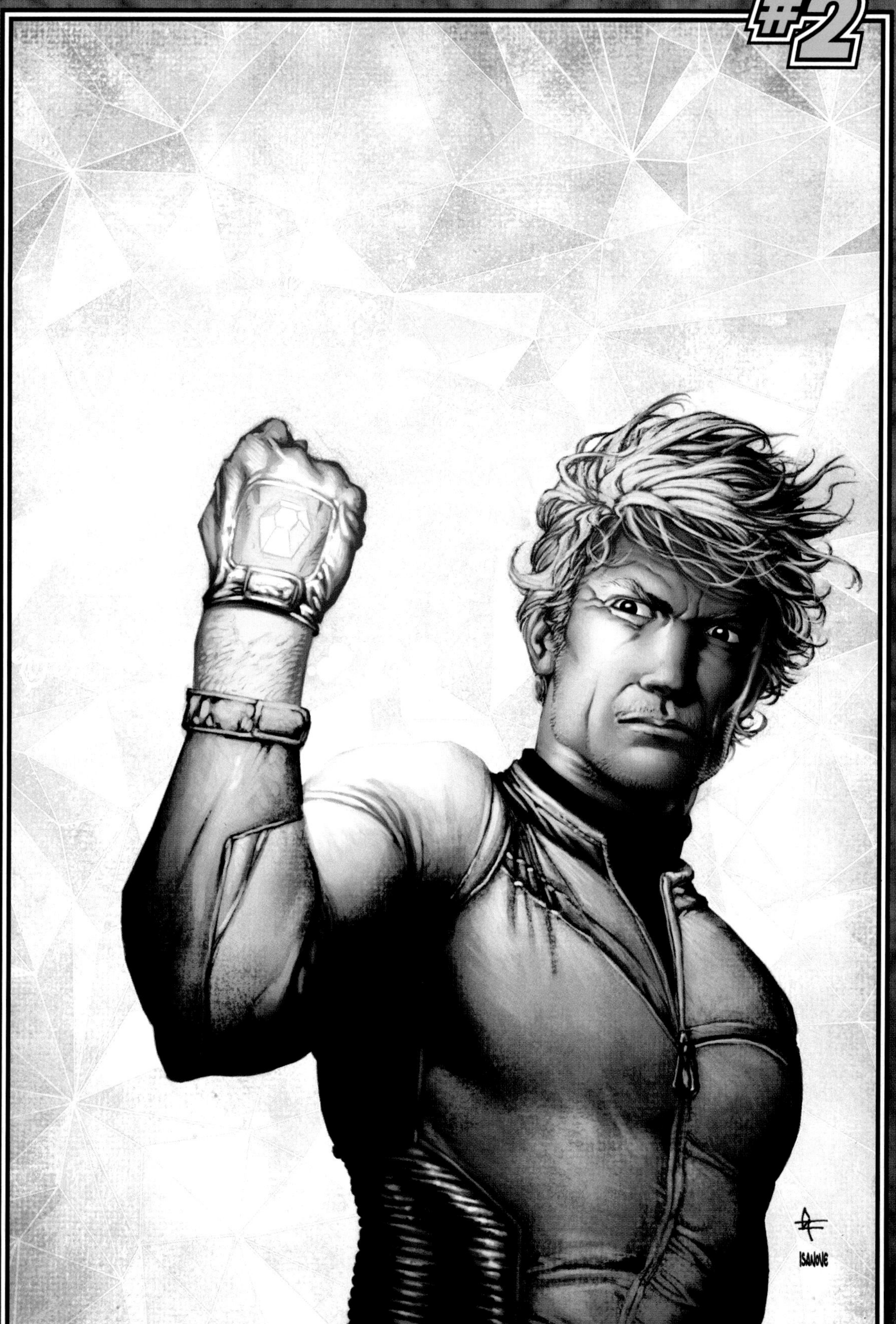
#2
ISANOVE

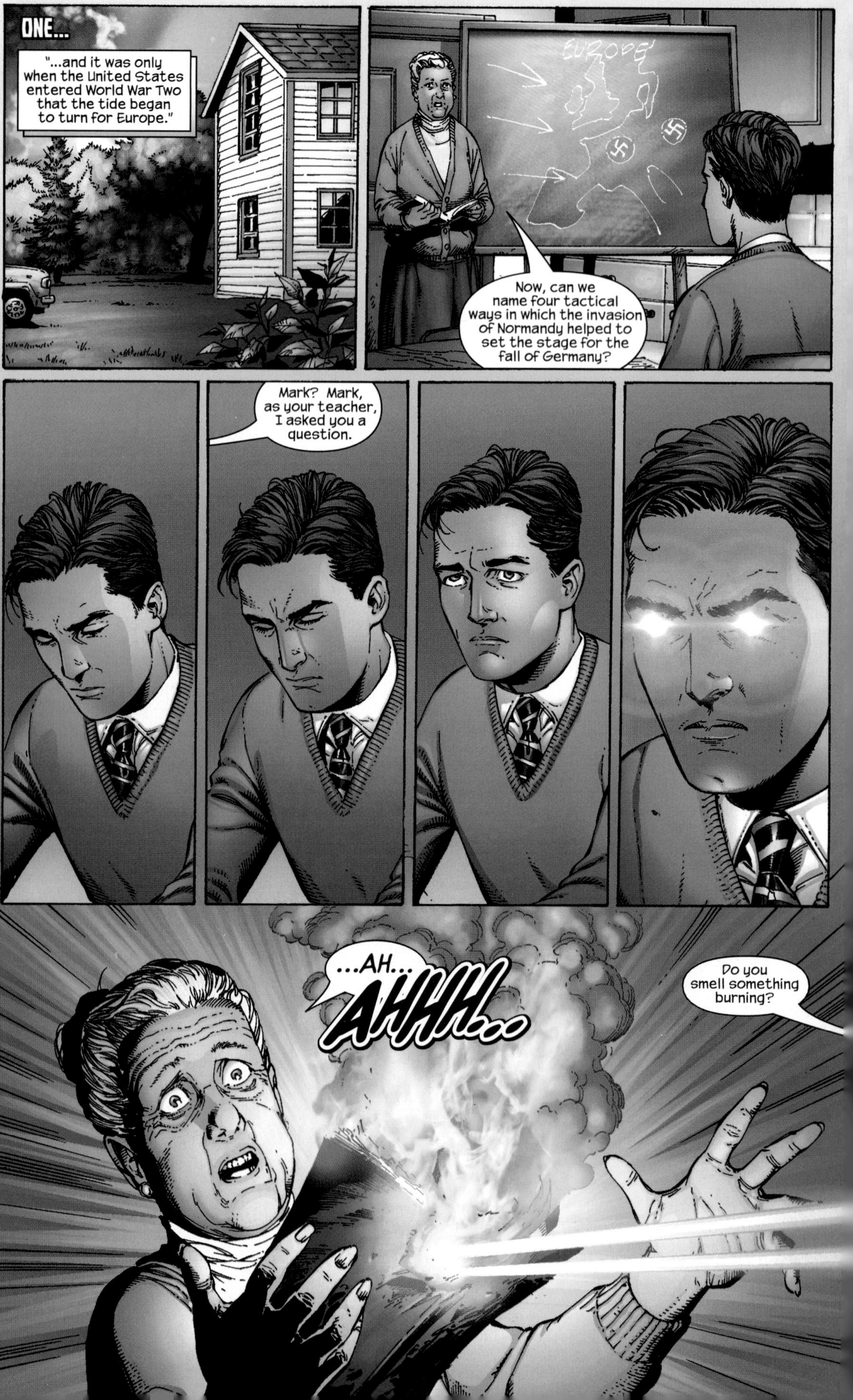
ONE...
"...and it was only when the United States entered World War Two that the tide began to turn for Europe."
EUROPE
Now, can we name four tactical ways in which the invasion of Normandy helped to set the stage for the fall of Germany?
Mark? Mark, as your teacher, I asked you a question.
...AH...
AHHH...
Do you smell something burning?

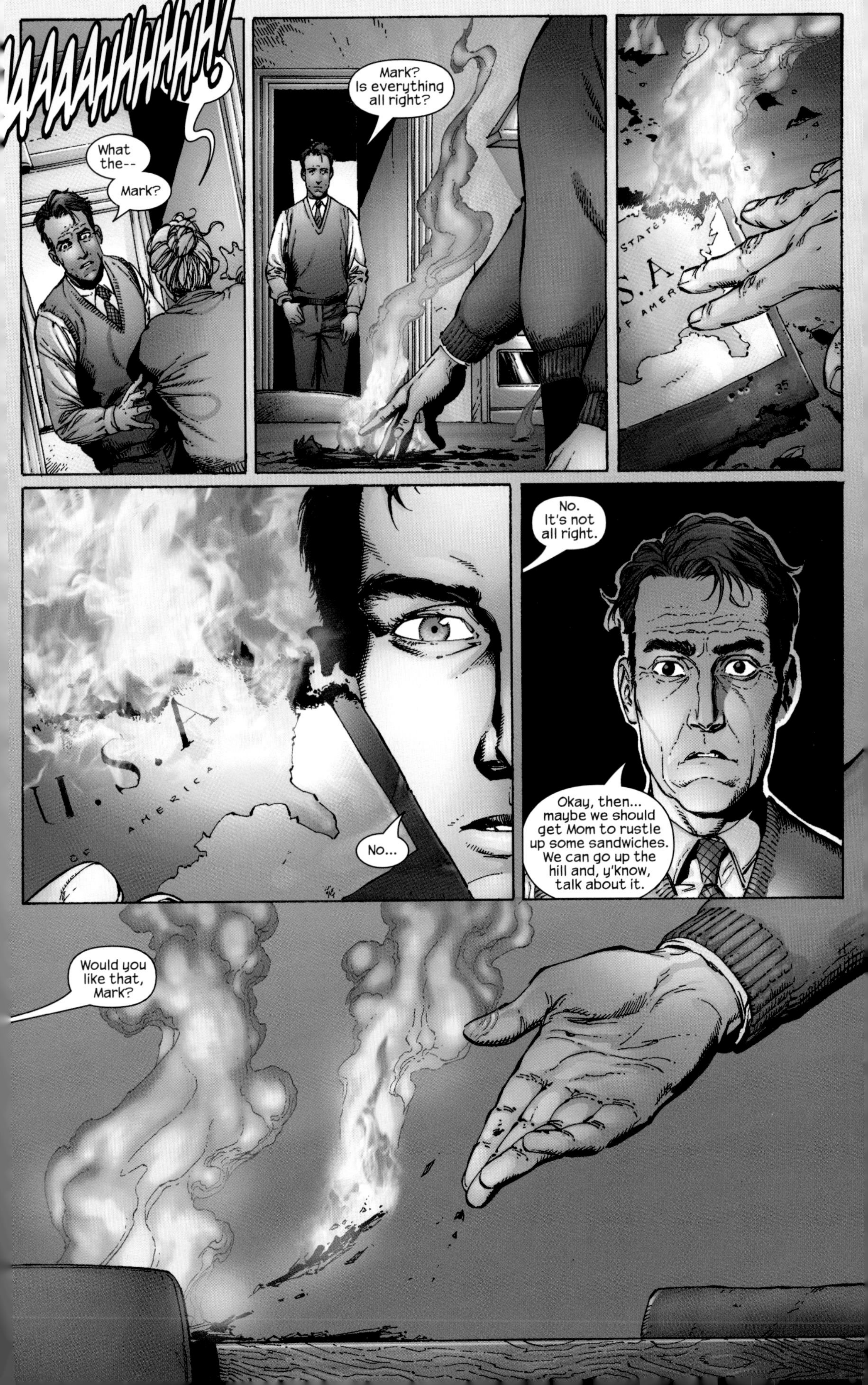
AAAAHHHHH!
What the--
Mark?
Mark?
Is everything all right?
S.A.
No...
No.
It's not all right.
Okay, then... maybe we should get Mom to rustle up some sandwiches. We can go up the hill and, y'know, talk about it.
Would you like that, Mark?

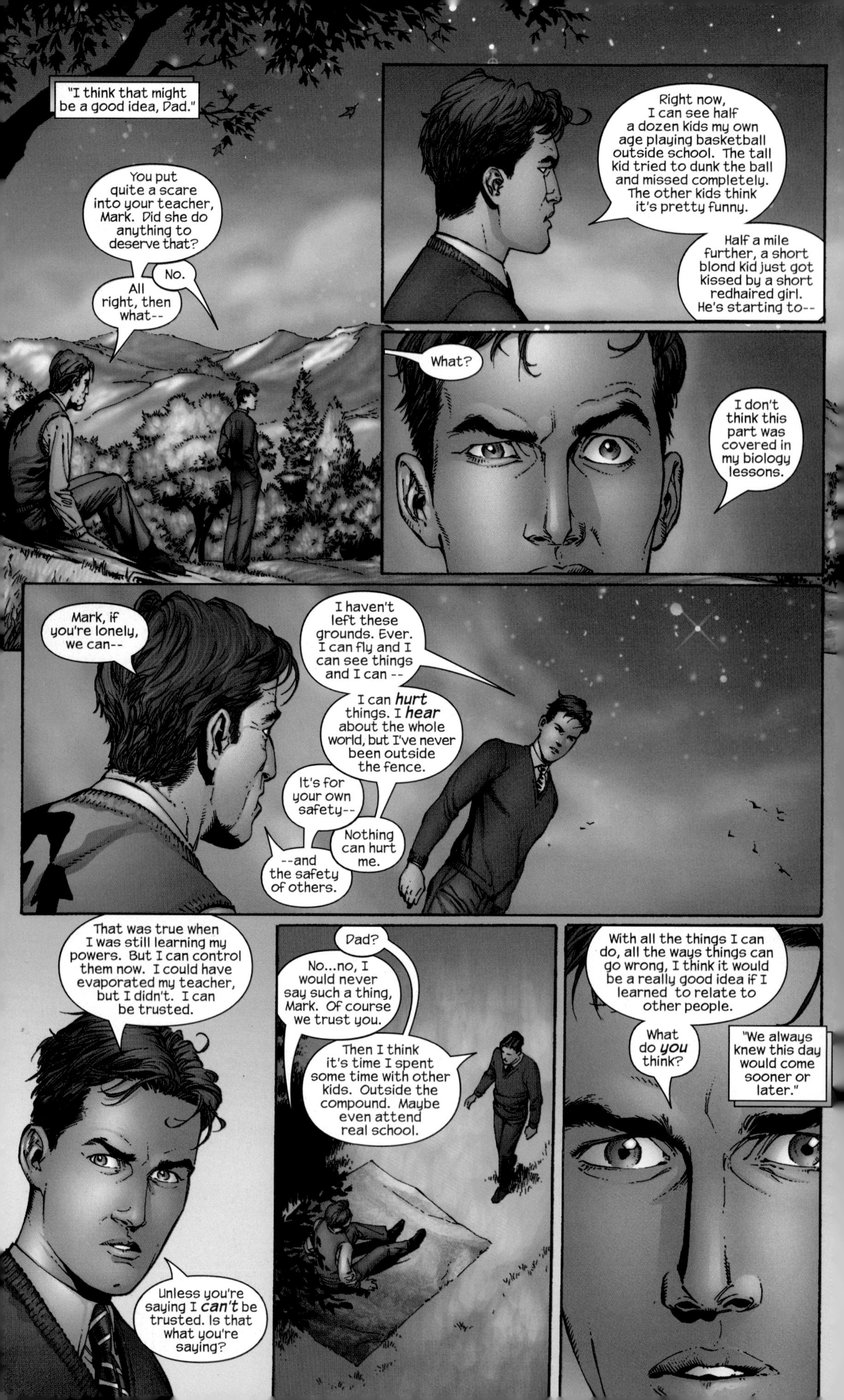
"I think that might be a good idea, Dad."
You put quite a scare into your teacher, Mark. Did she do anything to deserve that?
No.
All right, then what--
Right now, I can see half a dozen kids my own age playing basketball outside school. The tall kid tried to dunk the ball and missed completely. The other kids think it's pretty funny.
Half a mile further, a short blond kid just got kissed by a short redhaired girl. He's starting to--
What?
I don't think this part was covered in my biology lessons.
Mark, if you're lonely, we can--
I haven't left these grounds. Ever. I can fly and I can see things and I can --
I can hurt things. I hear about the whole world, but I've never been outside the fence.
It's for your own safety--
Nothing can hurt me.
--and the safety of others.
That was true when I was still learning my powers. But I can control them now. I could have evaporated my teacher, but I didn't. I can be trusted.
Unless you're saying I can't be trusted. Is that what you're saying?
Dad?
No...no, I would never say such a thing, Mark. Of course we trust you.
Then I think it's time I spent some time with other kids. Outside the compound. Maybe even attend real school.
With all the things I can do, all the ways things can go wrong, I think it would be a really good idea if I learned to relate to other people.
What do you think?
"We always knew this day would come sooner or later."

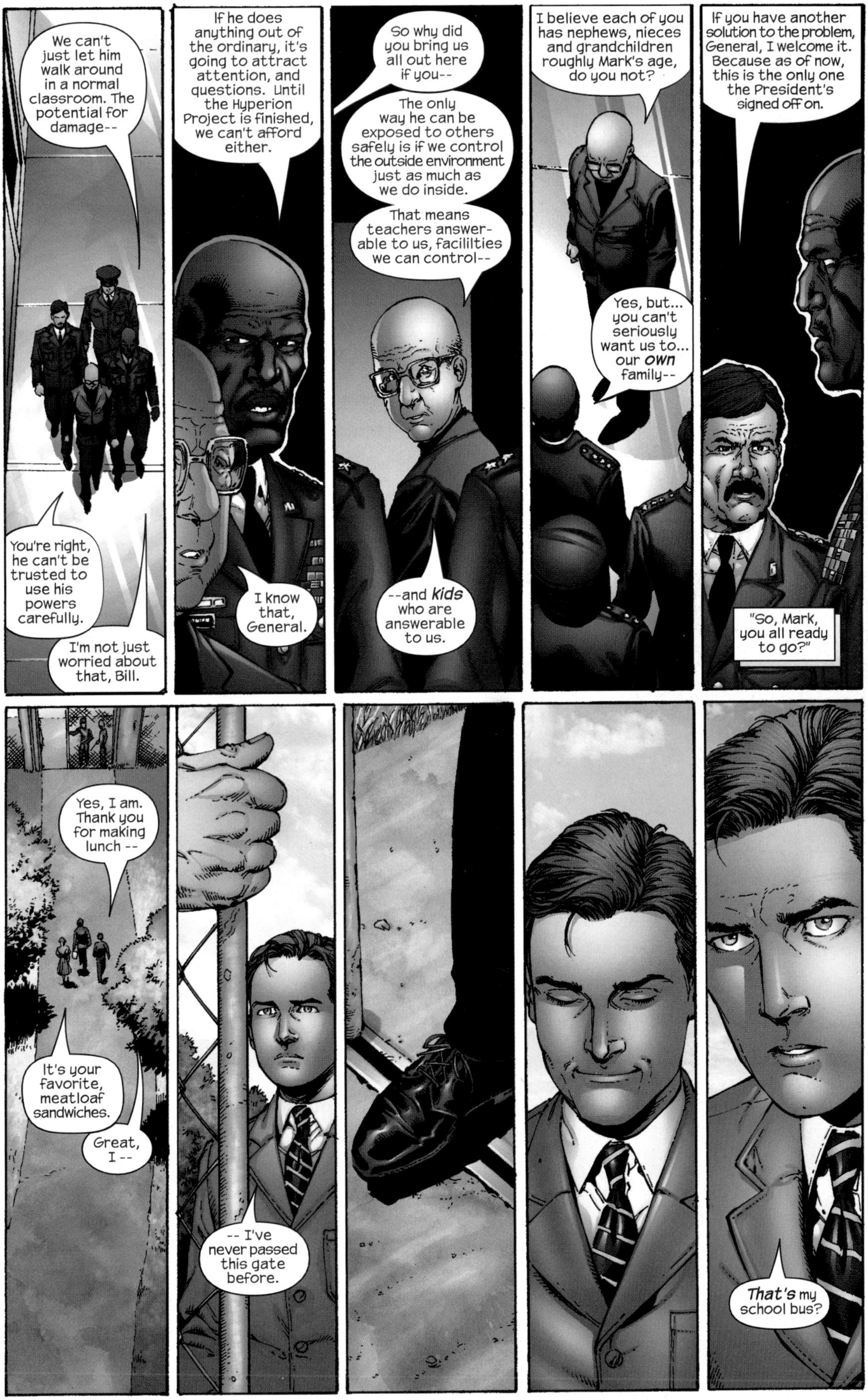

We can't just let him walk around in a normal classroom. The potential for damage--
You're right, he can't be trusted to use his powers carefully.
I'm not just worried about that, Bill.
If he does anything out of the ordinary, it's going to attract attention, and questions. Until the Hyperion Project is finished, we can't afford either.
I know that, General.
So why did you bring us all out here if you--
The only way he can be exposed to others safely is if we control the outside environment just as much as we do inside.
That means teachers answerable to us, facililties we can control--
--and kids who are answerable to us.
I believe each of you has nephews, nieces and grandchildren roughly Mark's age, do you not?
Yes, but... you can't seriously want us to... our own family--
If you have another solution to the problem, General, I welcome it. Because as of now, this is the only one the President's signed off on.
"So, Mark, you all ready to go?"
Yes, I am. Thank you for making lunch --
It's your favorite, meatloaf sandwiches.
Great, I --
-- I've never passed this gate before.
That's my school bus?

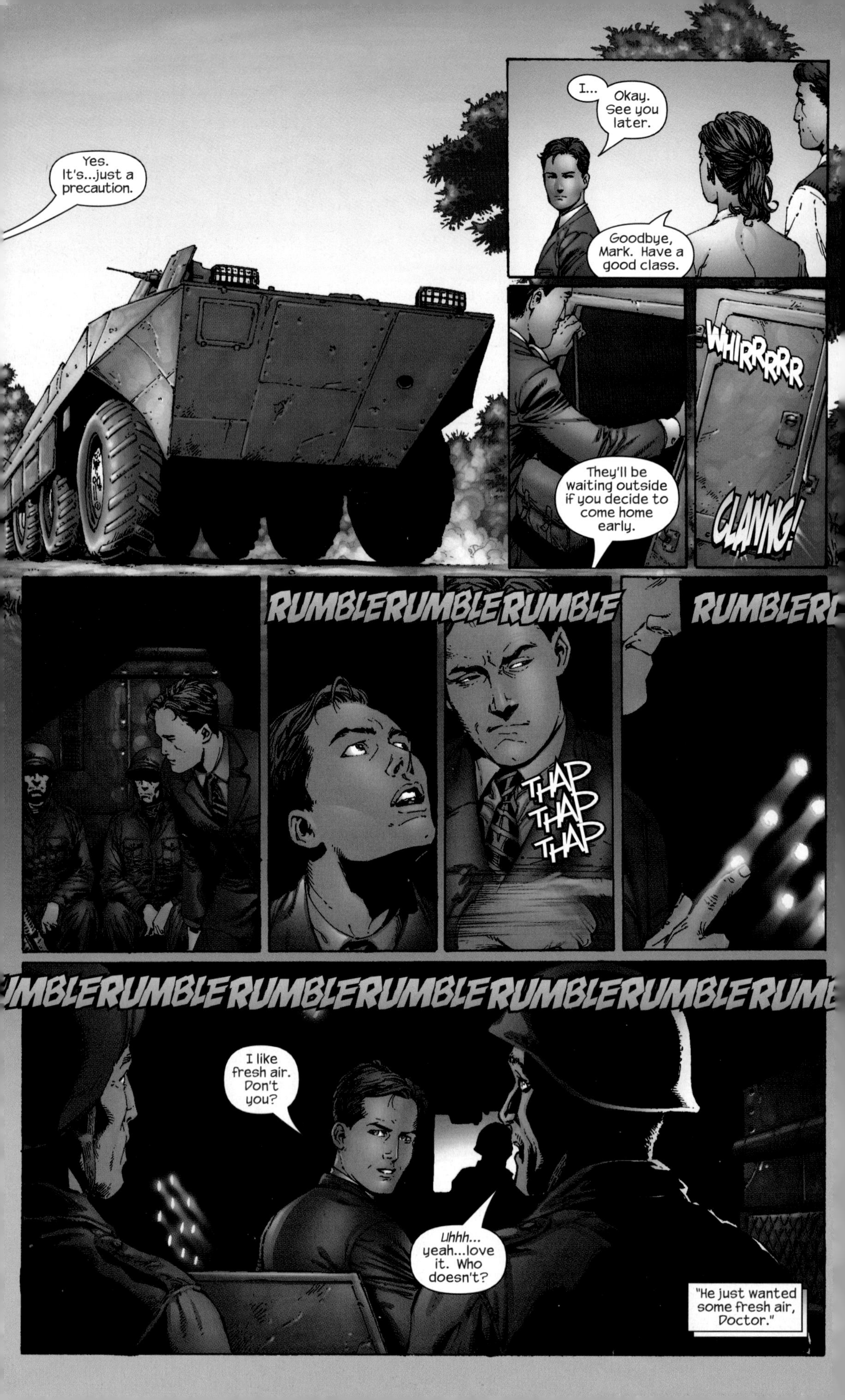
Yes. It's...just a precaution.
I...
Okay. See you later.
Goodbye, Mark. Have a good class.
They'll be waiting outside if you decide to come home early.
WHIRRRRR
CLANNG!
RUMBLERUMBLERUMBLE
THAP THAP THAP
I like fresh air. Don't you?
Uhhh... yeah...love it. Who doesn't?
"He just wanted some fresh air, Doctor."

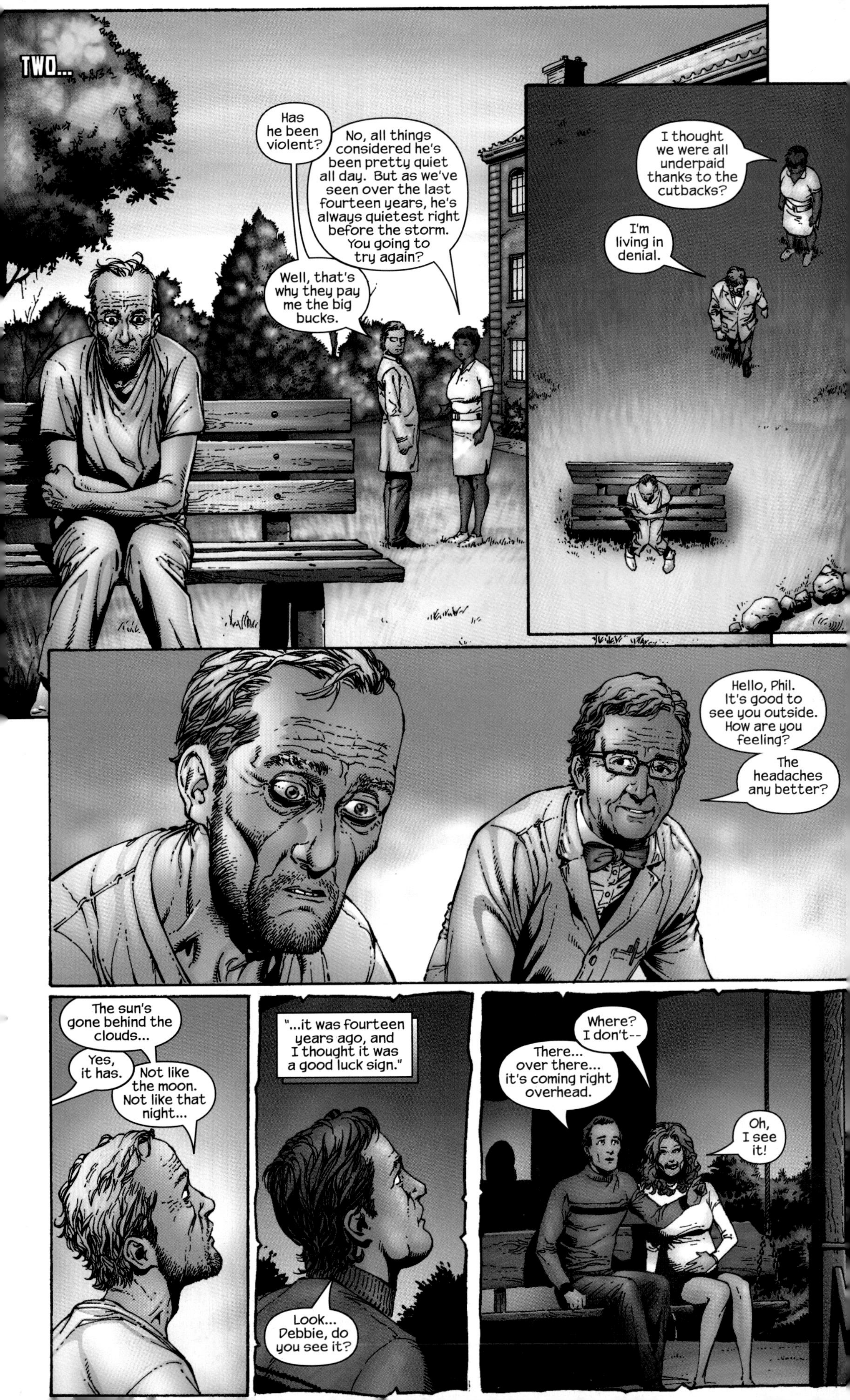
TWO...
Has he been violent?
No, all things considered he's been pretty quiet all day. But as we've seen over the last fourteen years, he's always quietest right before the storm. You going to try again?
Well, that's why they pay me the big bucks.
I thought we were all underpaid thanks to the cutbacks?
I'm living in denial.
Hello, Phil. It's good to see you outside. How are you feeling?
The headaches any better?
The sun's gone behind the clouds...
Yes, it has.
Not like the moon. Not like that night...
"...it was fourteen years ago, and I thought it was a good luck sign."
Look... Debbie, do you see it?
Where? I don't--
There... over there... it's coming right overhead.
Oh, I see it!

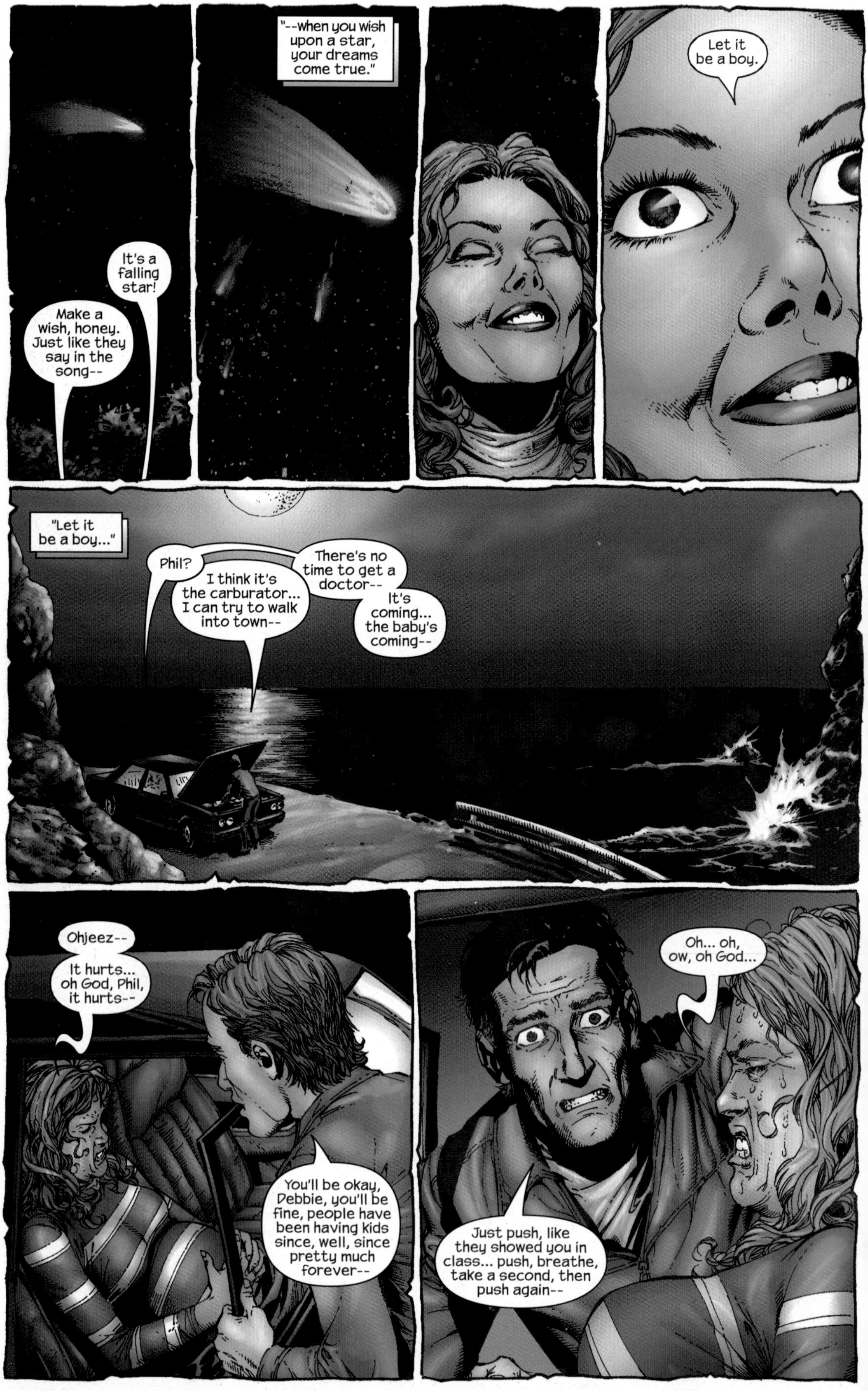
It's a falling star!
Make a wish, honey. Just like they say in the song--
"--when you wish upon a star, your dreams come true."
Let it be a boy.
"Let it be a boy..."
Phil?
I think it's the carburator... I can try to walk into town--
There's no time to get a doctor--
It's coming... the baby's coming--
Ohjeez--
It hurts... oh God, Phil, it hurts--
You'll be okay, Debbie, you'll be fine, people have been having kids since, well, since pretty much forever--
Oh... oh, ow, oh God...
Just push, like they showed you in class... push, breathe, take a second, then push again--

Hunh... hunh... *hunh*...

That's it... that's it, honey--

Oh...ah... owww....

Just a little further... that's it--

Hunh... Phil, I... hunh... HUUURRRKKK!

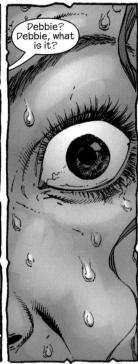

Debbie? Debbie, what is it?

Something... something's wrong...

Something's--

AAAIGGH!!

...oh, God...

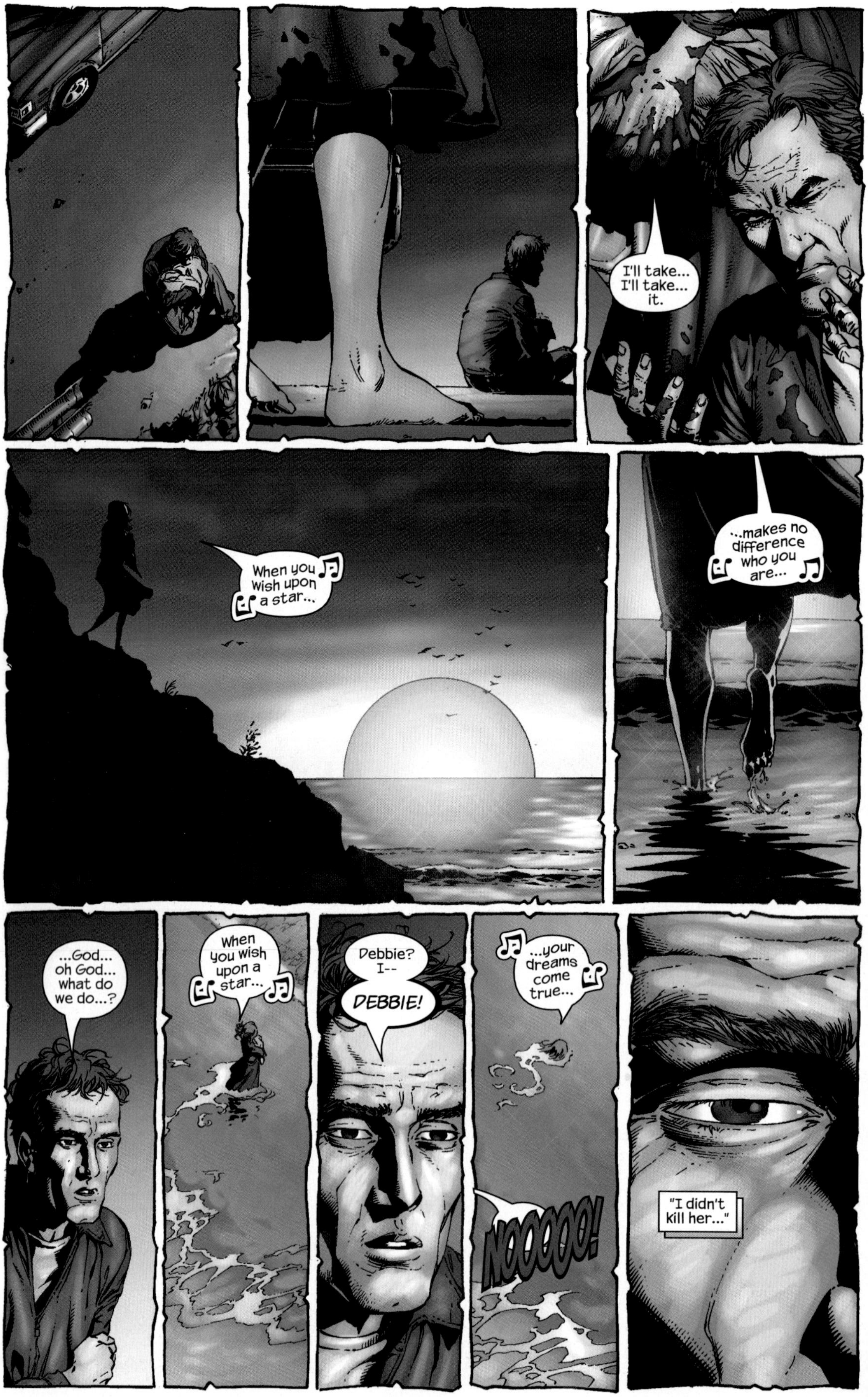

I'll take... I'll take... it.
When you wish upon a star...
...makes no difference who you are...
...God... oh God... what do we do...?
When you wish upon a star...
Debbie? I--
DEBBIE!
...your dreams come true...
NOOOOO!
"I didn't kill her..."

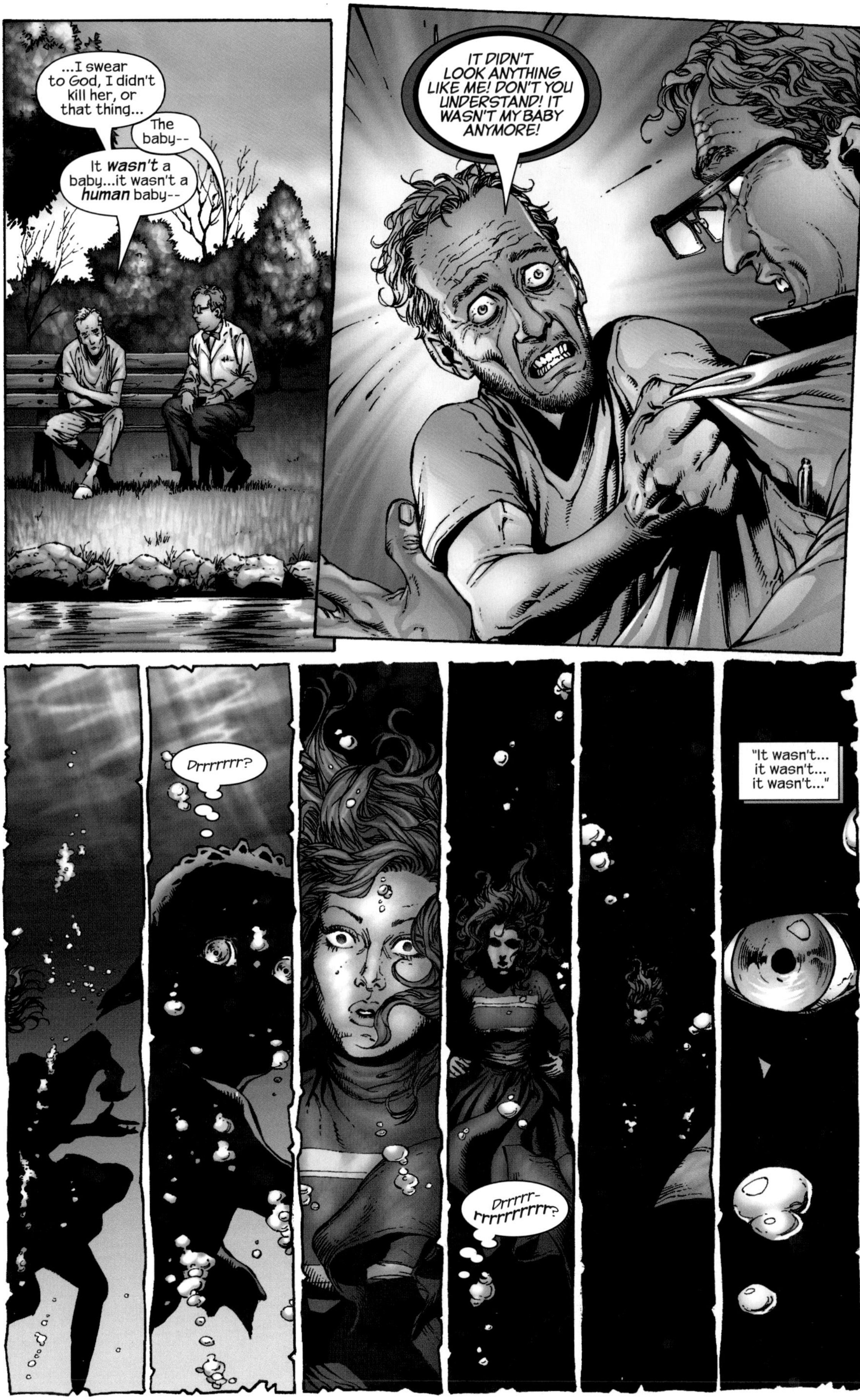
...I swear to God, I didn't kill her, or that thing...
The baby--
It wasn't a baby...it wasn't a human baby--
IT DIDN'T LOOK ANYTHING LIKE ME! DON'T YOU UNDERSTAND! IT WASN'T MY BABY ANYMORE!
Drrrrrrr?
Drrrrr-rrrrrrrrrr?
"It wasn't... it wasn't... it wasn't..."

THREE....

SKREECH!!

Hear that, Rosalie? You know what kind of bird that is?

Oh, and you do?

It's a nighthawk. See, most hawks hunt only during the day. But the prey they're chasing, well, they've got an advantage, because during the day, you can see the hawk's shadow.

Back when I was a boy at my uncle's ranch, we'd make cardboard cutouts of hawks, fly 'em over the chicken coops, and they'd run like the devil himself was after them.

But a hawk that hunts at night, well, you can't see it, can you? Can't see his shadow. Can't stop it.

You're making this up.

I've worked all my life to build up a business, to become successful enough to finally get out of Memphis, to marry a gorgeous wife, have a fine son, you think I'm going to *start* lying *now*?

Well-- Hell, I started that years ago, Rosalie, *years* ago.

Titus Richmond, you are a real pain, you know that?

Ha!

Kyle, you never listen to a word your father tells you about anything, you understand me?

Yes, Mom.

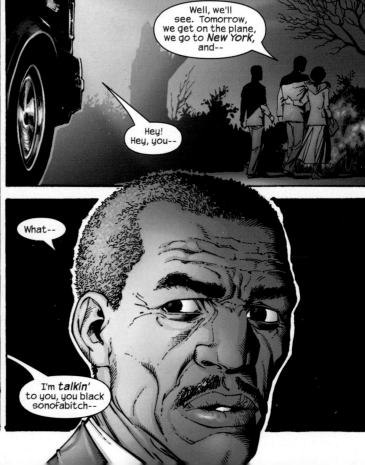

Well, we'll see. Tomorrow, we get on the plane, we go to *New York*, and--

Hey! Hey, you--

What--

I'm *talkin'* to you, you black sonofabitch--

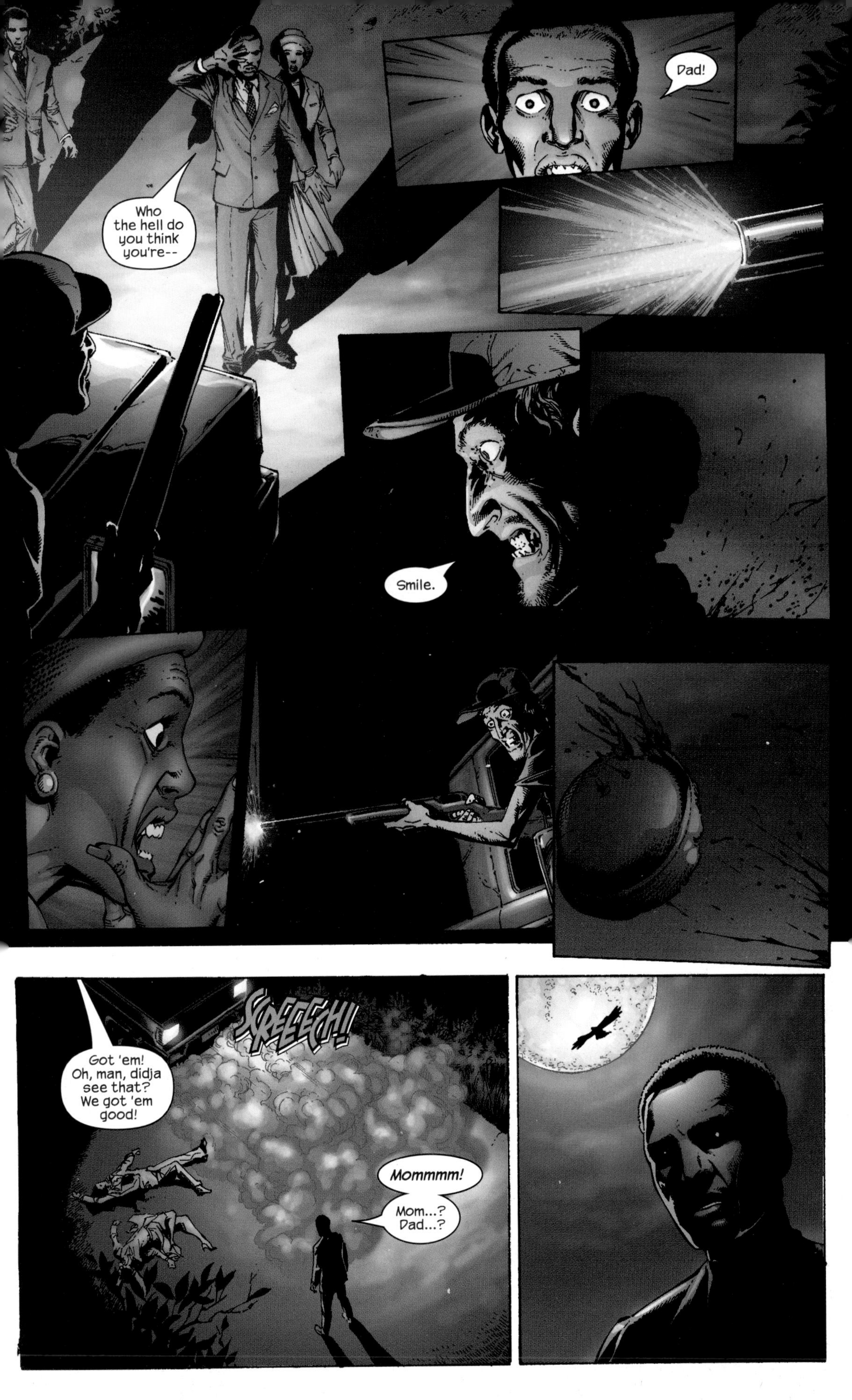
Who the hell do you think you're--
Dad!
Smile.
SCREEECH!
Got 'em! Oh, man, didja see that? We got 'em good!
Mommmm!
Mom...? Dad...?

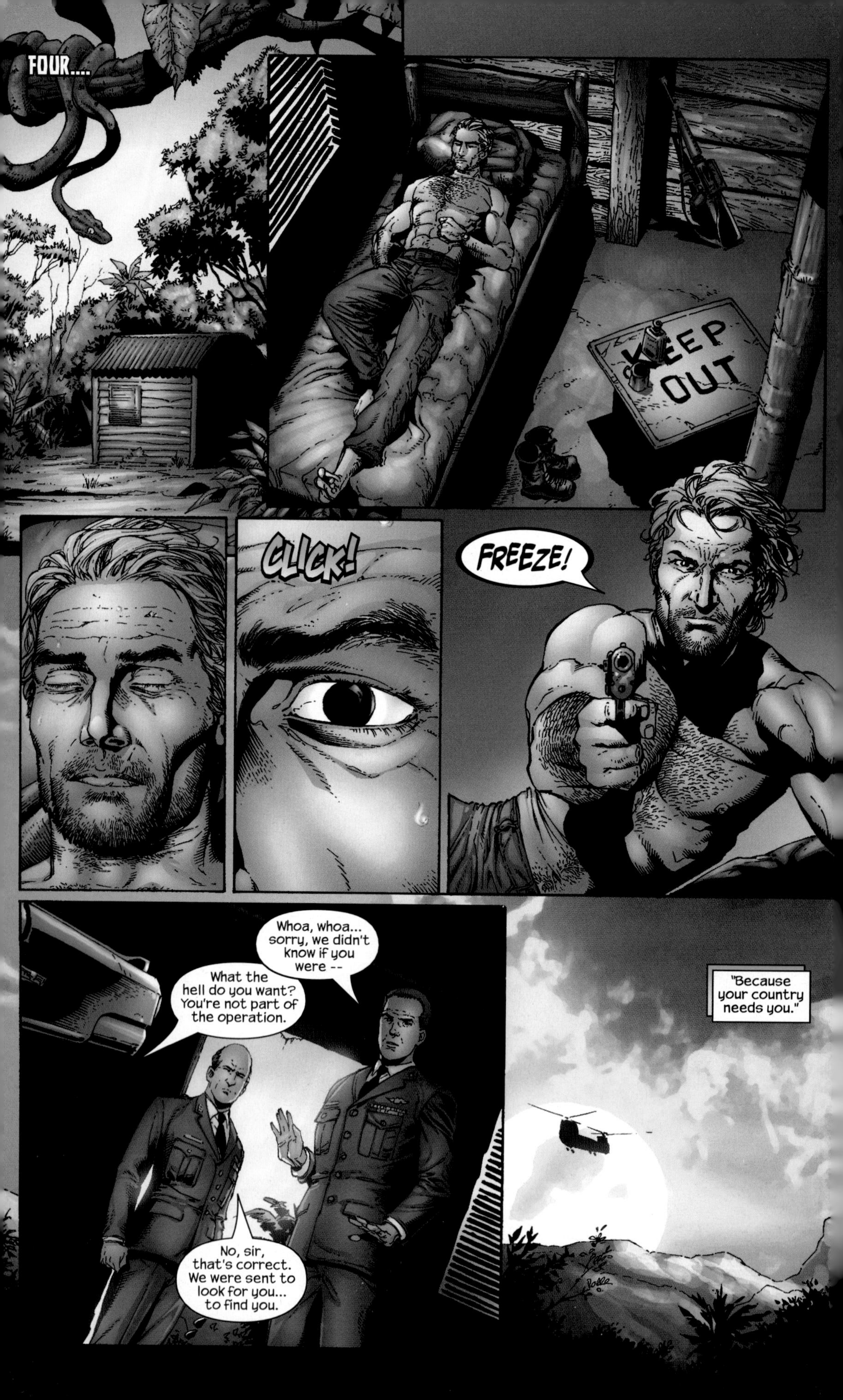
FOUR....
KEEP OUT
CLICK!
FREEZE!
Whoa, whoa... sorry, we didn't know if you were --
What the hell do you want? You're not part of the operation.
No, sir, that's correct. We were sent to look for you... to find you.
"Because your country needs you."

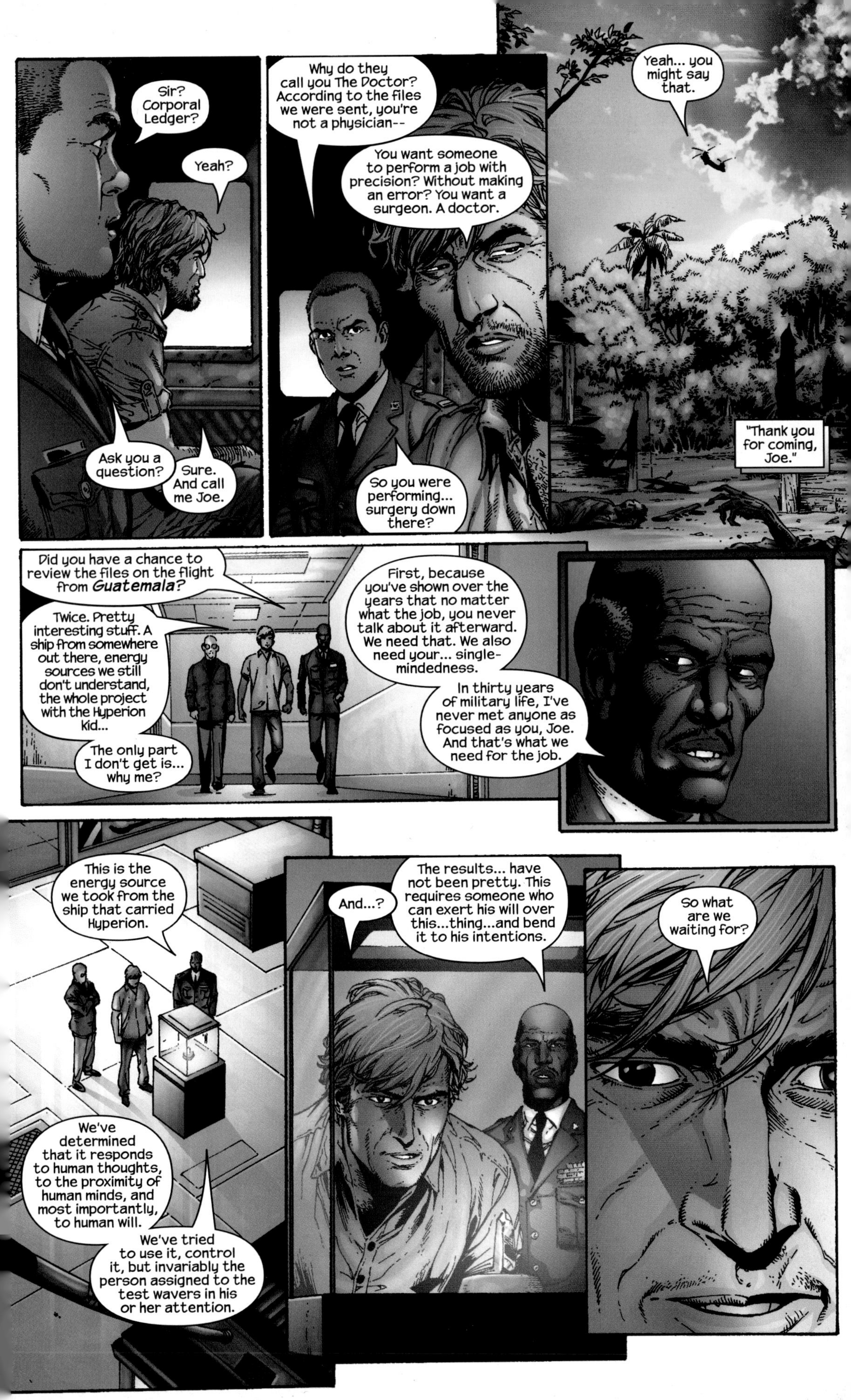
Sir? Corporal Ledger?
Yeah?
Ask you a question?
Sure. And call me Joe.
Why do they call you The Doctor? According to the files we were sent, you're not a physician--
You want someone to perform a job with precision? Without making an error? You want a surgeon. A doctor.
So you were performing... surgery down there?
Yeah... you might say that.
"Thank you for coming, Joe."
Did you have a chance to review the files on the flight from *Guatemala?*
Twice. Pretty interesting stuff. A ship from somewhere out there, energy sources we still don't understand, the whole project with the Hyperion kid...
The only part I don't get is... why me?
First, because you've shown over the years that no matter what the job, you never talk about it afterward. We need that. We also need your... single-mindedness.
In thirty years of military life, I've never met anyone as focused as you, Joe. And that's what we need for the job.
This is the energy source we took from the ship that carried Hyperion.
We've determined that it responds to human thoughts, to the proximity of human minds, and most importantly, to human will.
We've tried to use it, control it, but invariably the person assigned to the test wavers in his or her attention.
And...?
The results... have not been pretty. This requires someone who can exert his will over this...thing...and bend it to his intentions.
So what are we waiting for?

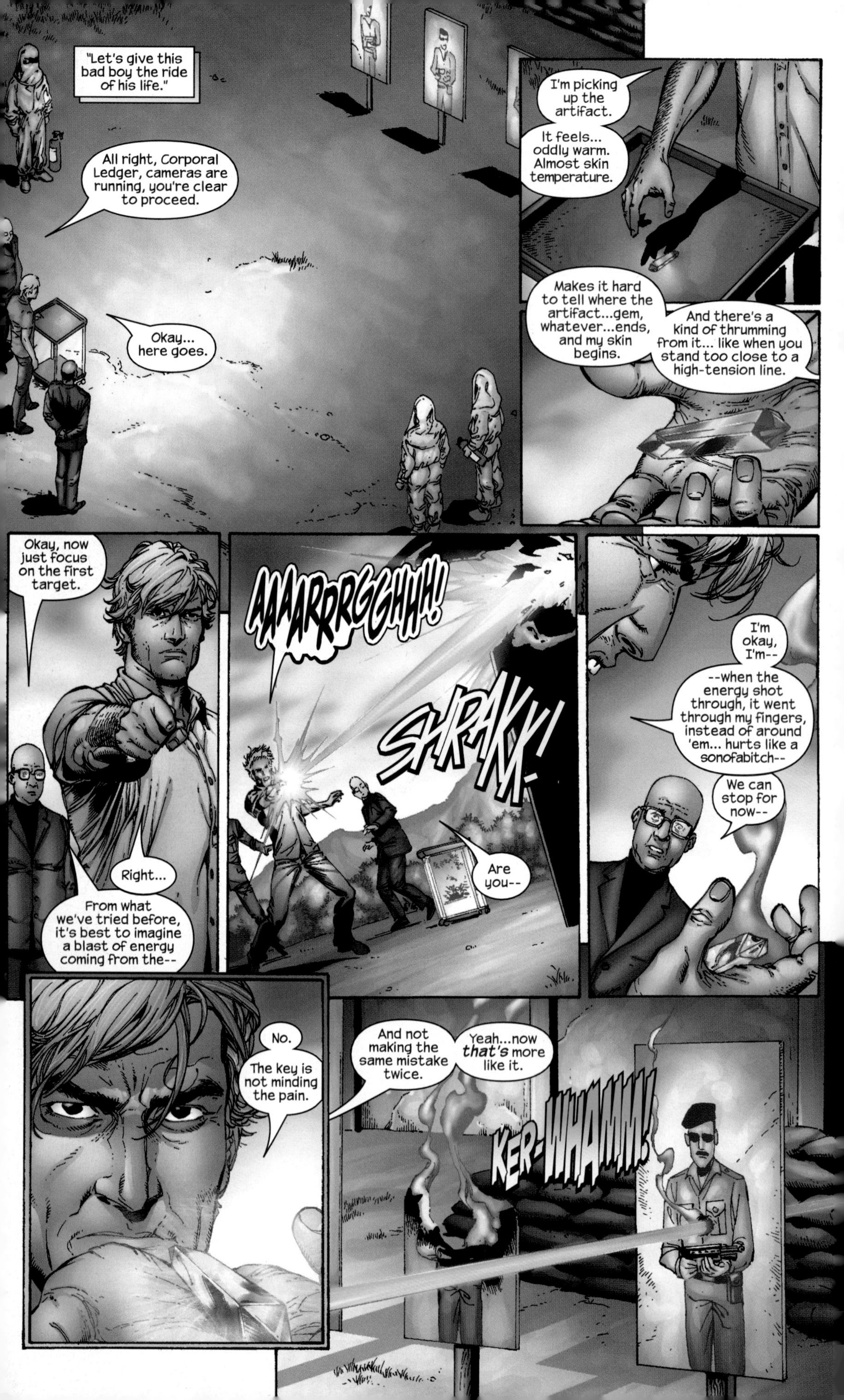
"Let's give this bad boy the ride of his life."
All right, Corporal Ledger, cameras are running, you're clear to proceed.
Okay... here goes.
I'm picking up the artifact.
It feels... oddly warm. Almost skin temperature.
Makes it hard to tell where the artifact...gem, whatever...ends, and my skin begins.
And there's a kind of thrumming from it... like when you stand too close to a high-tension line.
Okay, now just focus on the first target.
Right...
From what we've tried before, it's best to imagine a blast of energy coming from the--
AAAARRRGGHHH!
SHRAKK!
Are you--
I'm okay, I'm--
--when the energy shot through, it went through my fingers, instead of around 'em... hurts like a sonofabitch--
We can stop for now--
No.
The key is not minding the pain.
And not making the same mistake twice.
Yeah...now *that's* more like it.
KER-WHAMM!

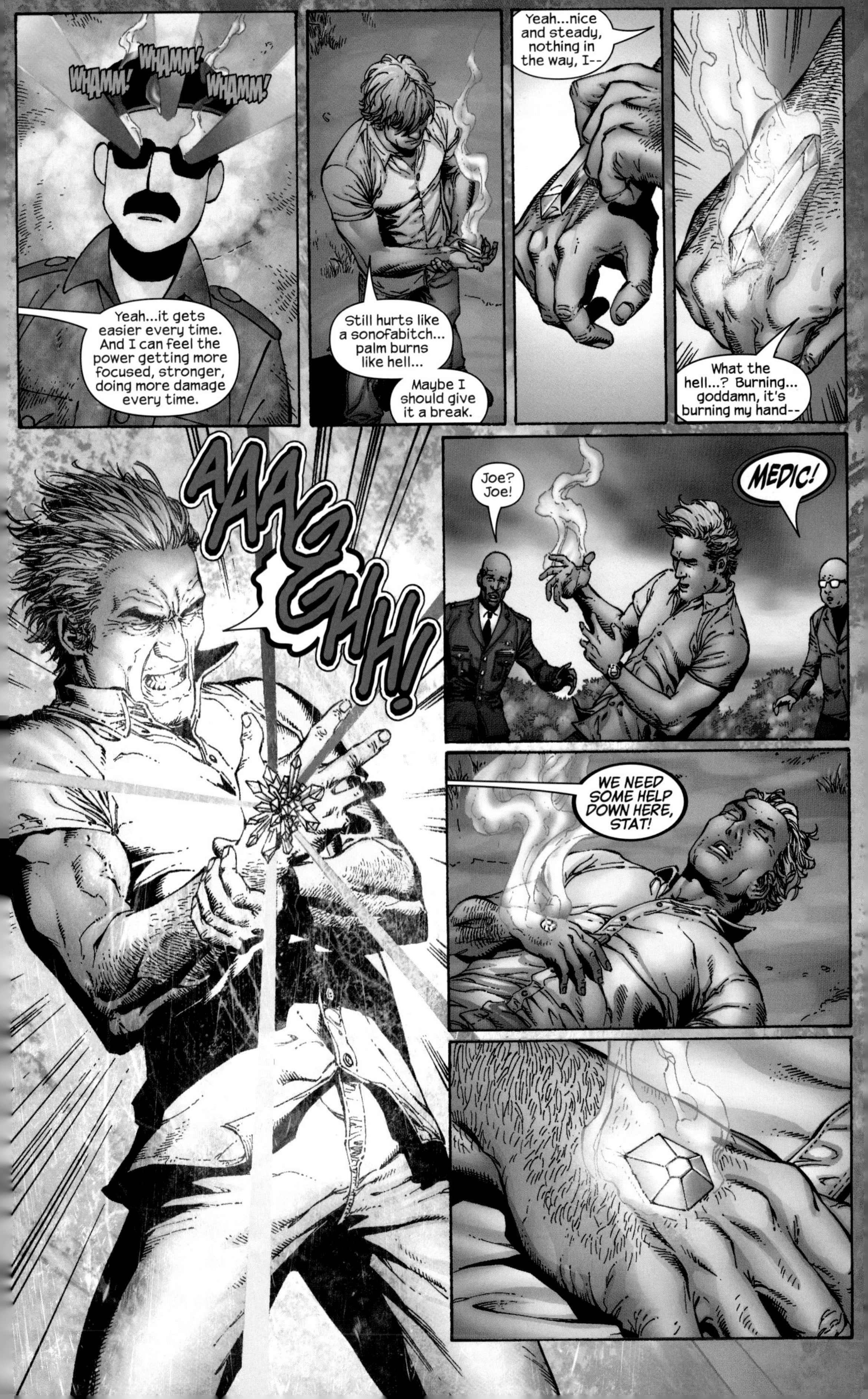
WHAMM! WHAMM! WHAMM!
Yeah...it gets easier every time. And I can feel the power getting more focused, stronger, doing more damage every time.
Still hurts like a sonofabitch... palm burns like hell...
Maybe I should give it a break.
Yeah...nice and steady, nothing in the way, I--
What the hell...? Burning... goddamn, it's burning my hand--
AAAGHH!
Joe? Joe!
MEDIC!
WE NEED SOME HELP DOWN HERE, STAT!

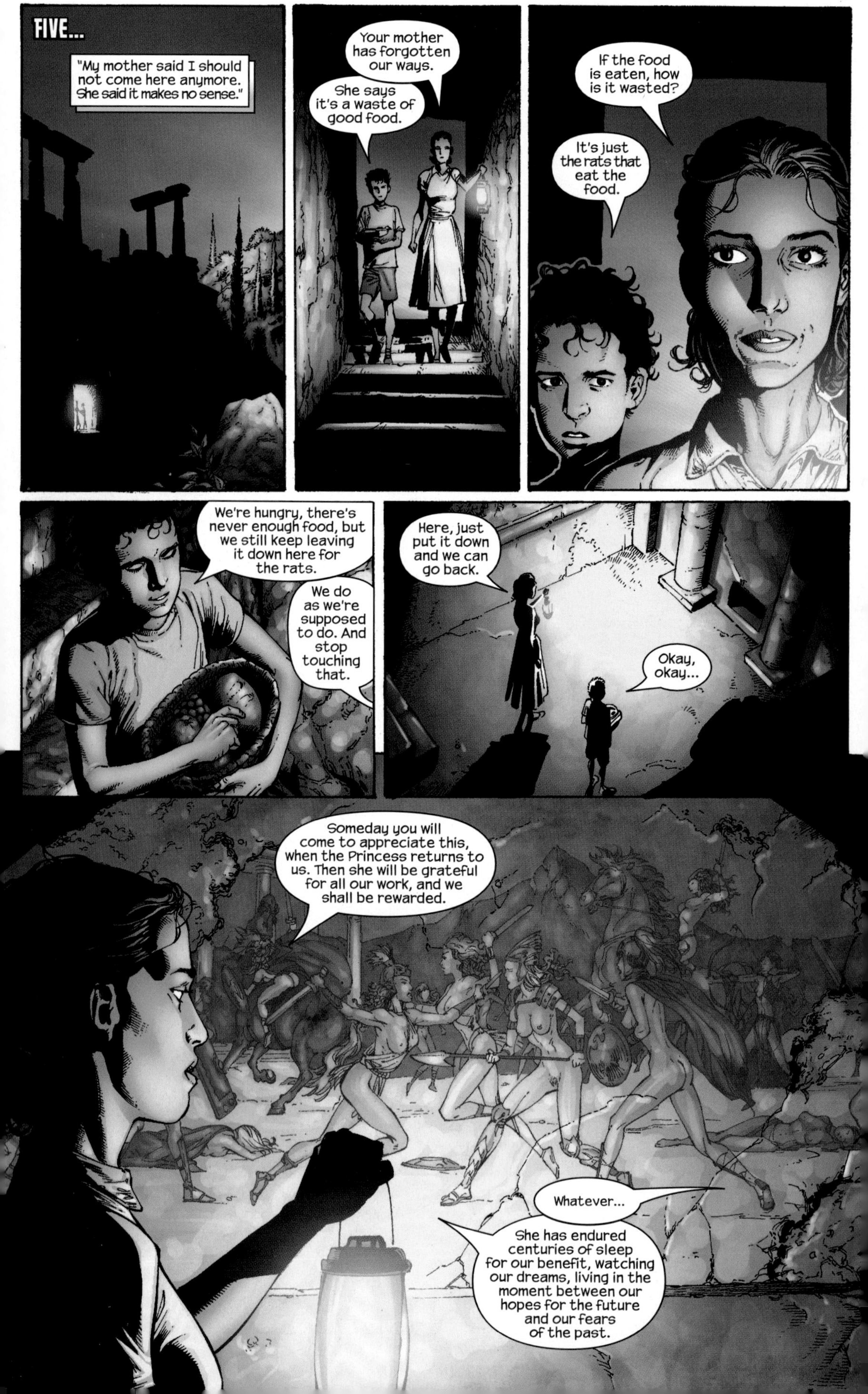

FIVE...
"My mother said I should not come here anymore. She said it makes no sense."
She says it's a waste of good food.
Your mother has forgotten our ways.
If the food is eaten, how is it wasted?
It's just the rats that eat the food.
We're hungry, there's never enough food, but we still keep leaving it down here for the rats.
We do as we're supposed to do. And stop touching that.
Here, just put it down and we can go back.
Okay, okay...
Someday you will come to appreciate this, when the Princess returns to us. Then she will be grateful for all our work, and we shall be rewarded.
Whatever...
She has endured centuries of sleep for our benefit, watching our dreams, living in the moment between our hopes for the future and our fears of the past.

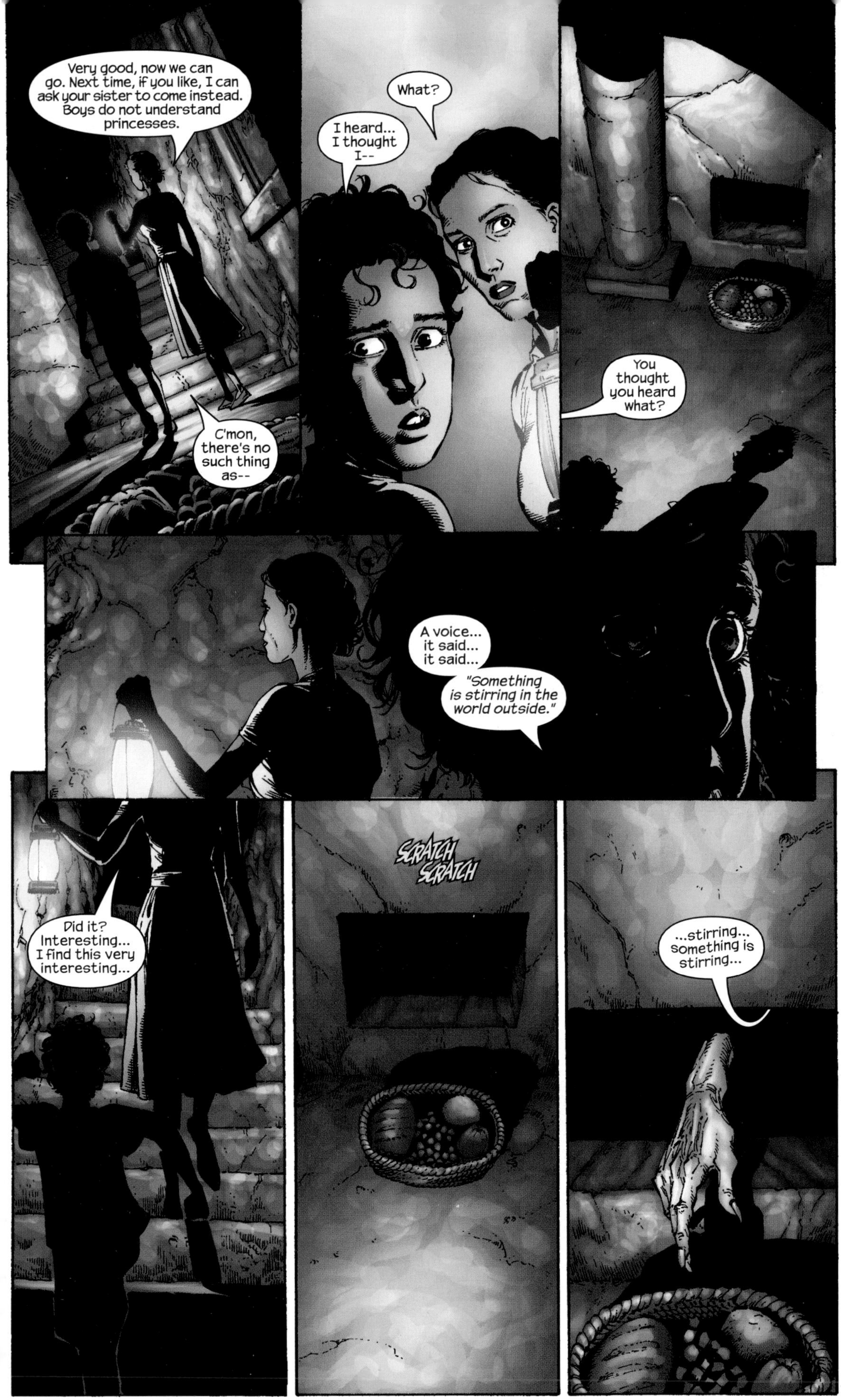
Very good, now we can go. Next time, if you like, I can ask your sister to come instead. Boys do not understand princesses.
C'mon, there's no such thing as--
What?
I heard... I thought I--
You thought you heard what?
A voice... it said... it said...
"Something is stirring in the world outside."
Did it? Interesting... I find this very interesting...
SCRATCH SCRATCH
...stirring... something is stirring...

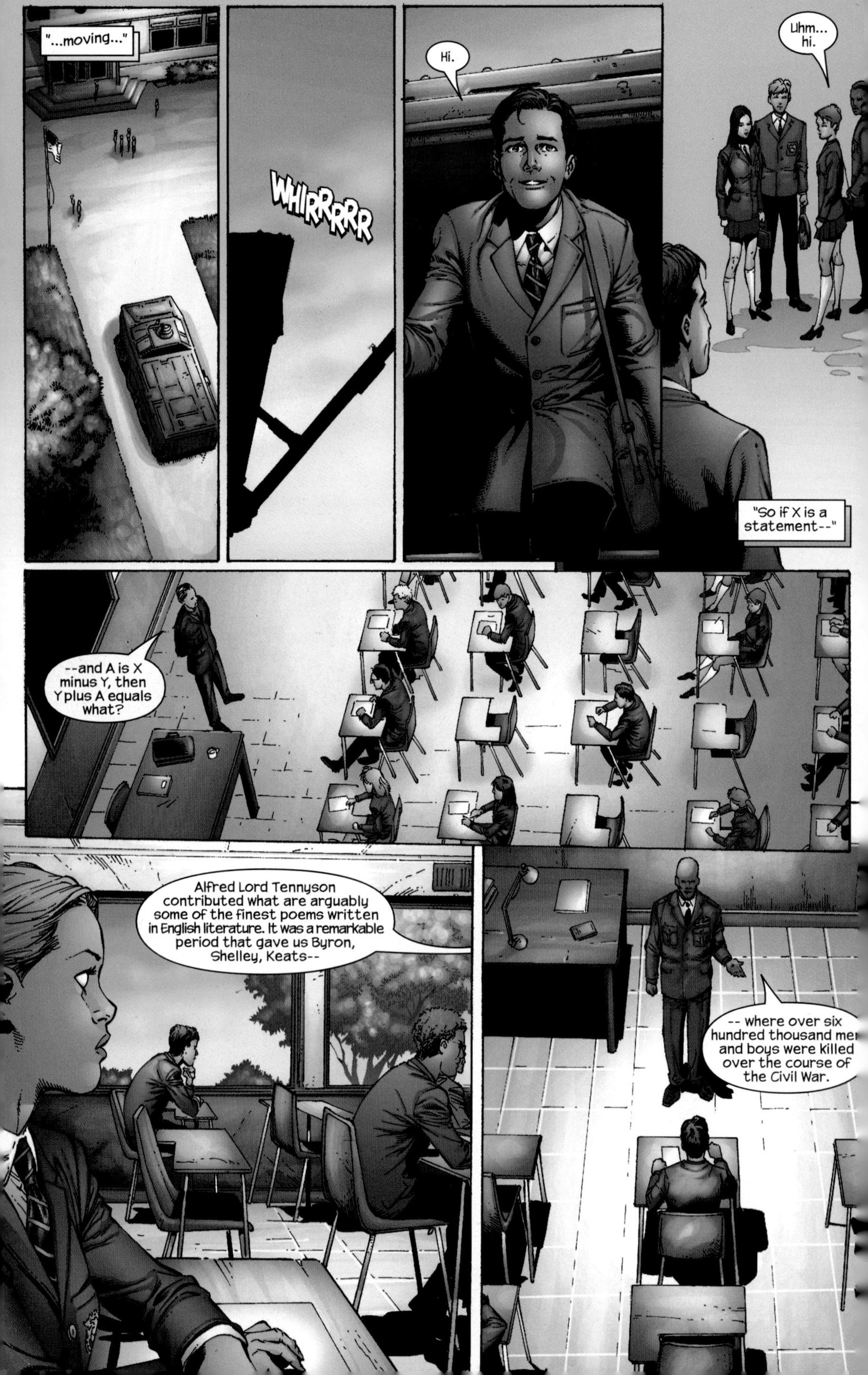
"...moving..."
WHIRRRRR
Hi.
Uhm... hi.
"So if X is a statement--"
--and A is X minus Y, then Y plus A equals what?
Alfred Lord Tennyson contributed what are arguably some of the finest poems written in English literature. It was a remarkable period that gave us Byron, Shelley, Keats--
-- where over six hundred thousand me
and boys were killed over the course of the Civil War.

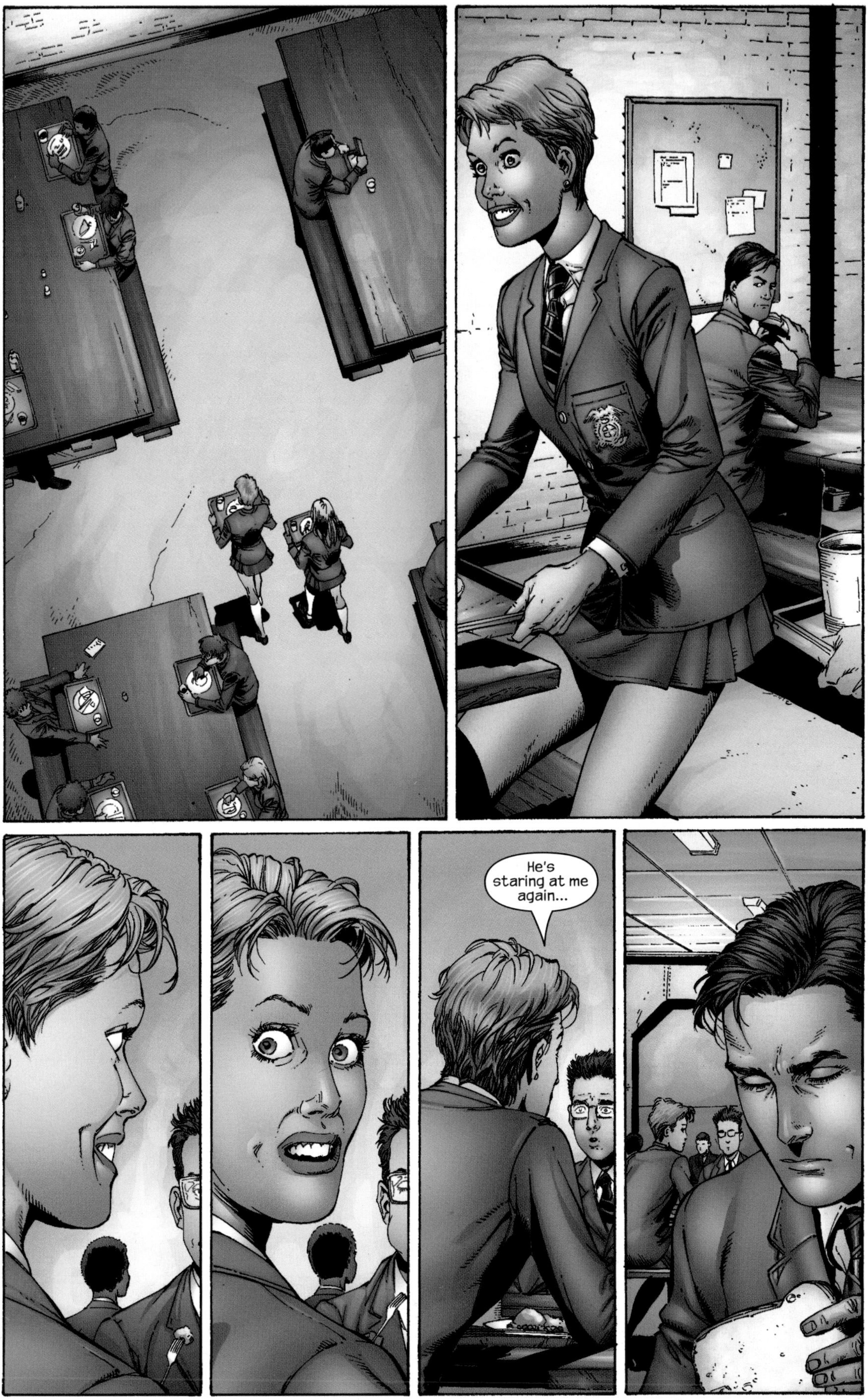
He's staring at me again...

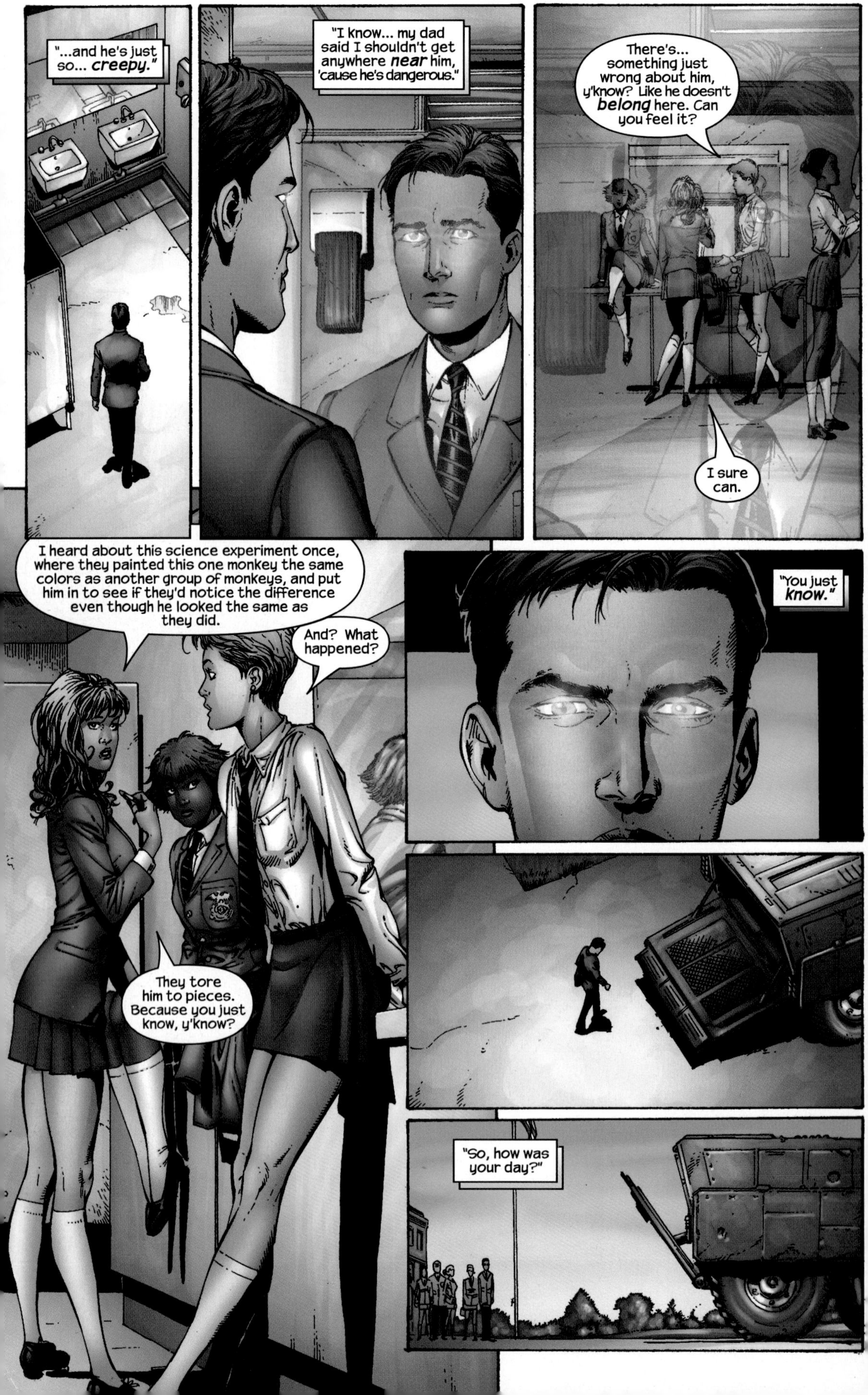
"...and he's just so... creepy."
"I know... my dad said I shouldn't get anywhere near him, 'cause he's dangerous."
There's... something just wrong about him, y'know? Like he doesn't belong here. Can you feel it?
I sure can.
I heard about this science experiment once, where they painted this one monkey the same colors as another group of monkeys, and put him in to see if they'd notice the difference even though he looked the same as they did.
And? What happened?
They tore him to pieces. Because you just know, y'know?
"You just know."
"So, how was your day?"

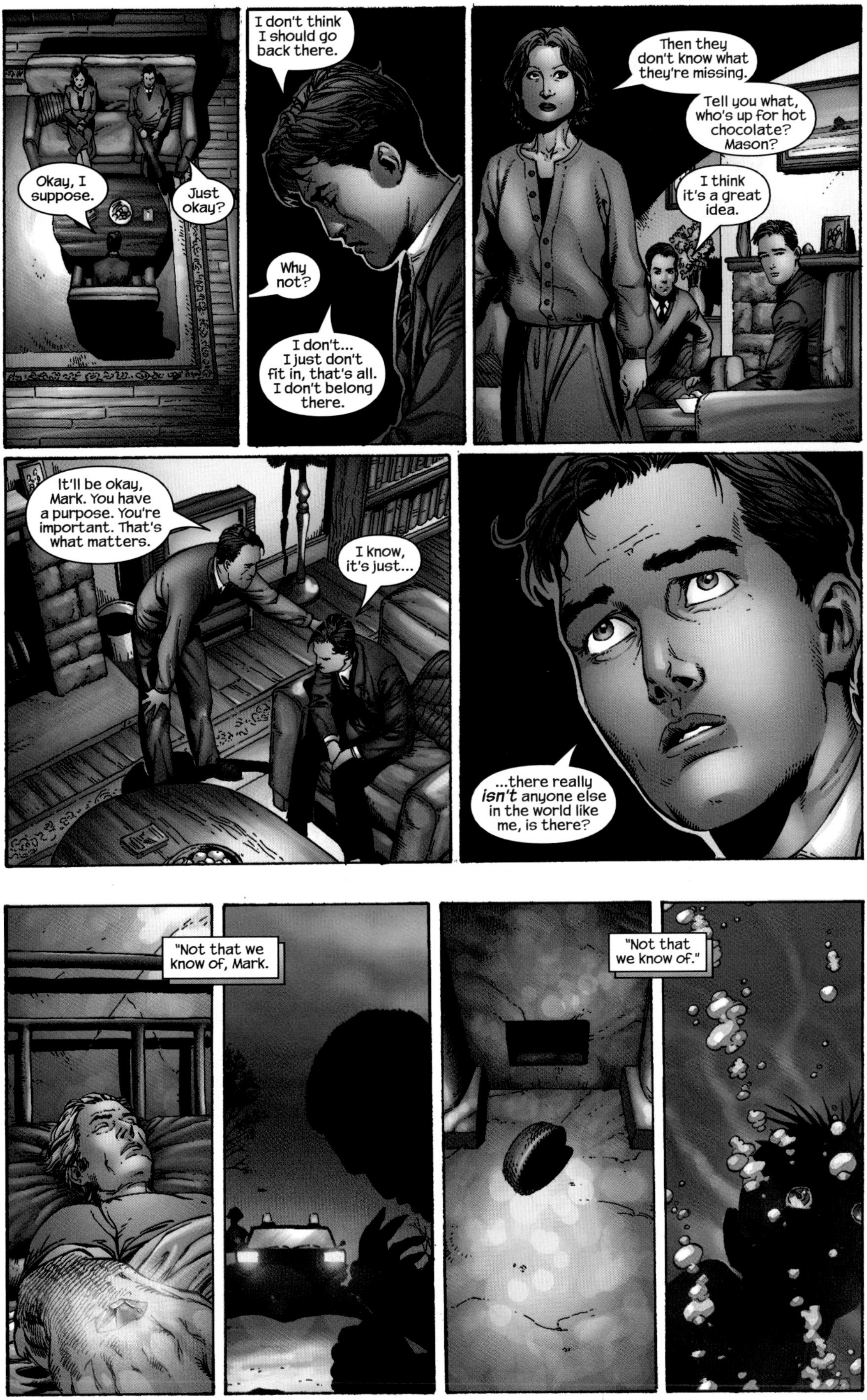
Okay, I suppose.
Just okay?
I don't think I should go back there.
Why not?
I don't... I just don't fit in, that's all. I don't belong there.
Then they don't know what they're missing.
Tell you what, who's up for hot chocolate? Mason?
I think it's a great idea.
It'll be okay, Mark. You have a purpose. You're important. That's what matters.
I know, it's just...
...there really *isn't* anyone else in the world like me, is there?
"Not that we know of, Mark.
"Not that we know of."

#3

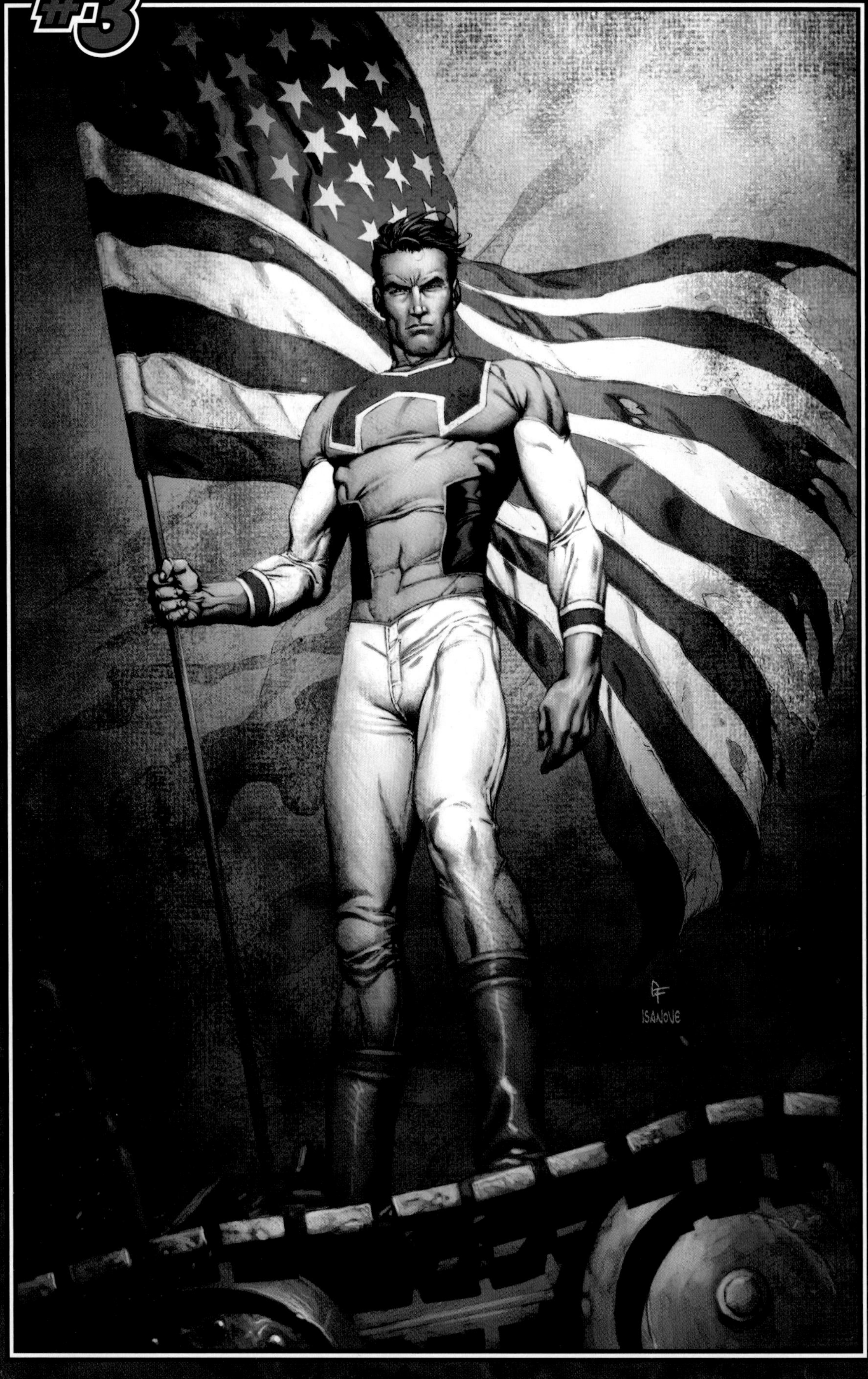
ISANOVE

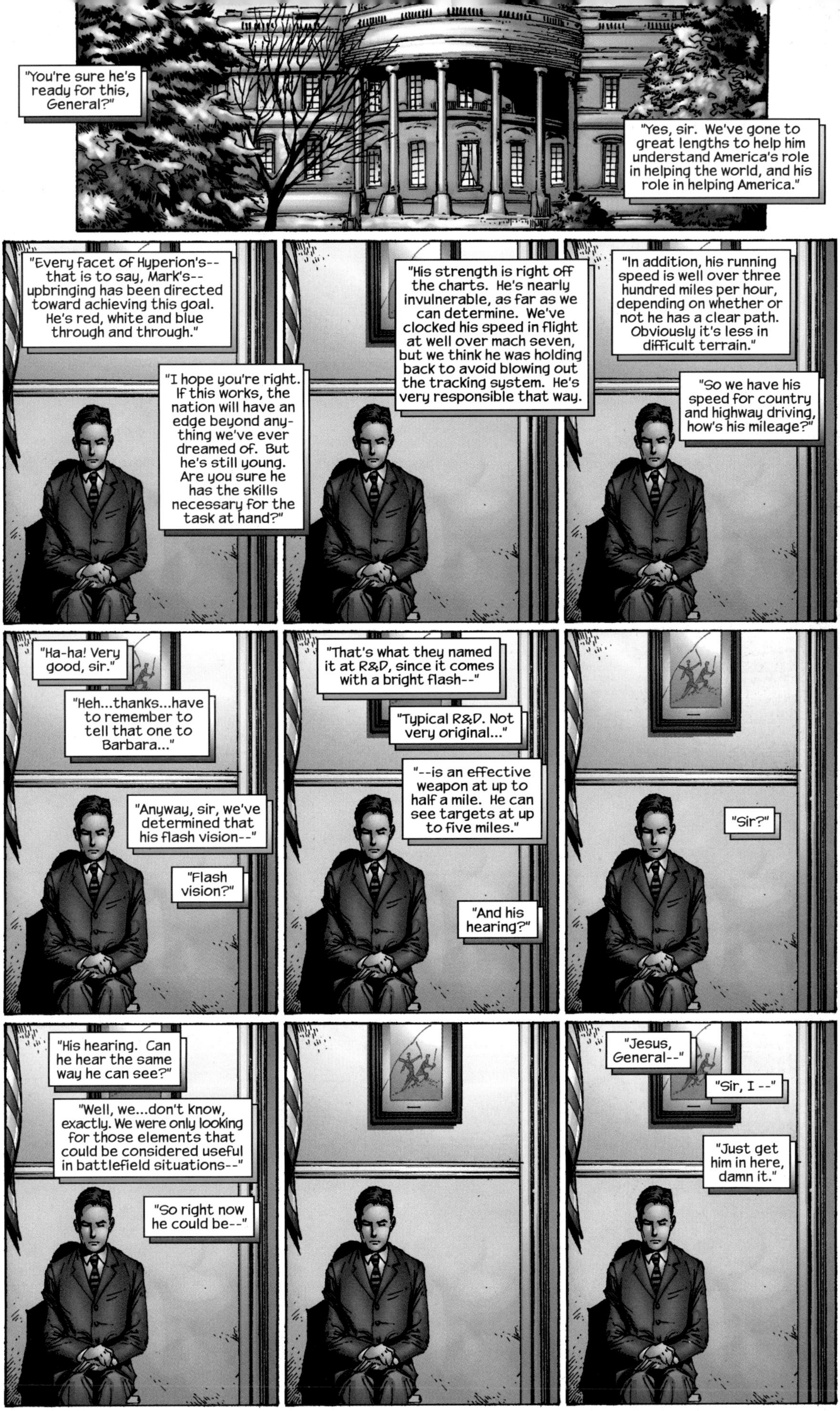
"You're sure he's ready for this, General?"
"Yes, sir. We've gone to great lengths to help him understand America's role in helping the world, and his role in helping America."
"Every facet of Hyperion's--that is to say, Mark's--upbringing has been directed toward achieving this goal. He's red, white and blue through and through."
"I hope you're right. If this works, the nation will have an edge beyond anything we've ever dreamed of. But he's still young. Are you sure he has the skills necessary for the task at hand?"
"His strength is right off the charts. He's nearly invulnerable, as far as we can determine. We've clocked his speed in flight at well over mach seven, but we think he was holding back to avoid blowing out the tracking system. He's very responsible that way.
"In addition, his running speed is well over three hundred miles per hour, depending on whether or not he has a clear path. Obviously it's less in difficult terrain."
"So we have his speed for country and highway driving, how's his mileage?"
"Ha-ha! Very good, sir."
"Heh...thanks...have to remember to tell that one to Barbara..."
"Anyway, sir, we've determined that his flash vision--"
"Flash vision?"
"That's what they named it at R&D, since it comes with a bright flash--"
"Typical R&D. Not very original..."
"--is an effective weapon at up to half a mile. He can see targets at up to five miles."
"And his hearing?"
"Sir?"
"His hearing. Can he hear the same way he can see?"
"Well, we...don't know, exactly. We were only looking for those elements that could be considered useful in battlefield situations--"
"So right now he could be--"
"Jesus, General--"
"Sir, I --"
"Just get him in here, damn it."

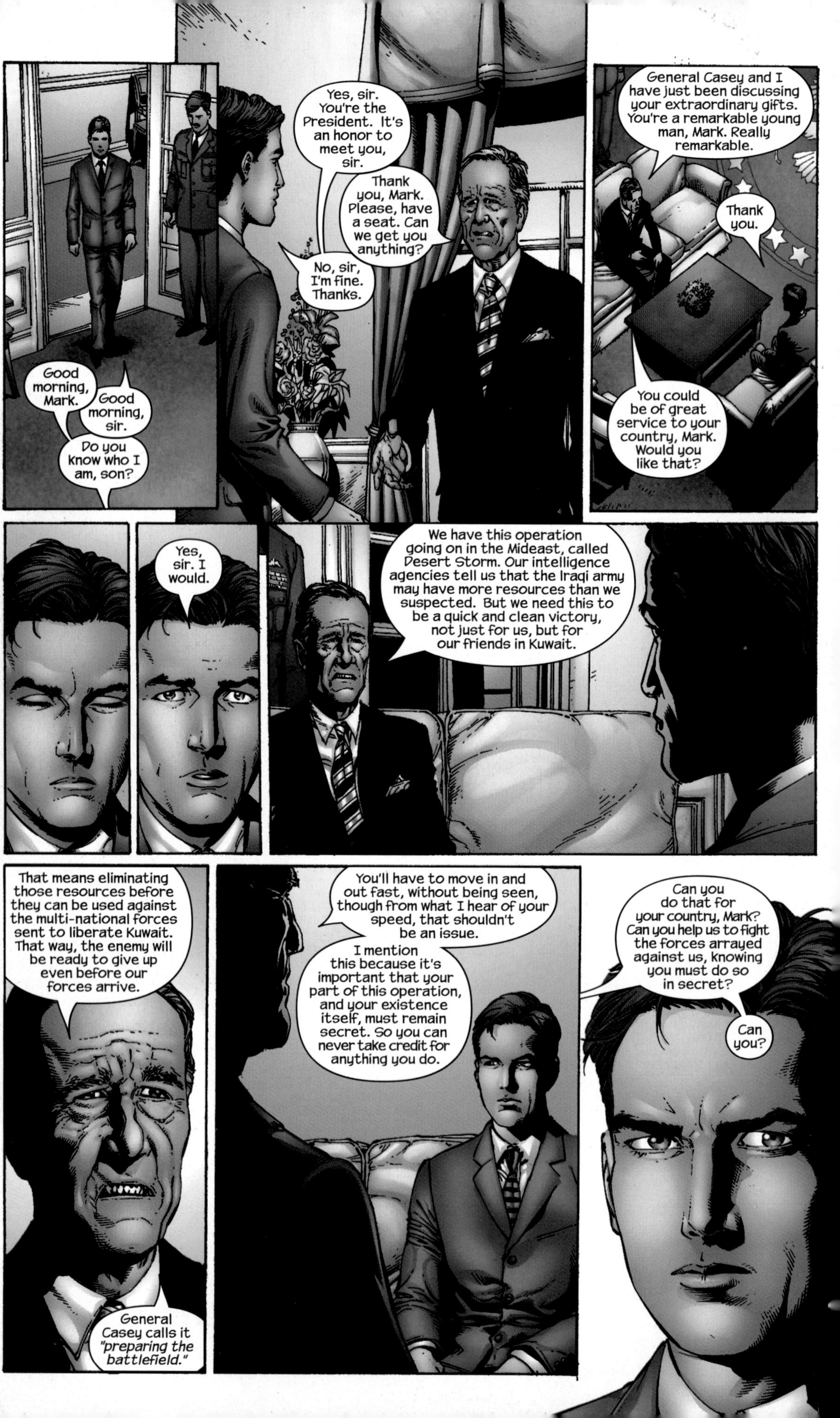
Good morning, Mark.
Good morning, sir.
Do you know who I am, son?
Yes, sir. You're the President. It's an honor to meet you, sir.
Thank you, Mark. Please, have a seat. Can we get you anything?
No, sir, I'm fine. Thanks.
General Casey and I have just been discussing your extraordinary gifts. You're a remarkable young man, Mark. Really remarkable.
Thank you.
You could be of great service to your country, Mark. Would you like that?
Yes, sir. I would.
We have this operation going on in the Mideast, called Desert Storm. Our intelligence agencies tell us that the Iraqi army may have more resources than we suspected. But we need this to be a quick and clean victory, not just for us, but for our friends in Kuwait.
That means eliminating those resources before they can be used against the multi-national forces sent to liberate Kuwait. That way, the enemy will be ready to give up even before our forces arrive.
General Casey calls it *"preparing the battlefield."*
You'll have to move in and out fast, without being seen, though from what I hear of your speed, that shouldn't be an issue.
I mention this because it's important that your part of this operation, and your existence itself, must remain secret. So you can never take credit for anything you do.
Can you do that for your country, Mark? Can you help us to fight the forces arrayed against us, knowing you must do so in secret?
Can you?

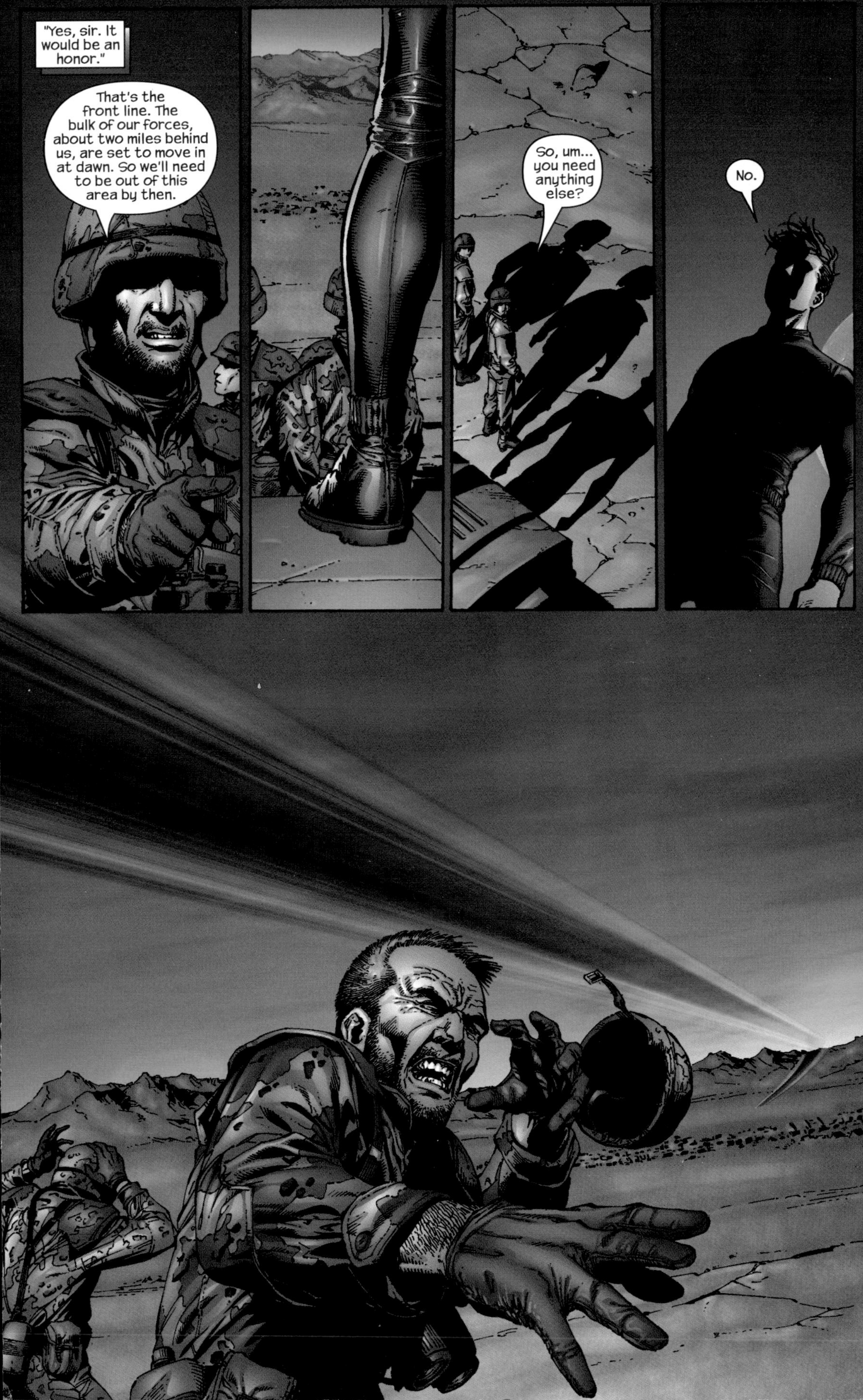
"Yes, sir. It would be an honor."
That's the front line. The bulk of our forces, about two miles behind us, are set to move in at dawn. So we'll need to be out of this area by then.
So, um... you need anything else?
No.

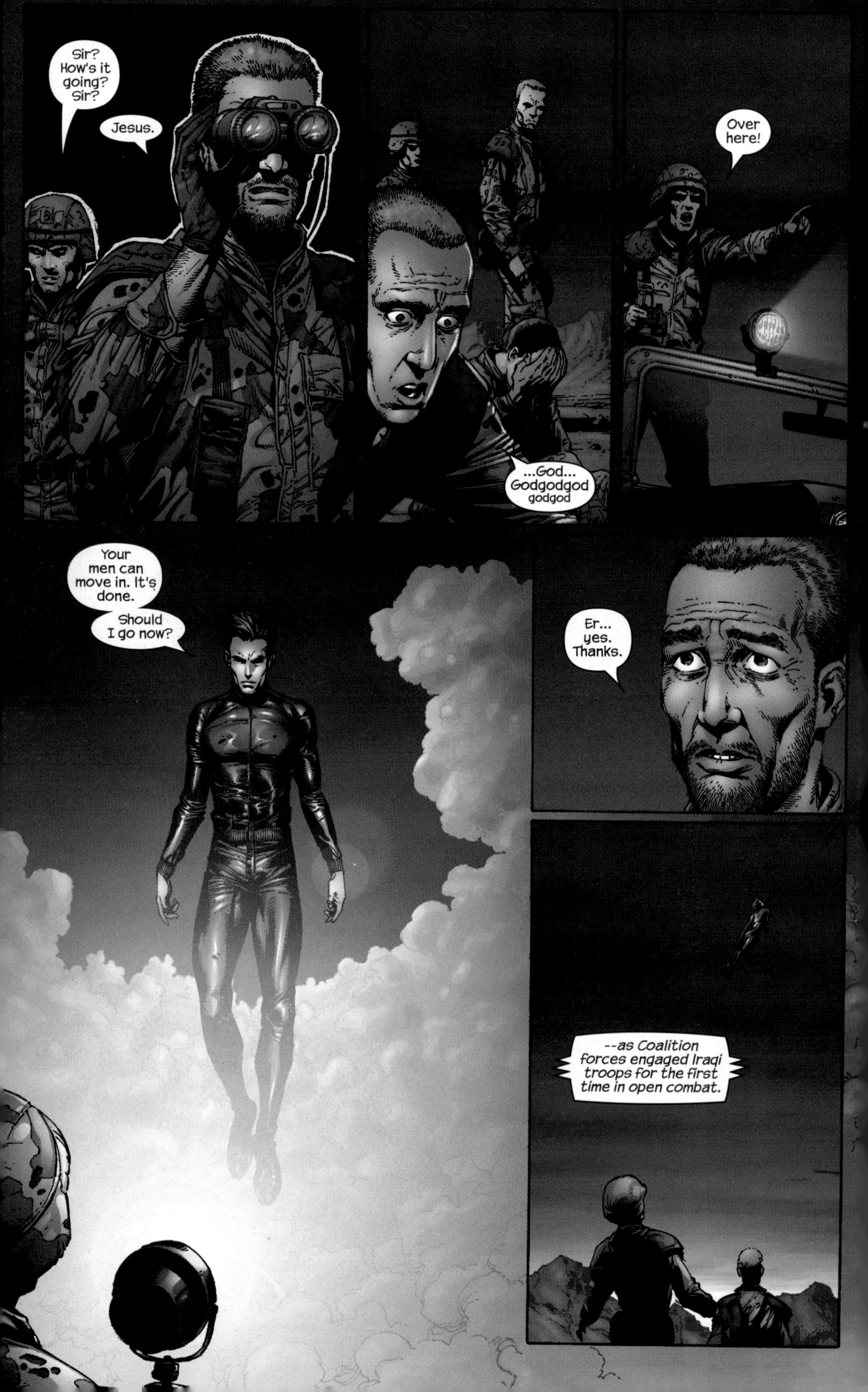
Sir? How's it going? Sir?
Jesus.
...God... Godgodgod godgod
Over here!
Your men can move in. It's done.
Should I go now?
Er... yes. Thanks.
--as Coalition forces engaged Iraqi troops for the first time in open combat.

To the astonishment of many American soldiers, opposition was surprisingly light, and the barely-armed Iraqi troops they encountered were quick to surrender.

This reconnaissance footage shows that what little armored vehicles and weaponry the Iraqi soldiers did possess had been eliminated during the night--

--presumably by laser-guided Cruise and Tomahawk Missiles launched by Coalition forces.

General Norman Schwartzkopf indicated that he was cautiously optimistic about the campaign based on successes to date.

RESISTANCE PRESUMABLY ELIMINATED BY CRUISE/TOMAHAWK MISSILES

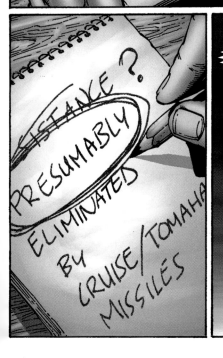

SISTANCE? PRESUMABLY ELIMINATED BY CRUISE/TOMAHAWK MISSILES

Schwartzkopf added, "There can be no question that today, American forces are in complete control of the skies over Iraq."

RESISTANCE PRESUMABLY ELIMINATED BY CRUISE/TOMAHAWK MISSILES

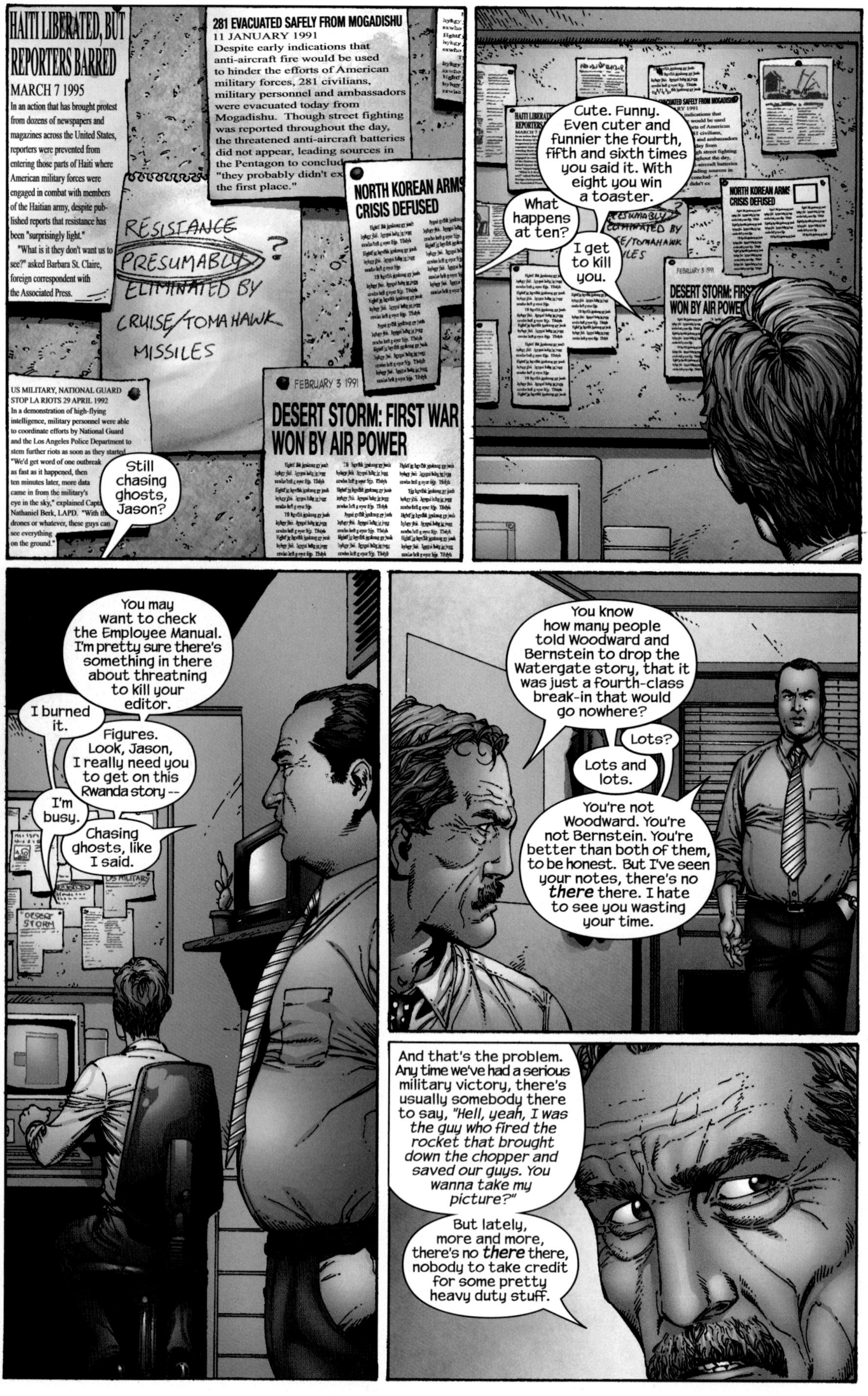
HAITI LIBERATED, BUT REPORTERS BARRED
MARCH 7 1995
In an action that has brought protest from dozens of newspapers and magazines across the United States, reporters were prevented from entering those parts of Haiti where American military forces were engaged in combat with members of the Haitian army, despite published reports that resistance has been "surprisingly light."
"What is it they don't want us to see?" asked Barbara St. Claire, foreign correspondent with the Associated Press.
281 EVACUATED SAFELY FROM MOGADISHU
11 JANUARY 1991
Despite early indications that anti-aircraft fire would be used to hinder the efforts of American military forces, 281 civilians, military personnel and ambassadors were evacuated today from Mogadishu. Though street fighting was reported throughout the day, the threatened anti-aircraft batteries did not appear, leading sources in the Pentagon to conclud "they probably didn't ex the first place."
RESISTANCE PRESUMABLY ? ELIMINATED BY CRUISE/TOMAHAWK MISSILES
NORTH KOREAN ARMS CRISIS DEFUSED
US MILITARY, NATIONAL GUARD STOP LA RIOTS 29 APRIL 1992
In a demonstration of high-flying intelligence, military personnel were able to coordinate efforts by National Guard and the Los Angeles Police Department to stem further riots as soon as they started. "We'd get word of one outbreak as fast as it happened, then ten minutes later, more data came in from the military's eye in the sky," explained Capta Nathaniel Berk, LAPD. "With th drones or whatever, these guys can see everything on the ground."
FEBRUARY 3 1991
DESERT STORM: FIRST WAR WON BY AIR POWER
Still chasing ghosts, Jason?
Cute. Funny. Even cuter and funnier the fourth, fifth and sixth times you said it. With eight you win a toaster.
What happens at ten?
I get to kill you.
You may want to check the Employee Manual. I'm pretty sure there's something in there about threatning to kill your editor.
I burned it.
Figures. Look, Jason, I really need you to get on this Rwanda story --
I'm busy.
Chasing ghosts, like I said.
You know how many people told Woodward and Bernstein to drop the Watergate story, that it was just a fourth-class break-in that would go nowhere?
Lots?
Lots and lots.
You're not Woodward. You're not Bernstein. You're better than both of them, to be honest. But I've seen your notes, there's no *there* there. I hate to see you wasting your time.
And that's the problem. Any time we've had a serious military victory, there's usually somebody there to say, *"Hell, yeah, I was the guy who fired the rocket that brought down the chopper and saved our guys. You wanna take my picture?"*
But lately, more and more, there's no *there* there, nobody to take credit for some pretty heavy duty stuff.

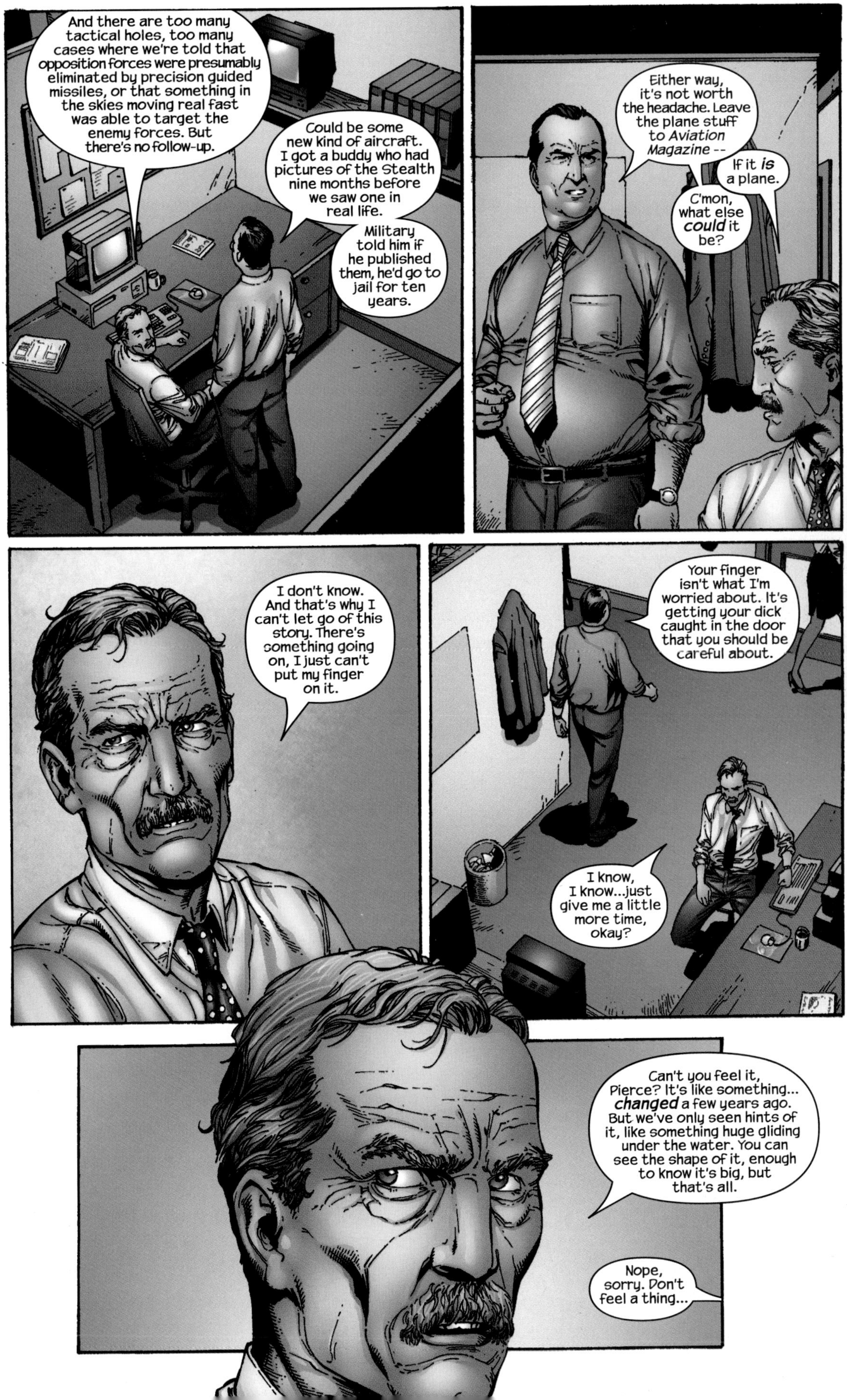

And there are too many tactical holes, too many cases where we're told that opposition forces were presumably eliminated by precision guided missiles, or that something in the skies moving real fast was able to target the enemy forces. But there's no follow-up.
Could be some new kind of aircraft. I got a buddy who had pictures of the Stealth nine months before we saw one in real life.
Military told him if he published them, he'd go to jail for ten years.
Either way, it's not worth the headache. Leave the plane stuff to *Aviation Magazine* --
If it **is** a plane.
C'mon, what else **could** it be?
I don't know. And that's why I can't let go of this story. There's something going on, I just can't put my finger on it.
Your finger isn't what I'm worried about. It's getting your dick caught in the door that you should be careful about.
I know, I know...just give me a little more time, okay?
Can't you feel it, Pierce? It's like something... ***changed*** a few years ago. But we've only seen hints of it, like something huge gliding under the water. You can see the shape of it, enough to know it's big, but that's all.
Nope, sorry. Don't feel a thing...

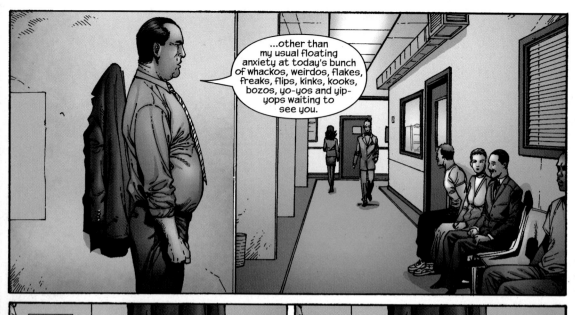

...other than my usual floating anxiety at today's bunch of whackos, weirdos, flakes, freaks, flips, kinks, kooks, bozos, yo-yos and yip-yops waiting to see you.

"Happy hunting, Ahab..."

--which is when me and Jimmy were taken up by the aliens. They said they were gonna help us bring the world to the next level by telling us the meaning of life so we could sell it and make a lot of money. You got any donuts?

It's all strictly black ops, and if I tell you, they'll have to kill *both* of us, and I've been dead once already, and I didn't like it. Don't ask, I can't tell you about that one either.

Desert Storm was a hoax, designed to let the U.S. take over huge parts of the Mideast. Same with the moon landing. C'mon, you think we're gonna send guys that far for rocks?

I got a friend of a friend who said he heard somebody he knows in the military talking about something called Project Hyperion. It may be nothing, but --

--and the military's got these bases in the earth's core, which is hollow, and that's why we get so many earthquakes lately --

I've written a rather scholarly work on this very subject, "*The Psychological Impact of America as a Proto-Empire on Strategic Allies in the Twentieth Century.*" I can send you a copy if you mention the book in your article.

-- and when the alien ship crashed, we found this baby in the wreck, not even hurt. We took him with us, but then the military came in black helicopters and took him away. We think they may still have him. My doctor says I shouldn't talk about these things, but --

Yeah, now that you mention it, I did hear something about a Project Hyperion while I was stationed in Kuwait a few years ago. They seemed awfully hush-hush about it.

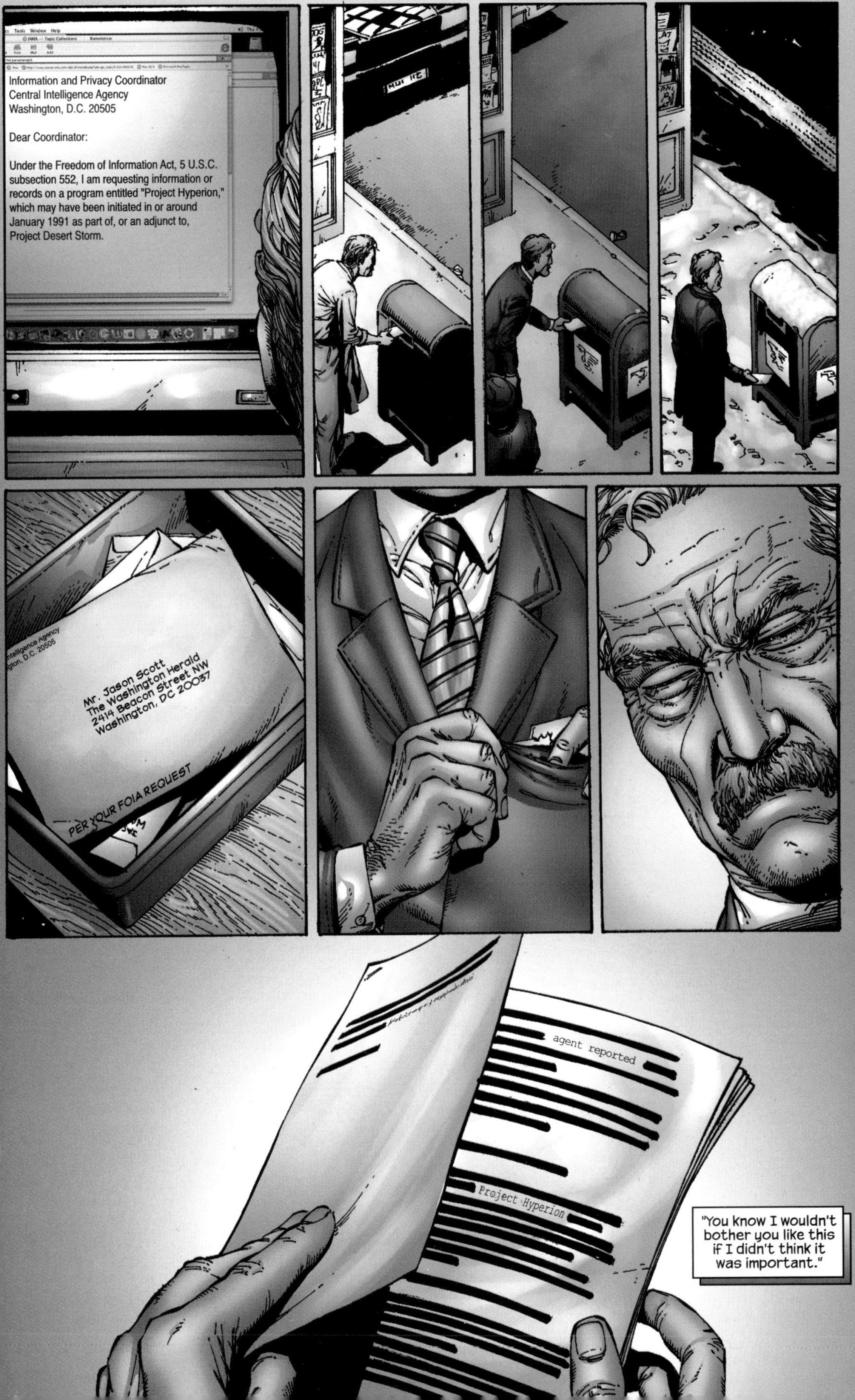

Information and Privacy Coordinator
Central Intelligence Agency
Washington, D.C. 20505
Dear Coordinator:
Under the Freedom of Information Act, 5 U.S.C. subsection 552, I am requesting information or records on a program entitled "Project Hyperion," which may have been initiated in or around January 1991 as part of, or an adjunct to, Project Desert Storm.
ntelligence Agency
gton, D.C. 20505
Mr. Jason Scott
The Washington Herald
2414 Beacon Street NW
Washington, DC 20037
PER YOUR FOIA REQUEST
[redacted] agent reported [redacted]
[redacted] Project Hyperion [redacted]
"You know I wouldn't bother you like this if I didn't think it was important."

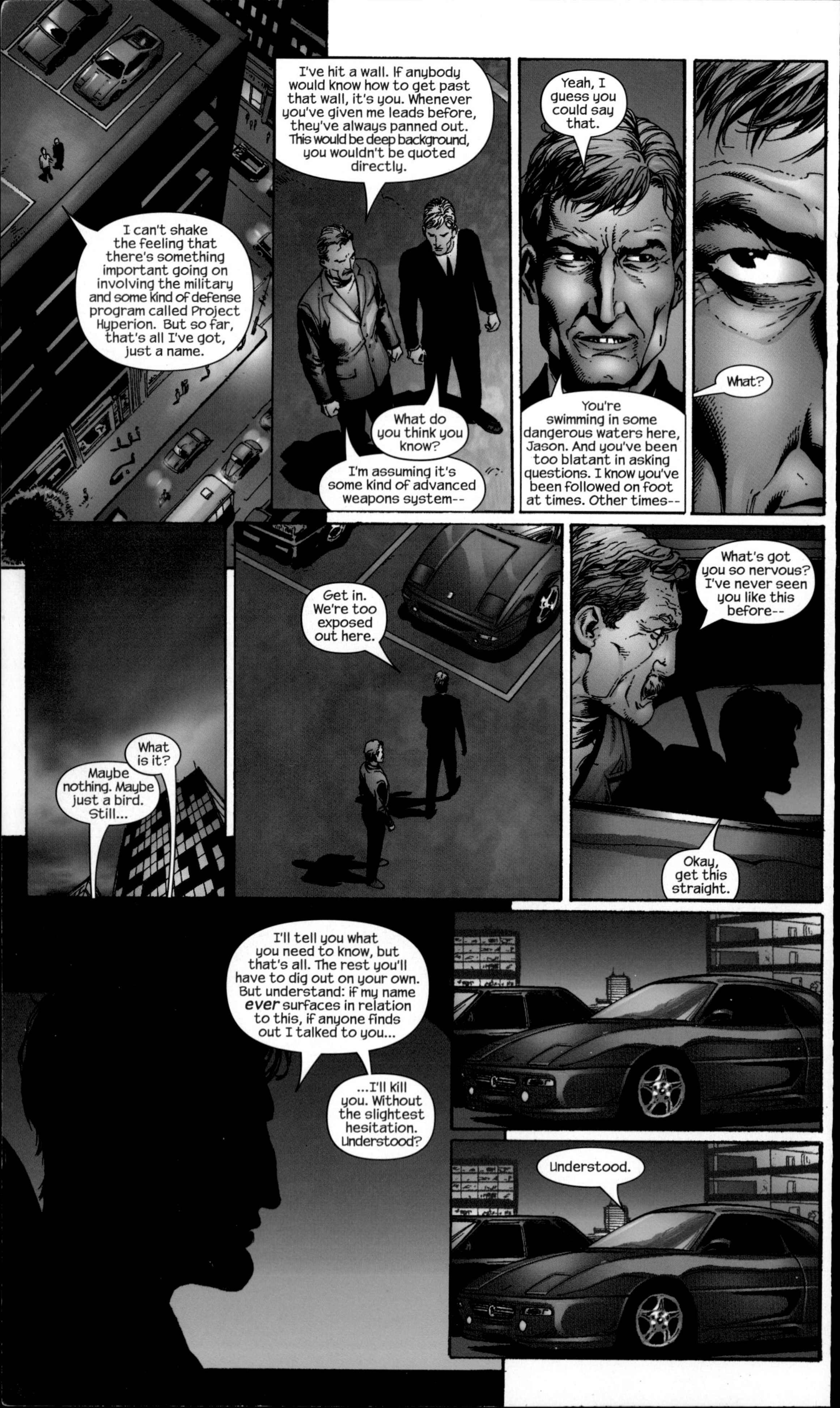
I can't shake the feeling that there's something important going on involving the military and some kind of defense program called Project Hyperion. But so far, that's all I've got, just a name.
I've hit a wall. If anybody would know how to get past that wall, it's you. Whenever you've given me leads before, they've always panned out. This would be deep background, you wouldn't be quoted directly.
What do you think you know?
I'm assuming it's some kind of advanced weapons system--
Yeah, I guess you could say that.
You're swimming in some dangerous waters here, Jason. And you've been too blatant in asking questions. I know you've been followed on foot at times. Other times--
What?
What is it?
Maybe nothing. Maybe just a bird. Still...
Get in. We're too exposed out here.
What's got you so nervous? I've never seen you like this before--
Okay, get this straight.
I'll tell you what you need to know, but that's all. The rest you'll have to dig out on your own. But understand: if my name ever surfaces in relation to this, if anyone finds out I talked to you...
...I'll kill you. Without the slightest hesitation. Understood?
Understood.

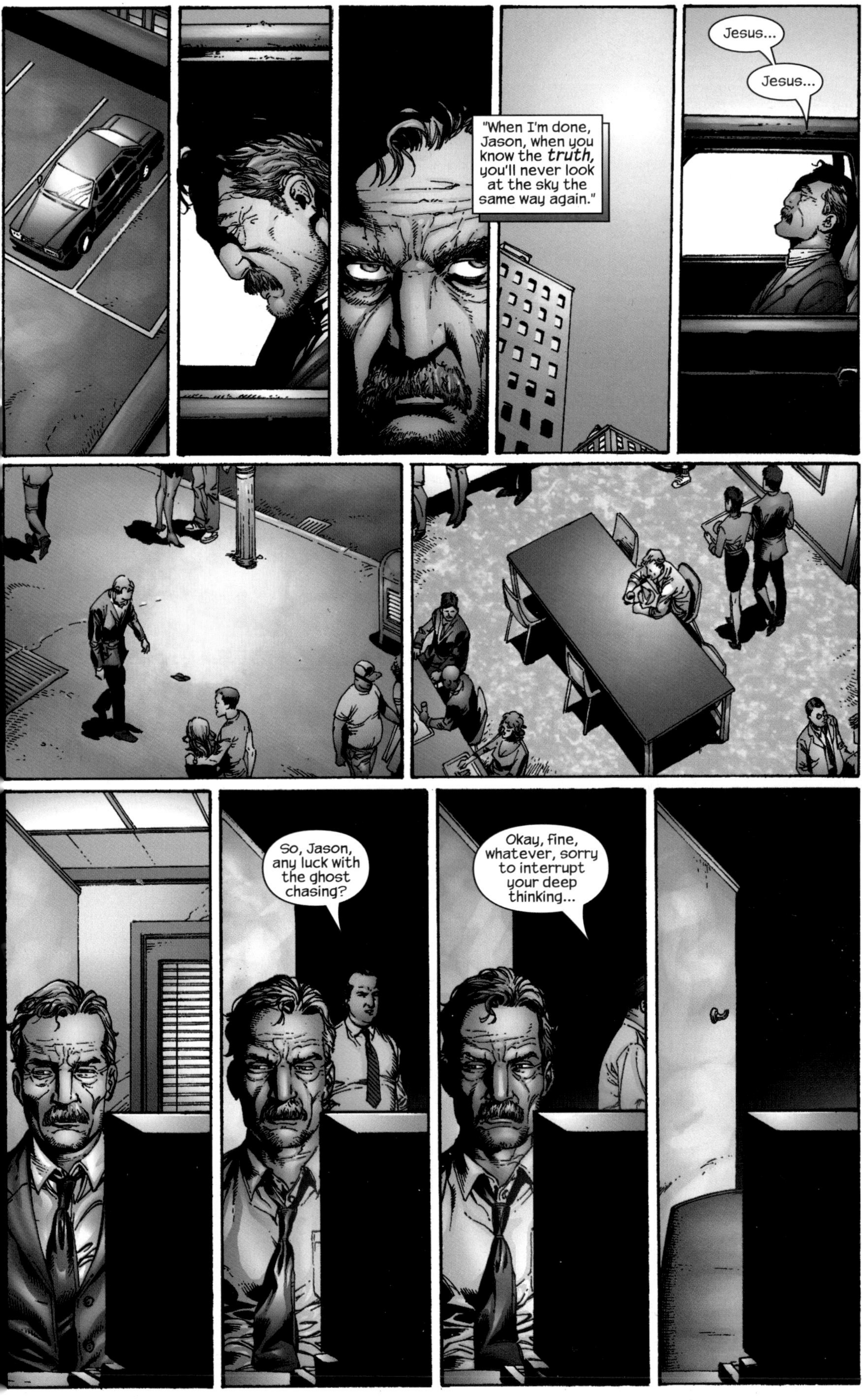
"When I'm done, Jason, when you know the *truth*, you'll never look at the sky the same way again."
Jesus...
Jesus...
So, Jason, any luck with the ghost chasing?
Okay, fine, whatever, sorry to interrupt your deep thinking...

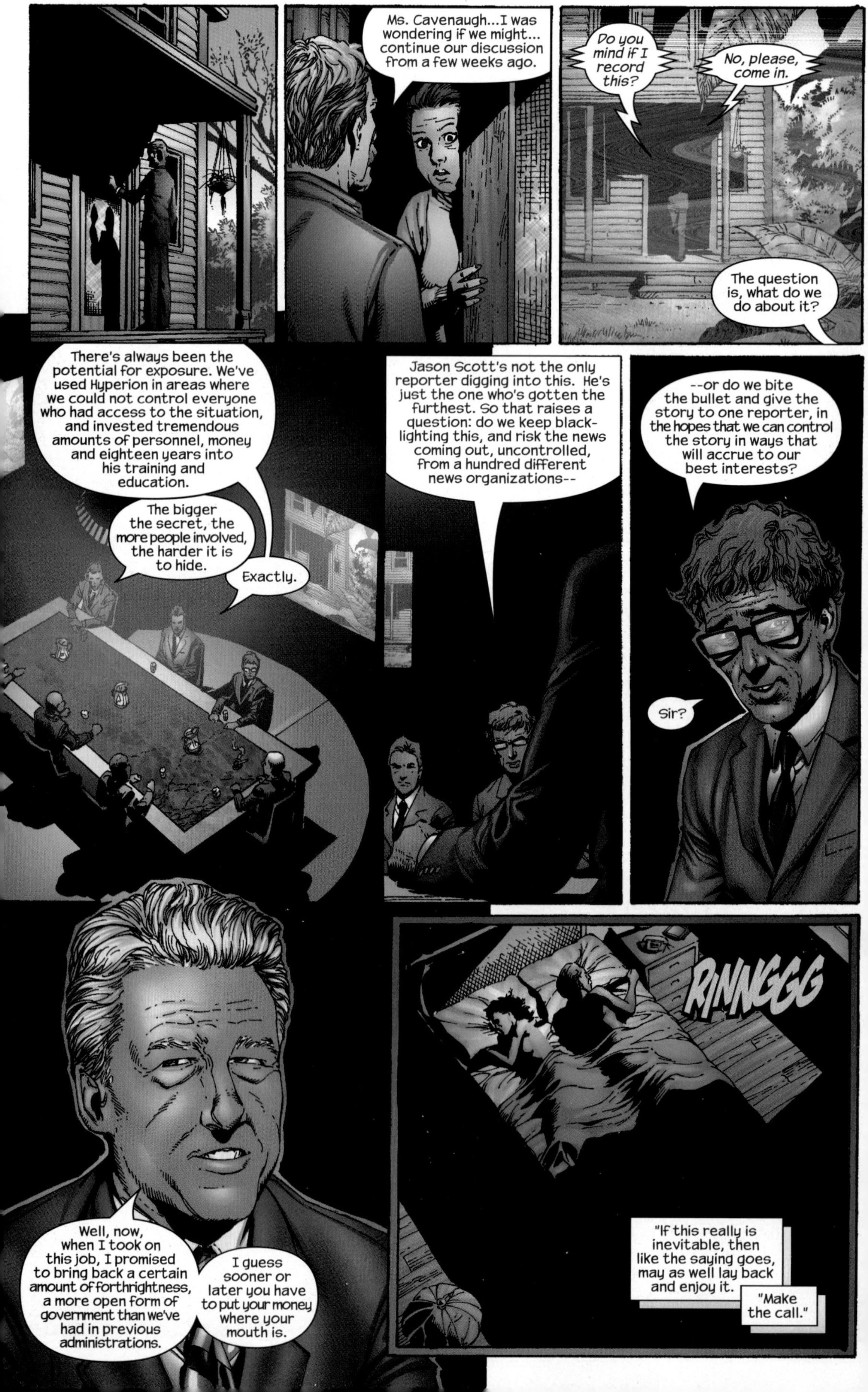
Ms. Cavenaugh...I was wondering if we might... continue our discussion from a few weeks ago.
Do you mind if I record this?
No, please, come in.
The question is, what do we do about it?
There's always been the potential for exposure. We've used Hyperion in areas where we could not control everyone who had access to the situation, and invested tremendous amounts of personnel, money and eighteen years into his training and education.
The bigger the secret, the more people involved, the harder it is to hide.
Exactly.
Jason Scott's not the only reporter digging into this. He's just the one who's gotten the furthest. So that raises a question: do we keep black-lighting this, and risk the news coming out, uncontrolled, from a hundred different news organizations--
--or do we bite the bullet and give the story to one reporter, in the hopes that we can control the story in ways that will accrue to our best interests?
Sir?
Well, now, when I took on this job, I promised to bring back a certain amount of forthrightness, a more open form of government than we've had in previous administrations.
I guess sooner or later you have to put your money where your mouth is.
RINNGGG
"If this really is inevitable, then like the saying goes, may as well lay back and enjoy it.
"Make the call."

...yeah?

Jason Scott?

Yeah...?

Go to the balcony.

CLICK

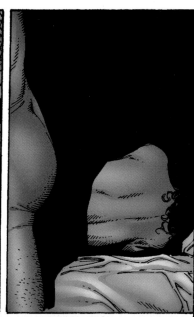

Who is this?

Go to the balcony.

Good evening, Mr. Scott.

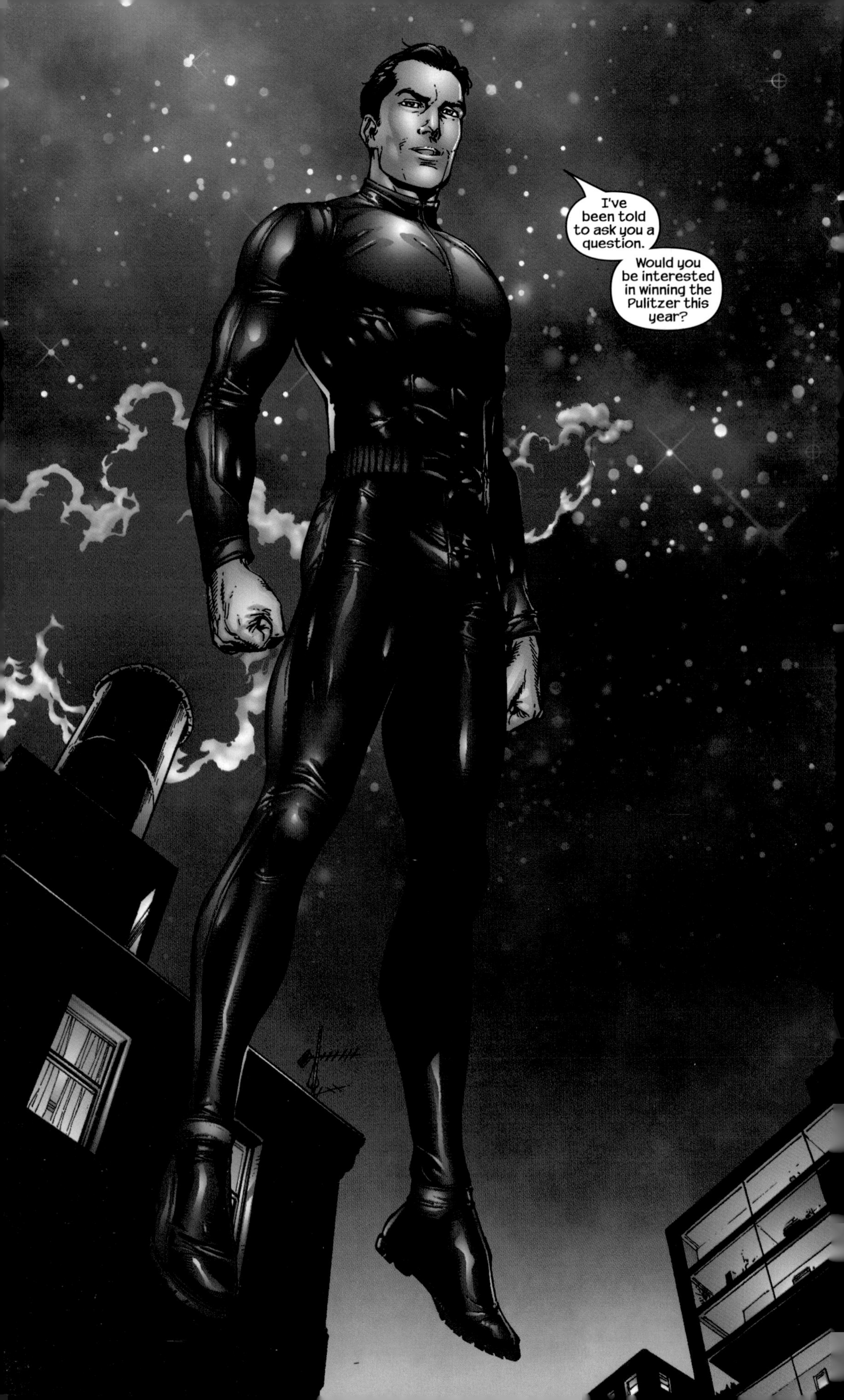
I've been told to ask you a question.
Would you be interested in winning the Pulitzer this year?

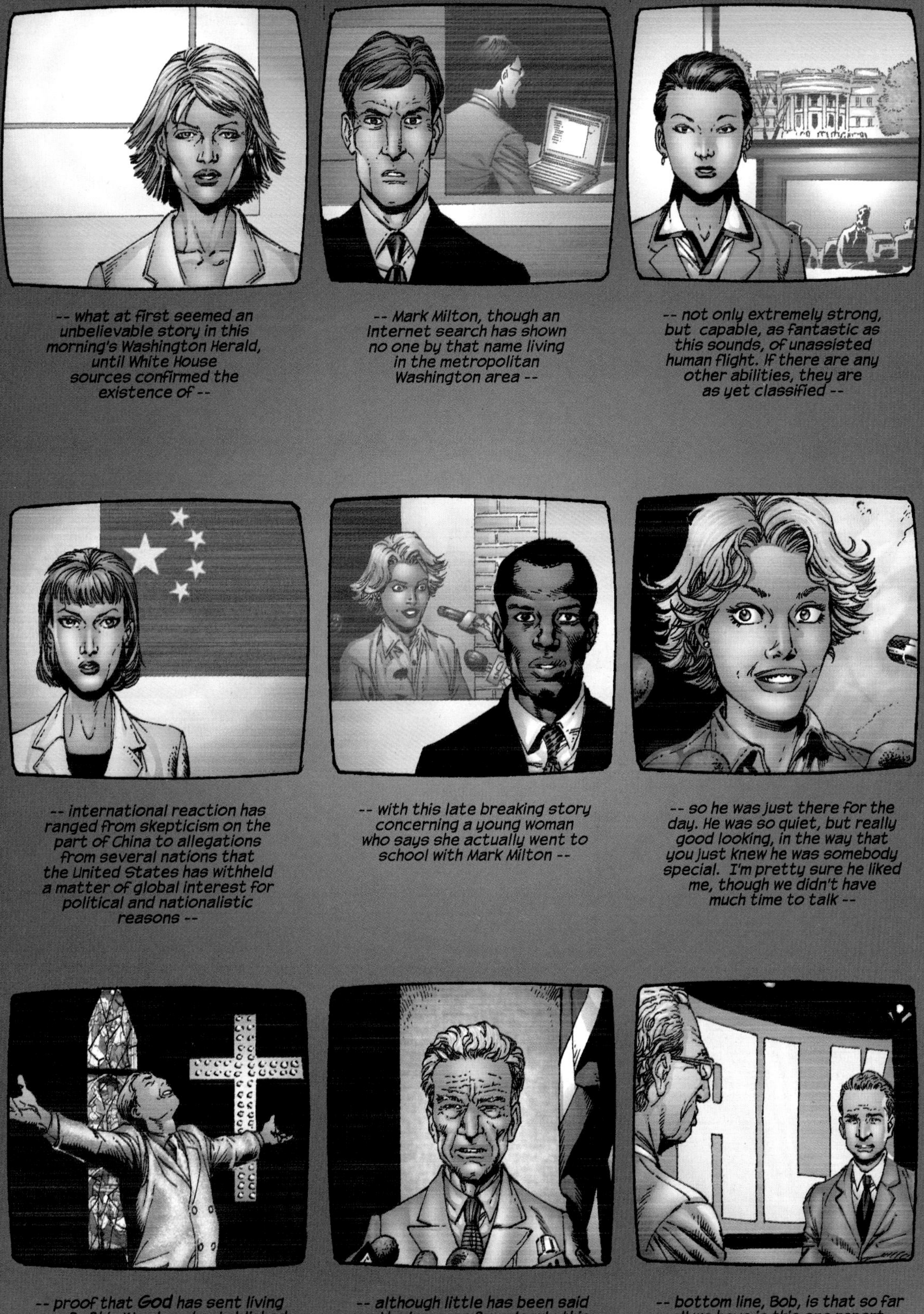
-- what at first seemed an unbelievable story in this morning's Washington Herald, until White House sources confirmed the existence of --
-- Mark Milton, though an internet search has shown no one by that name living in the metropolitan Washington area --
-- not only extremely strong, but capable, as fantastic as this sounds, of unassisted human flight. If there are any other abilities, they are as yet classified --
-- international reaction has ranged from skepticism on the part of China to allegations from several nations that the United States has withheld a matter of global interest for political and nationalistic reasons --
-- with this late breaking story concerning a young woman who says she actually went to school with Mark Milton --
-- so he was just there for the day. He was so quiet, but really good looking, in the way that you just knew he was somebody special. I'm pretty sure he liked me, though we didn't have much time to talk --
-- proof that God has sent living proof of his Word, and established heavenly guardians for America against the forces of evil --
-- although little has been said on the issue so far, clearly this individual has been used to give America an unfair strategic advantage, typical of its covert activities in the past--
-- bottom line, Bob, is that so far all we have is this one report. The White House has confirmed the story, but without producing an inch of proof.

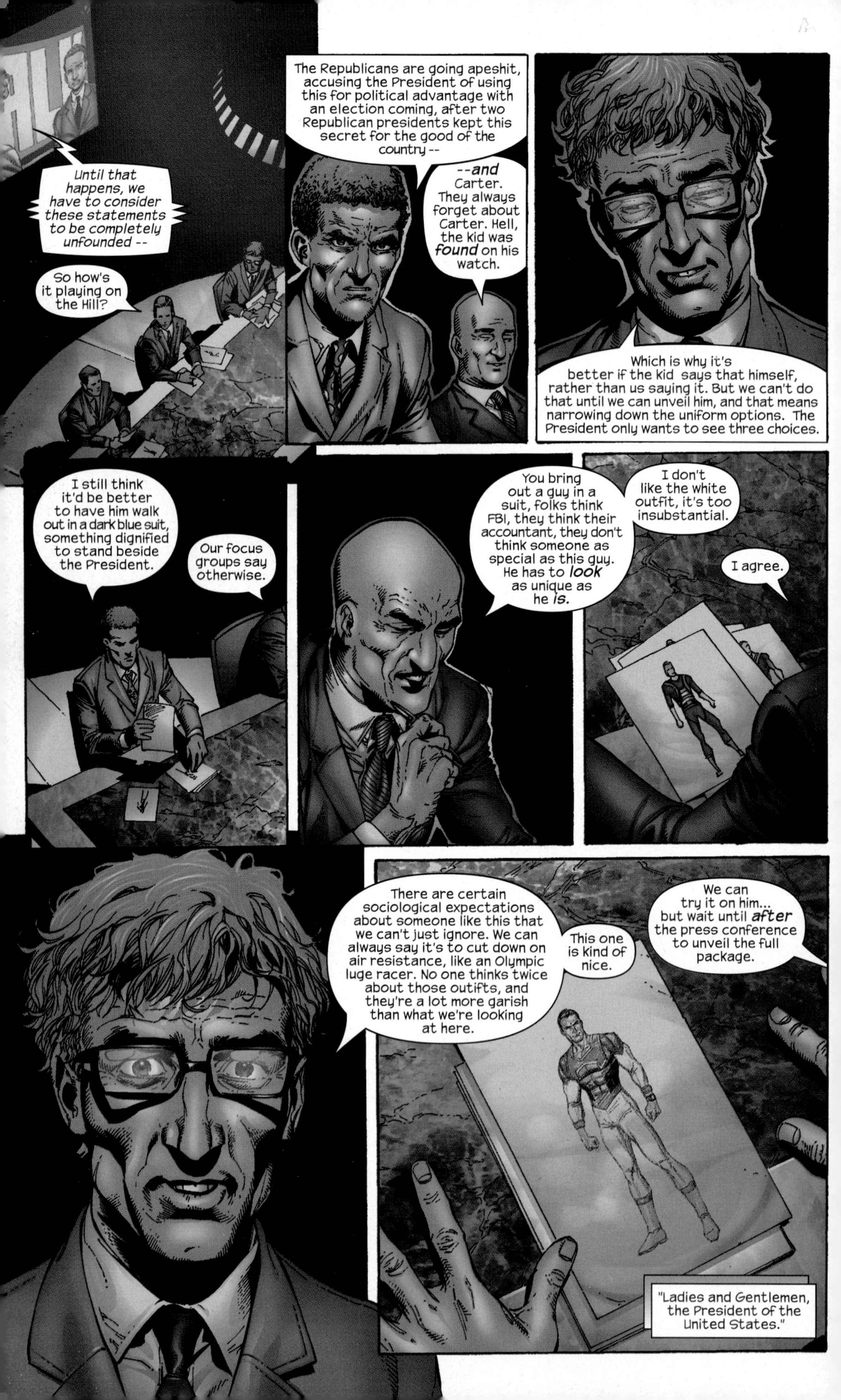

Until that happens, we have to consider these statements to be completely unfounded --
So how's it playing on the Hill?
The Republicans are going apeshit, accusing the President of using this for political advantage with an election coming, after two Republican presidents kept this secret for the good of the country --
--and Carter. They always forget about Carter. Hell, the kid was found on his watch.
Which is why it's better if the kid says that himself, rather than us saying it. But we can't do that until we can unveil him, and that means narrowing down the uniform options. The President only wants to see three choices.
I still think it'd be better to have him walk out in a dark blue suit, something dignified to stand beside the President.
Our focus groups say otherwise.
You bring out a guy in a suit, folks think FBI, they think their accountant, they don't think someone as special as this guy. He has to look as unique as he is.
I don't like the white outfit, it's too insubstantial.
I agree.
There are certain sociological expectations about someone like this that we can't just ignore. We can always say it's to cut down on air resistance, like an Olympic luge racer. No one thinks twice about those outfits, and they're a lot more garish than what we're looking at here.
This one is kind of nice.
We can try it on him... but wait until after the press conference to unveil the full package.
"Ladies and Gentlemen, the President of the United States."

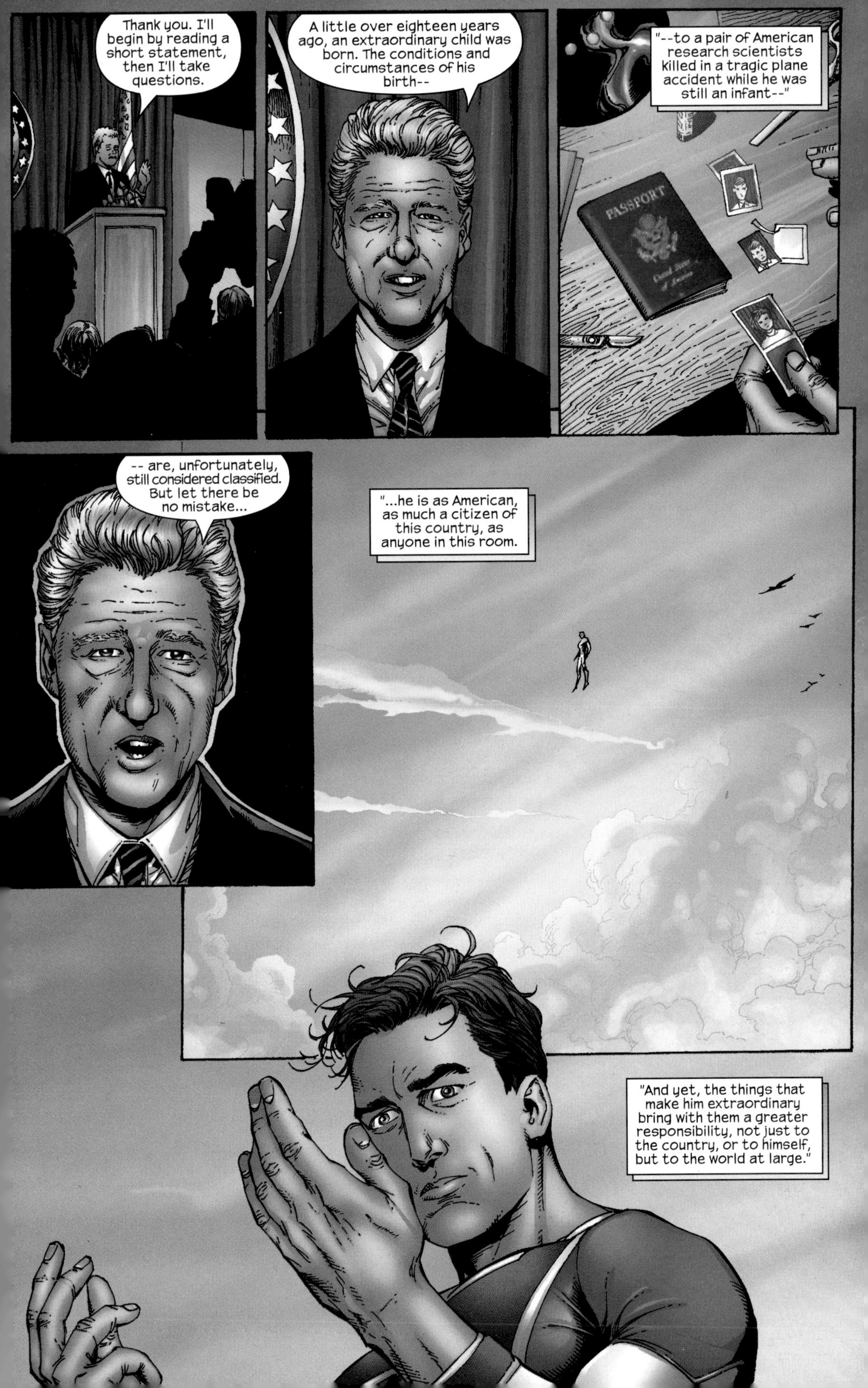

Thank you. I'll begin by reading a short statement, then I'll take questions.
A little over eighteen years ago, an extraordinary child was born. The conditions and circumstances of his birth--
"--to a pair of American research scientists killed in a tragic plane accident while he was still an infant--"
PASSPORT
-- are, unfortunately, still considered classified. But let there be no mistake...
"...he is as American, as much a citizen of this country, as anyone in this room.
"And yet, the things that make him extraordinary bring with them a greater responsibility, not just to the country, or to himself, but to the world at large."

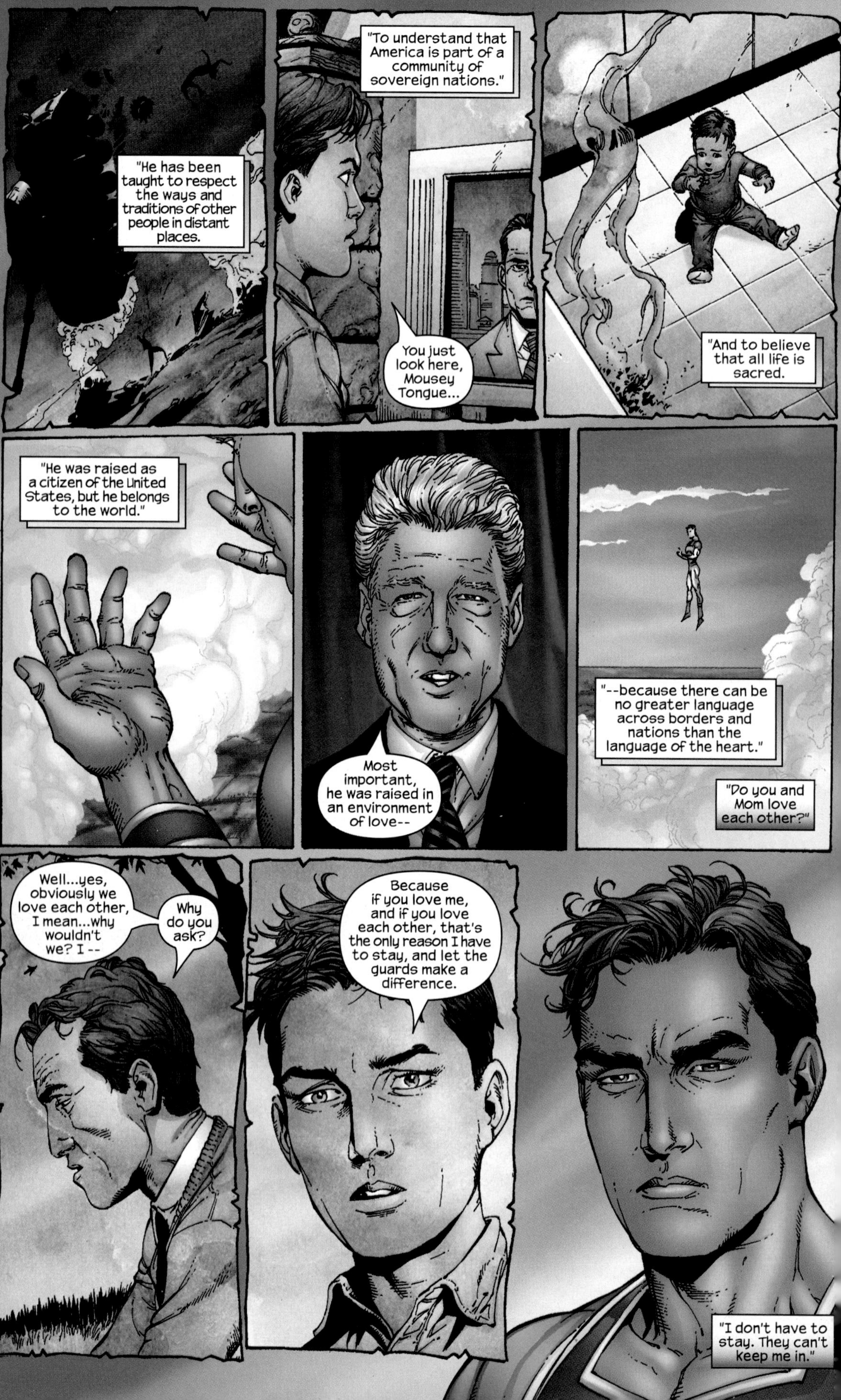

"He has been taught to respect the ways and traditions of other people in distant places.
"To understand that America is part of a community of sovereign nations."
You just look here, Mousey Tongue...
"And to believe that all life is sacred.
"He was raised as a citizen of the United States, but he belongs to the world."
Most important, he was raised in an environment of love--
"--because there can be no greater language across borders and nations than the language of the heart."
"Do you and Mom love each other?"
Well...yes, obviously we love each other, I mean...why wouldn't we? I --
Why do you ask?
Because if you love me, and if you love each other, that's the only reason I have to stay, and let the guards make a difference.
"I don't have to stay. They can't keep me in."

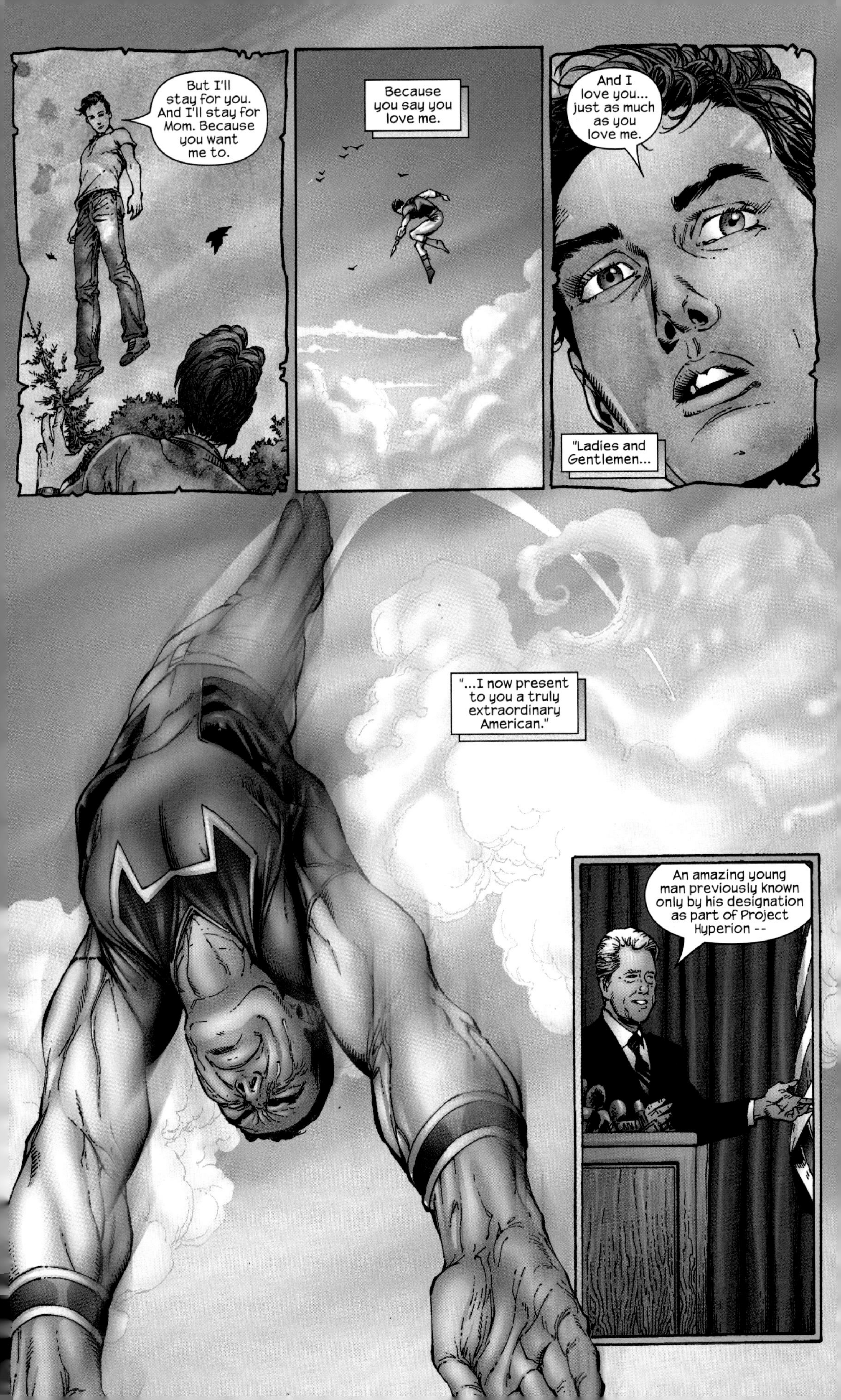
But I'll stay for you. And I'll stay for Mom. Because you want me to.
Because you say you love me.
And I love you... just as much as you love me.
"Ladies and Gentlemen...
"...I now present to you a truly extraordinary American."
An amazing young man previously known only by his designation as part of Project Hyperion --

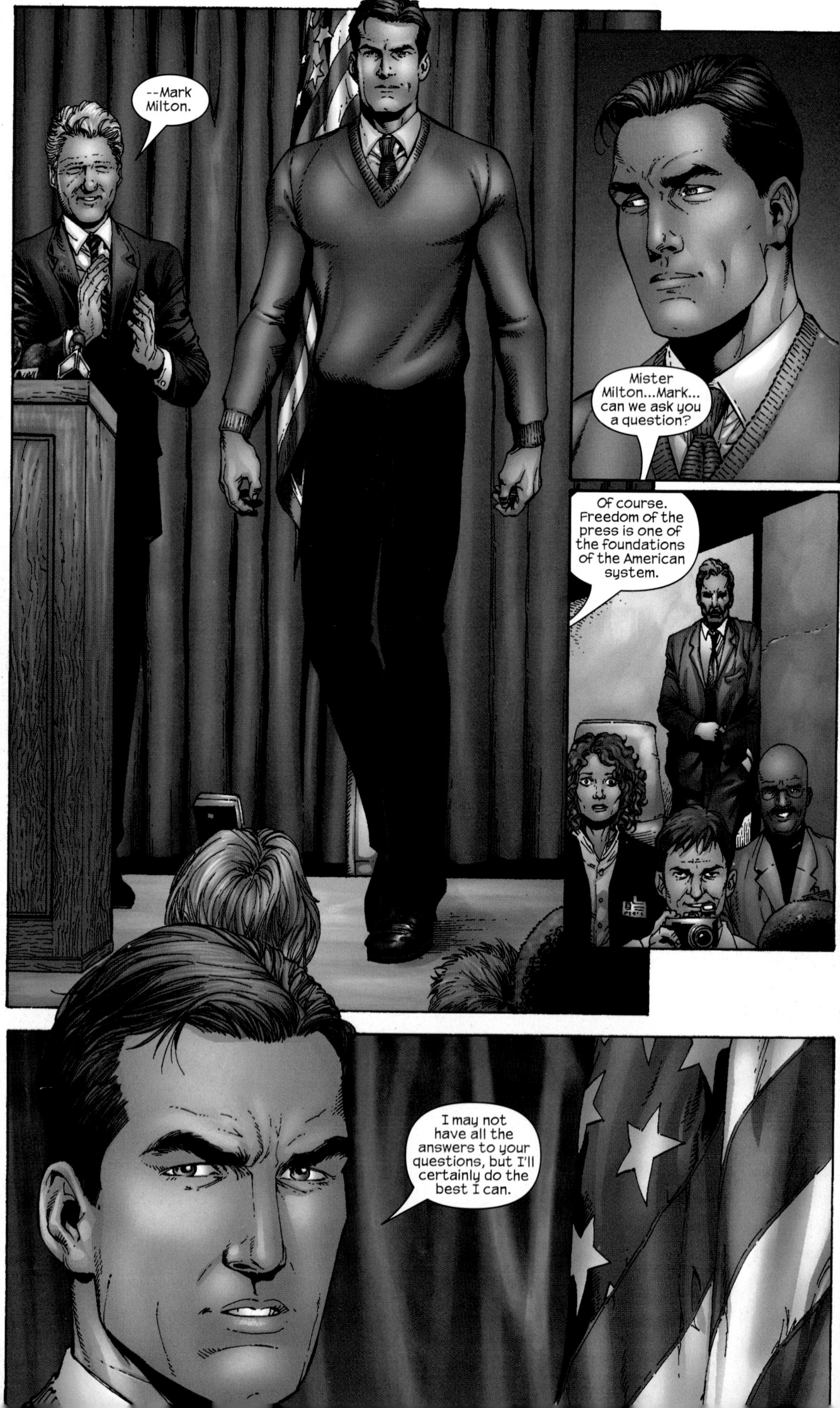

--Mark Milton.
Mister Milton...Mark... can we ask you a question?
Of course. Freedom of the press is one of the foundations of the American system.
I may not have all the answers to your questions, but I'll certainly do the best I can.

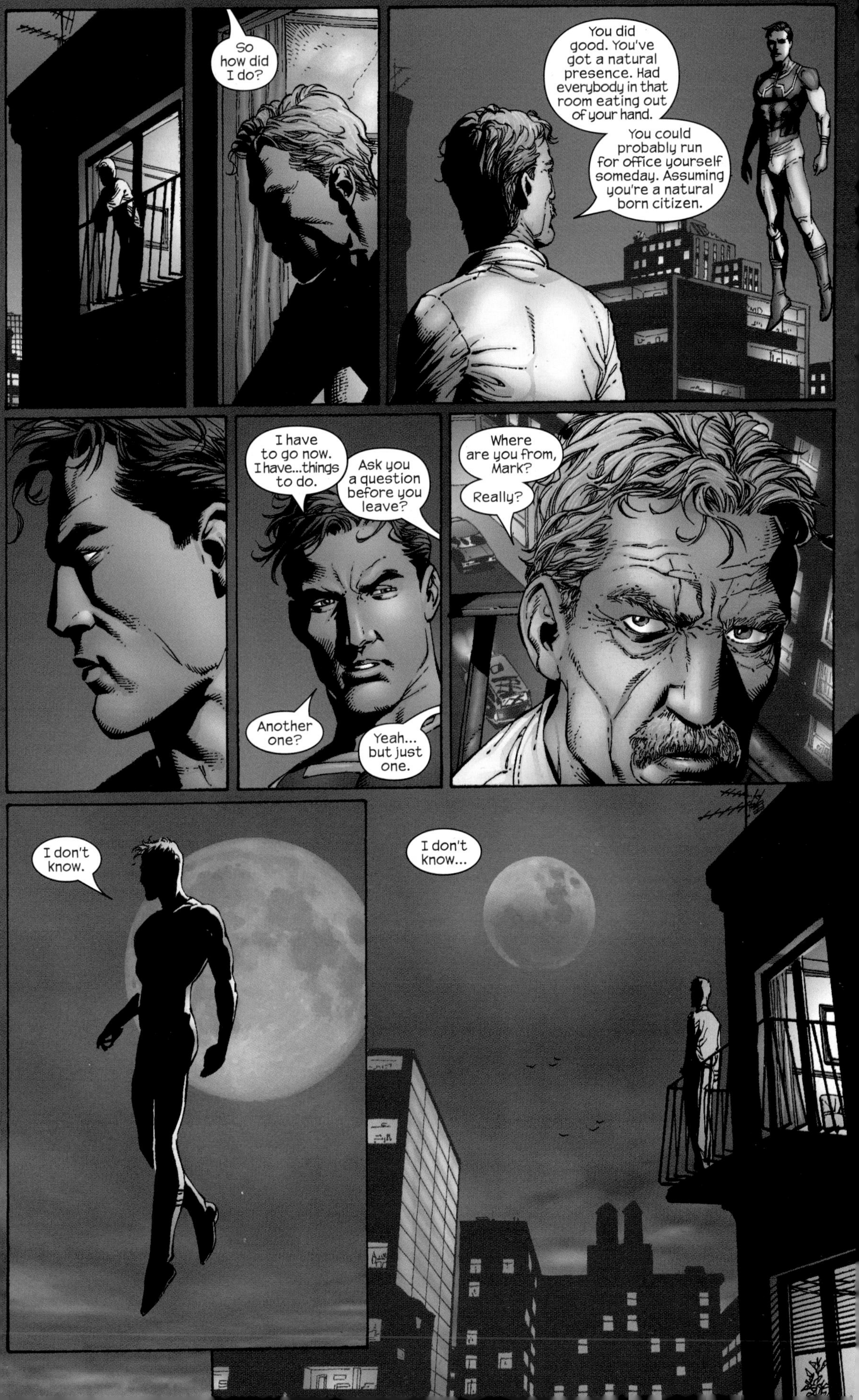

So how did I do?
You did good. You've got a natural presence. Had everybody in that room eating out of your hand.
You could probably run for office yourself someday. Assuming you're a natural born citizen.
I have to go now. I have...things to do.
Ask you a question before you leave?
Another one?
Yeah... but just one.
Where are you from, Mark?
Really?
I don't know.
I don't know...

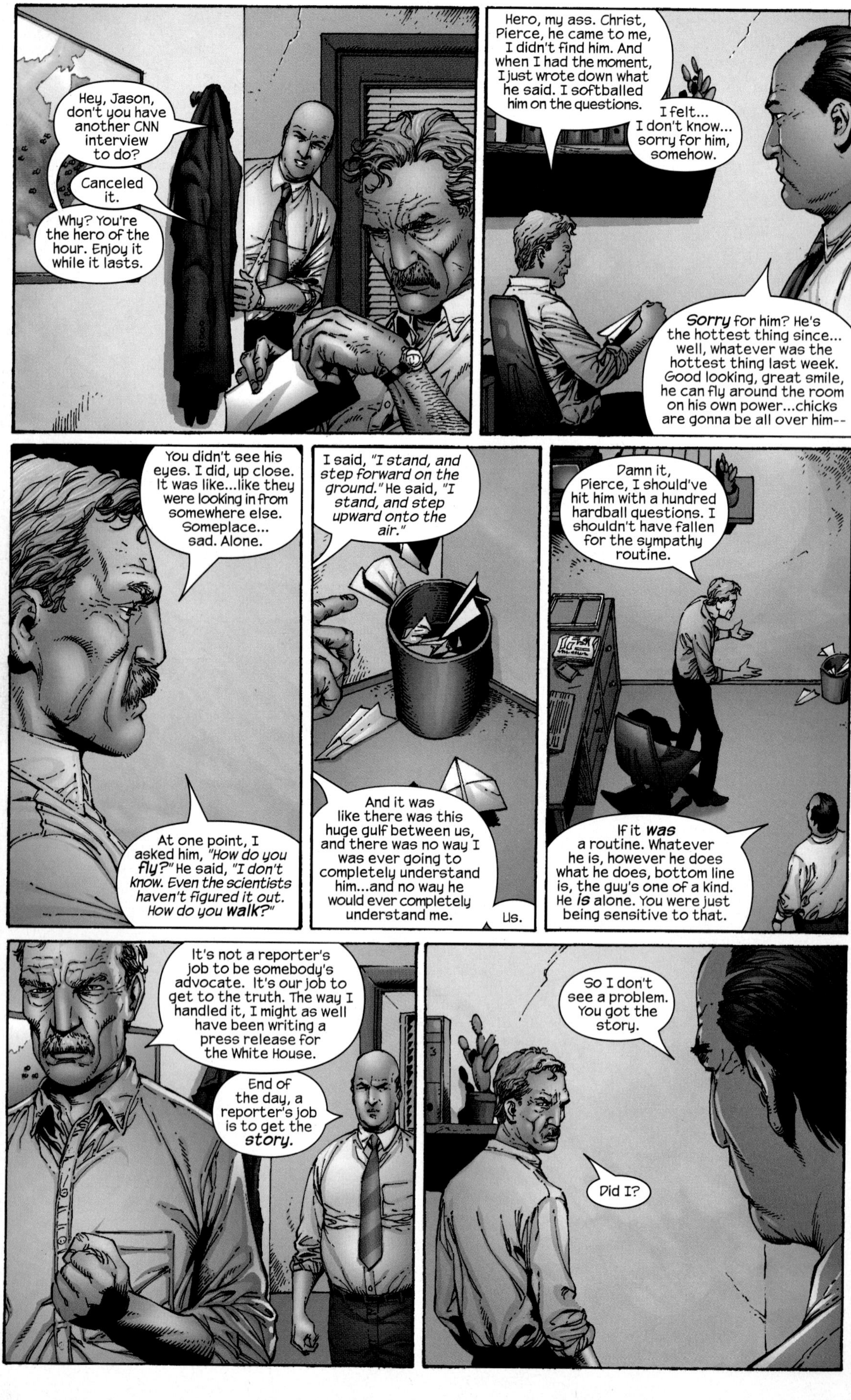
Hey, Jason, don't you have another CNN interview to do?
Canceled it.
Why? You're the hero of the hour. Enjoy it while it lasts.
Hero, my ass. Christ, Pierce, he came to me, I didn't find him. And when I had the moment, I just wrote down what he said. I softballed him on the questions.
I felt... I don't know... sorry for him, somehow.
Sorry for him? He's the hottest thing since... well, whatever was the hottest thing last week. Good looking, great smile, he can fly around the room on his own power...chicks are gonna be all over him--
You didn't see his eyes. I did, up close. It was like...like they were looking in from somewhere else. Someplace... sad. Alone.
At one point, I asked him, "How do you fly?" He said, "I don't know. Even the scientists haven't figured it out. How do you walk?"
I said, "I stand, and step forward on the ground." He said, "I stand, and step upward onto the air."
And it was like there was this huge gulf between us, and there was no way I was ever going to completely understand him...and no way he would ever completely understand me.
Us.
Damn it, Pierce, I should've hit him with a hundred hardball questions. I shouldn't have fallen for the sympathy routine.
If it was a routine. Whatever he is, however he does what he does, bottom line is, the guy's one of a kind. He is alone. You were just being sensitive to that.
It's not a reporter's job to be somebody's advocate. It's our job to get to the truth. The way I handled it, I might as well have been writing a press release for the White House.
End of the day, a reporter's job is to get the story.
So I don't see a problem. You got the story.
Did I?

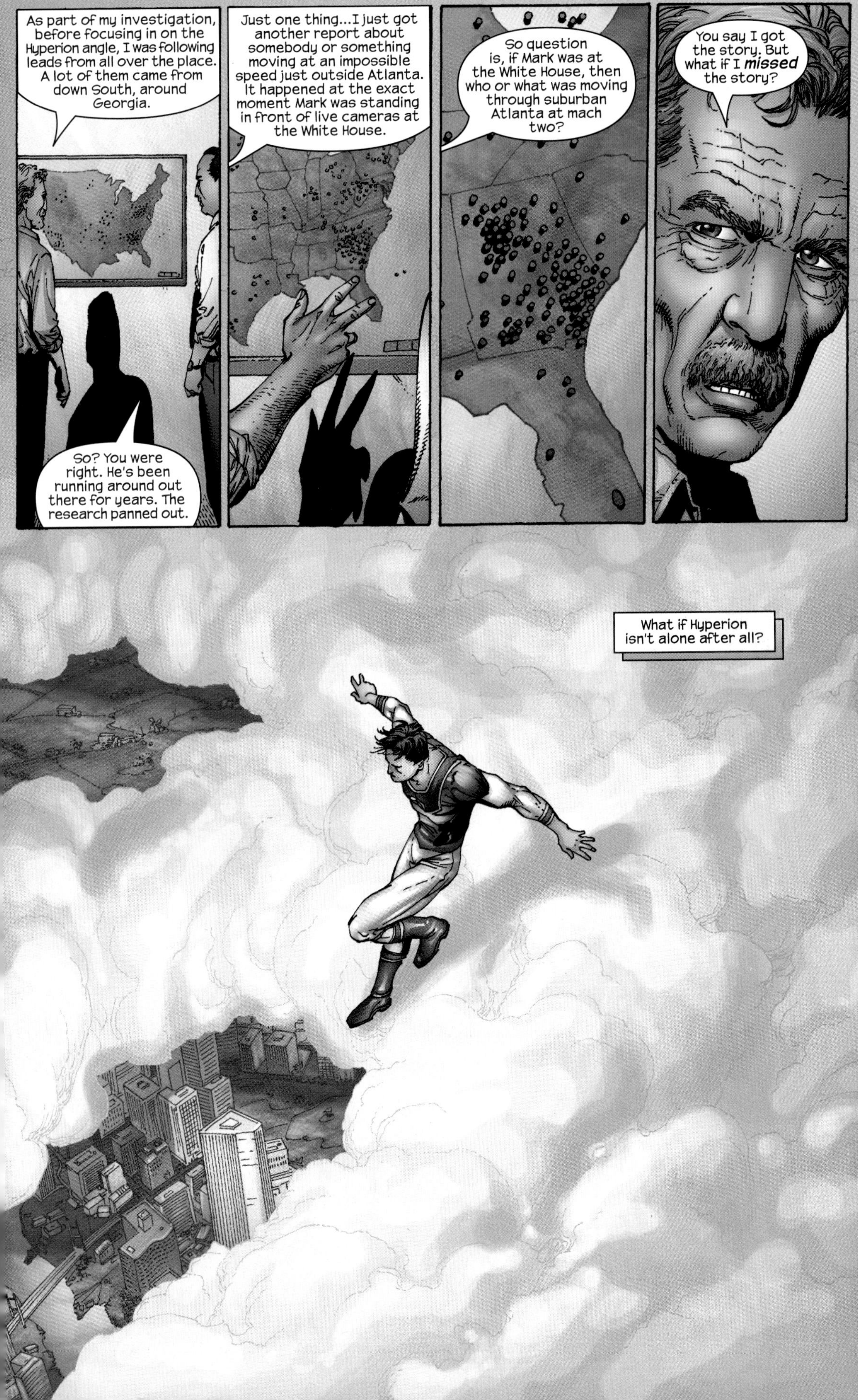
As part of my investigation, before focusing in on the Hyperion angle, I was following leads from all over the place. A lot of them came from down South, around Georgia.
So? You were right. He's been running around out there for years. The research panned out.
Just one thing...I just got another report about somebody or something moving at an impossible speed just outside Atlanta. It happened at the exact moment Mark was standing in front of live cameras at the White House.
So question is, if Mark was at the White House, then who or what was moving through suburban Atlanta at mach two?
You say I got the story. But what if I *missed* the story?
What if Hyperion isn't alone after all?

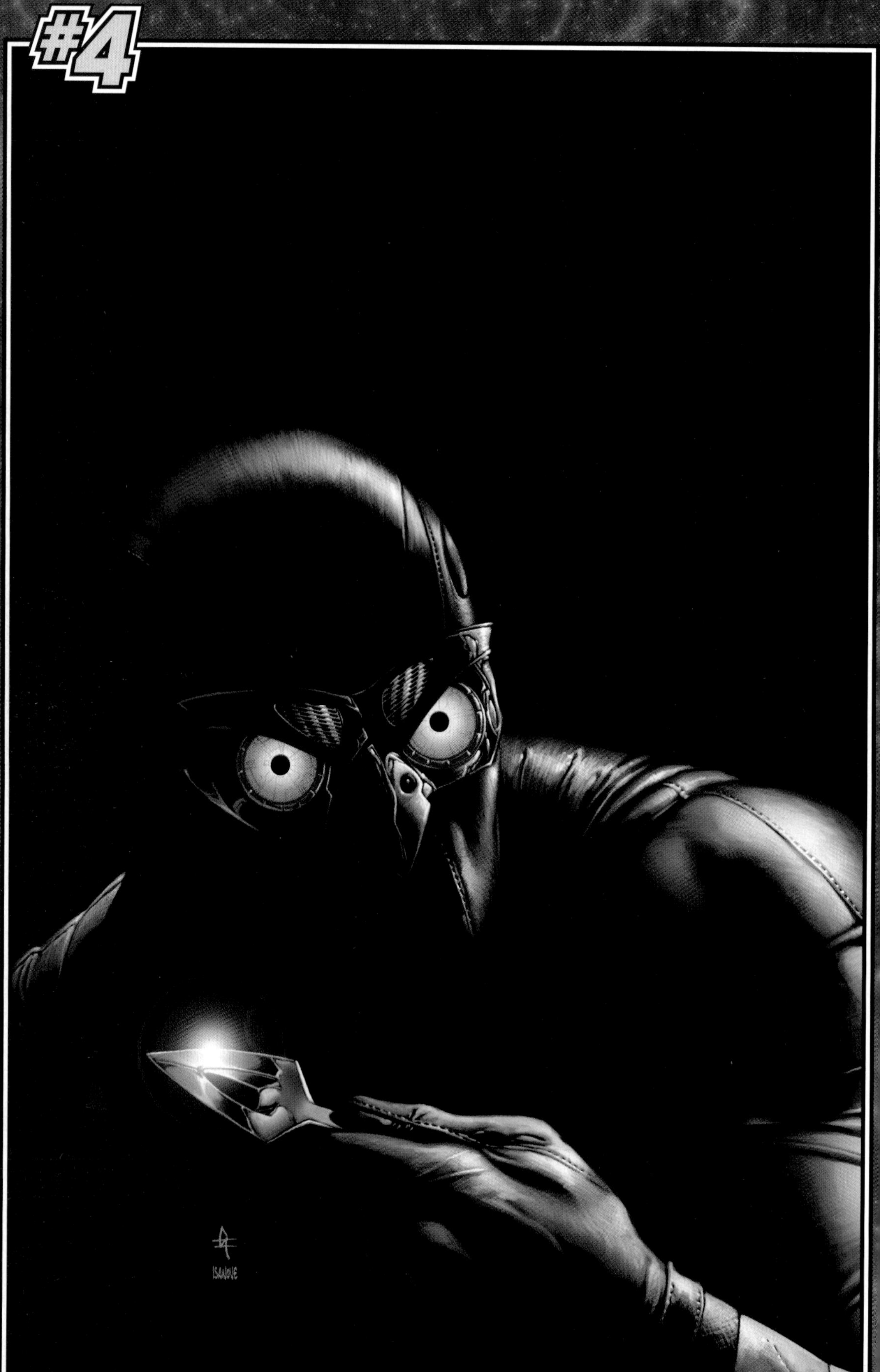

#4
ISANOVE

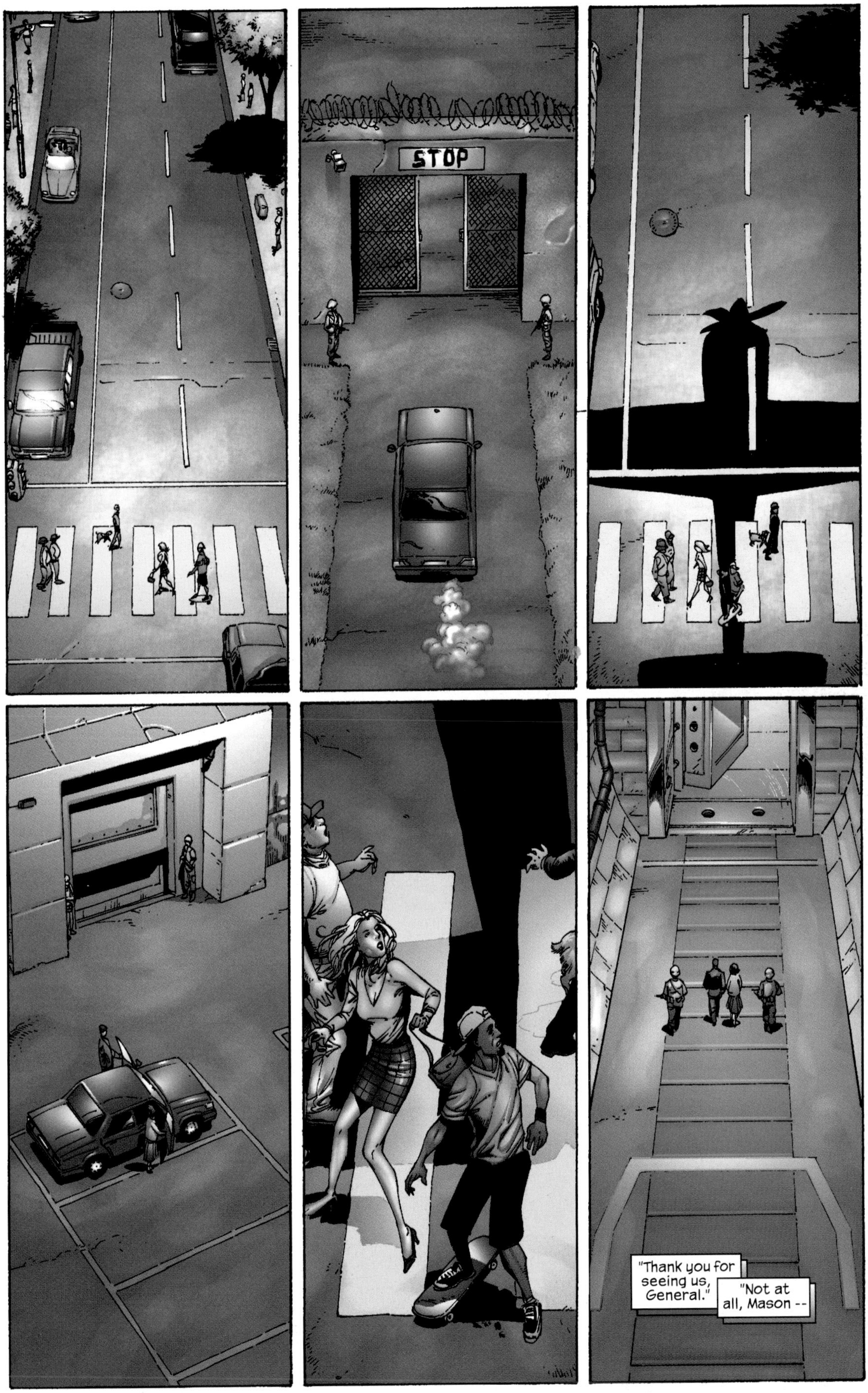
STOP
"Thank you for seeing us, General."
"Not at all, Mason --

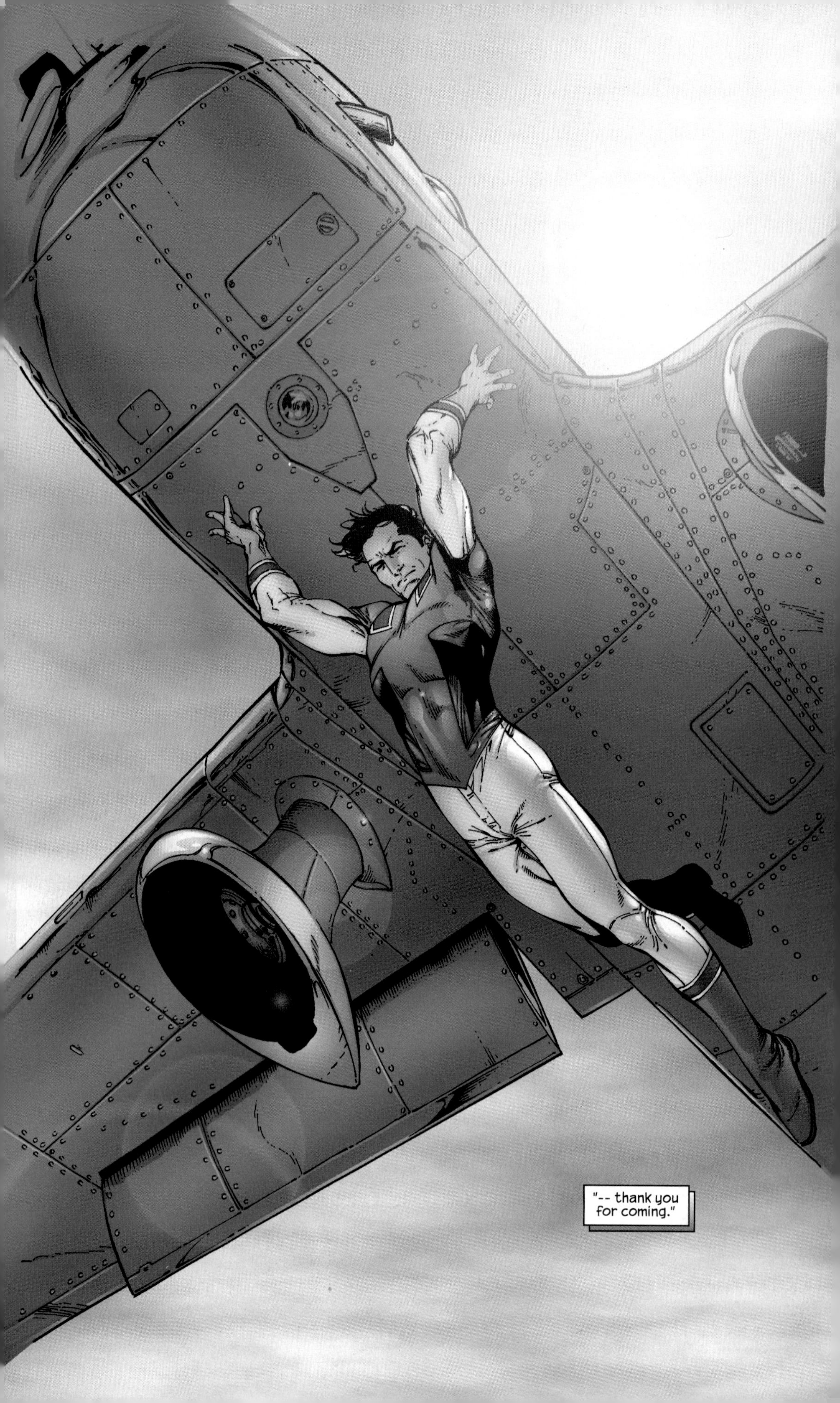
"-- thank you
for coming."

Can I get you anything?

No, thanks, we're fine.

Are you sure it's safe to talk here?

There's two hundred feet of dirt, rock, lead, steel and concrete between this office and the outside world. We can't be overheard, even by Mark.

"Just to be extra safe, however, we arranged for a small plane to run out of fuel in his vicinity right about now."

"He'll have plenty to keep him occupied until we're done."

I just wanted you to know that the process has been started. We've scheduled your extraction for Thursday night.

That quickly? We'd only just made the request...I thought we'd have longer--

No point to it, really. Less time to think about it means less chance for something to go wrong.

Besides, our research shows that a sudden loss of his parents at this delicate time of his life, coming into full adulthood, would cause Mark to rely even more on the country as his spiritual mother and father--

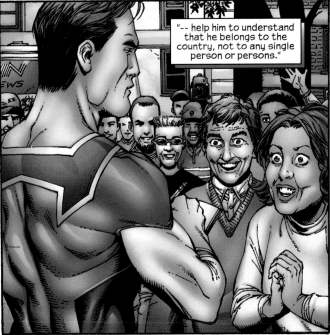

"-- help him to understand that he belongs to the country, not to any single person or persons."

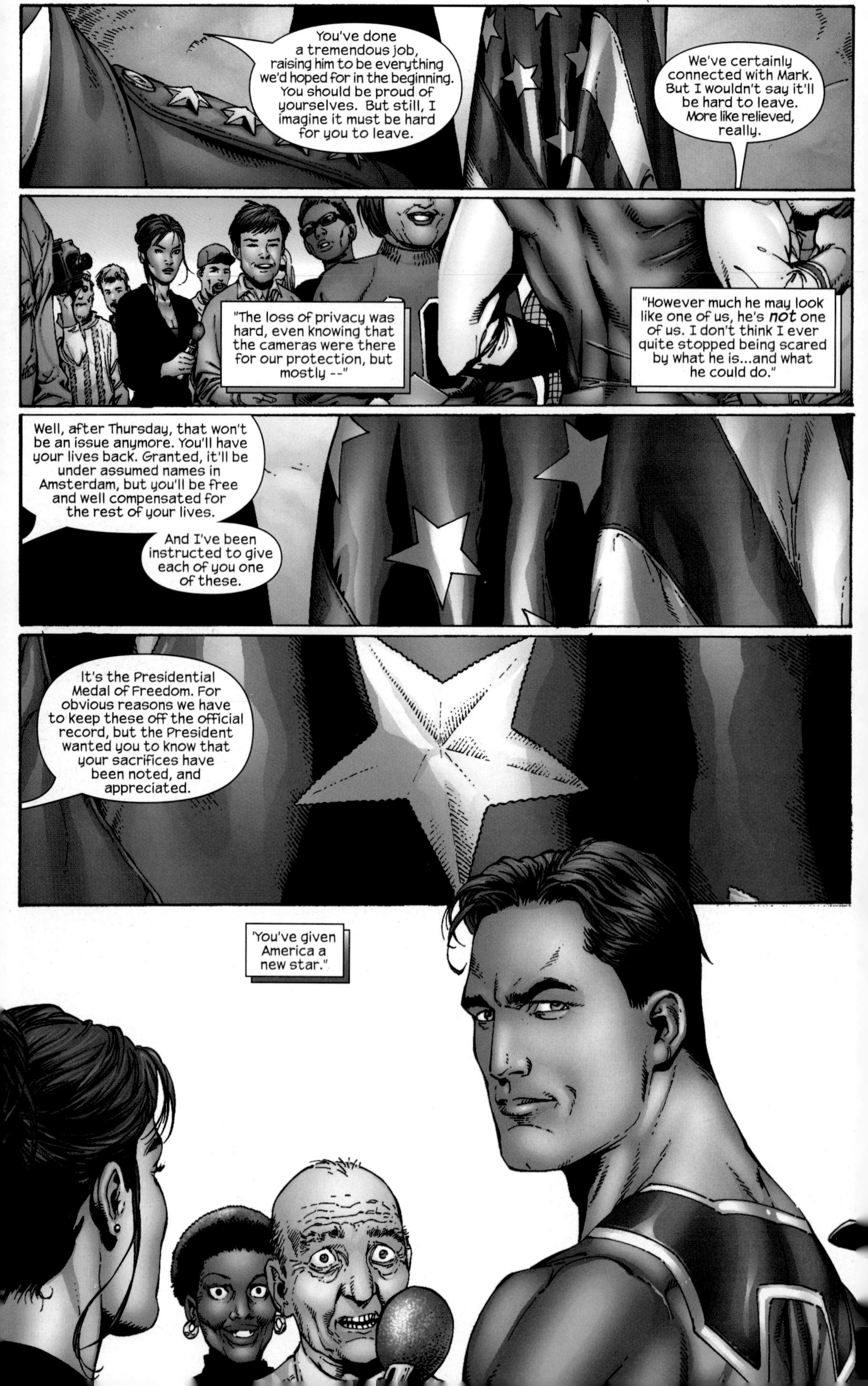

You've done a tremendous job, raising him to be everything we'd hoped for in the beginning. You should be proud of yourselves. But still, I imagine it must be hard for you to leave.
We've certainly connected with Mark. But I wouldn't say it'll be hard to leave. More like relieved, really.
"The loss of privacy was hard, even knowing that the cameras were there for our protection, but mostly --"
"However much he may look like one of us, he's *not* one of us. I don't think I ever quite stopped being scared by what he is...and what he could do."
Well, after Thursday, that won't be an issue anymore. You'll have your lives back. Granted, it'll be under assumed names in Amsterdam, but you'll be free and well compensated for the rest of your lives.
And I've been instructed to give each of you one of these.
It's the Presidential Medal of Freedom. For obvious reasons we have to keep these off the official record, but the President wanted you to know that your sacrifices have been noted, and appreciated.
"You've given America a new star."

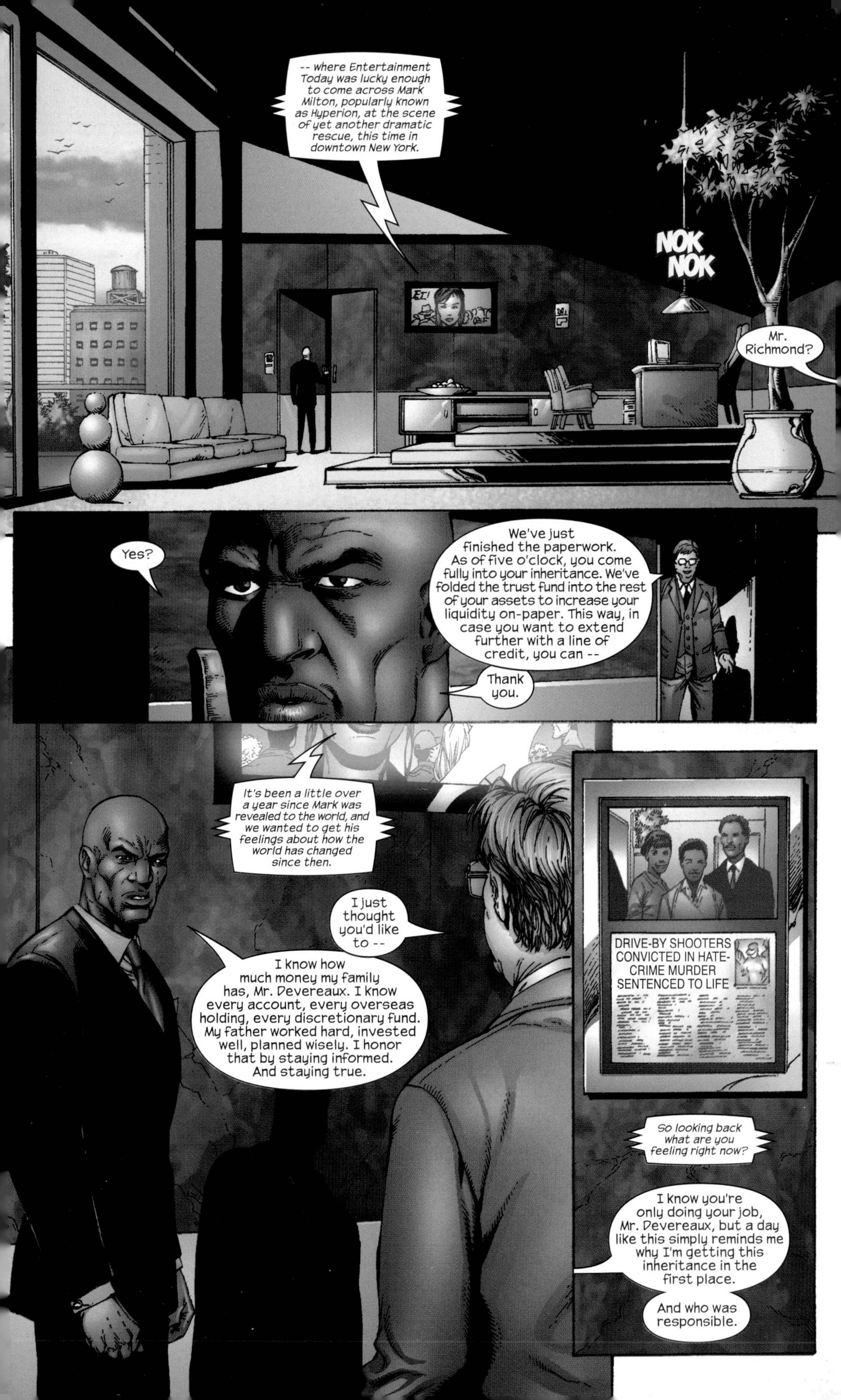

-- where Entertainment Today was lucky enough to come across Mark Milton, popularly known as Hyperion, at the scene of yet another dramatic rescue, this time in downtown New York.
NOK NOK
Mr. Richmond?
Yes?
We've just finished the paperwork. As of five o'clock, you come fully into your inheritance. We've folded the trust fund into the rest of your assets to increase your liquidity on-paper. This way, in case you want to extend further with a line of credit, you can --
Thank you.
It's been a little over a year since Mark was revealed to the world, and we wanted to get his feelings about how the world has changed since then.
I just thought you'd like to --
I know how much money my family has, Mr. Devereaux. I know every account, every overseas holding, every discretionary fund. My father worked hard, invested well, planned wisely. I honor that by staying informed. And staying true.
DRIVE-BY SHOOTERS CONVICTED IN HATE-CRIME MURDER SENTENCED TO LIFE
So looking back what are you feeling right now?
I know you're only doing your job, Mr. Devereaux, but a day like this simply reminds me why I'm getting this inheritance in the first place.
And who was responsible.

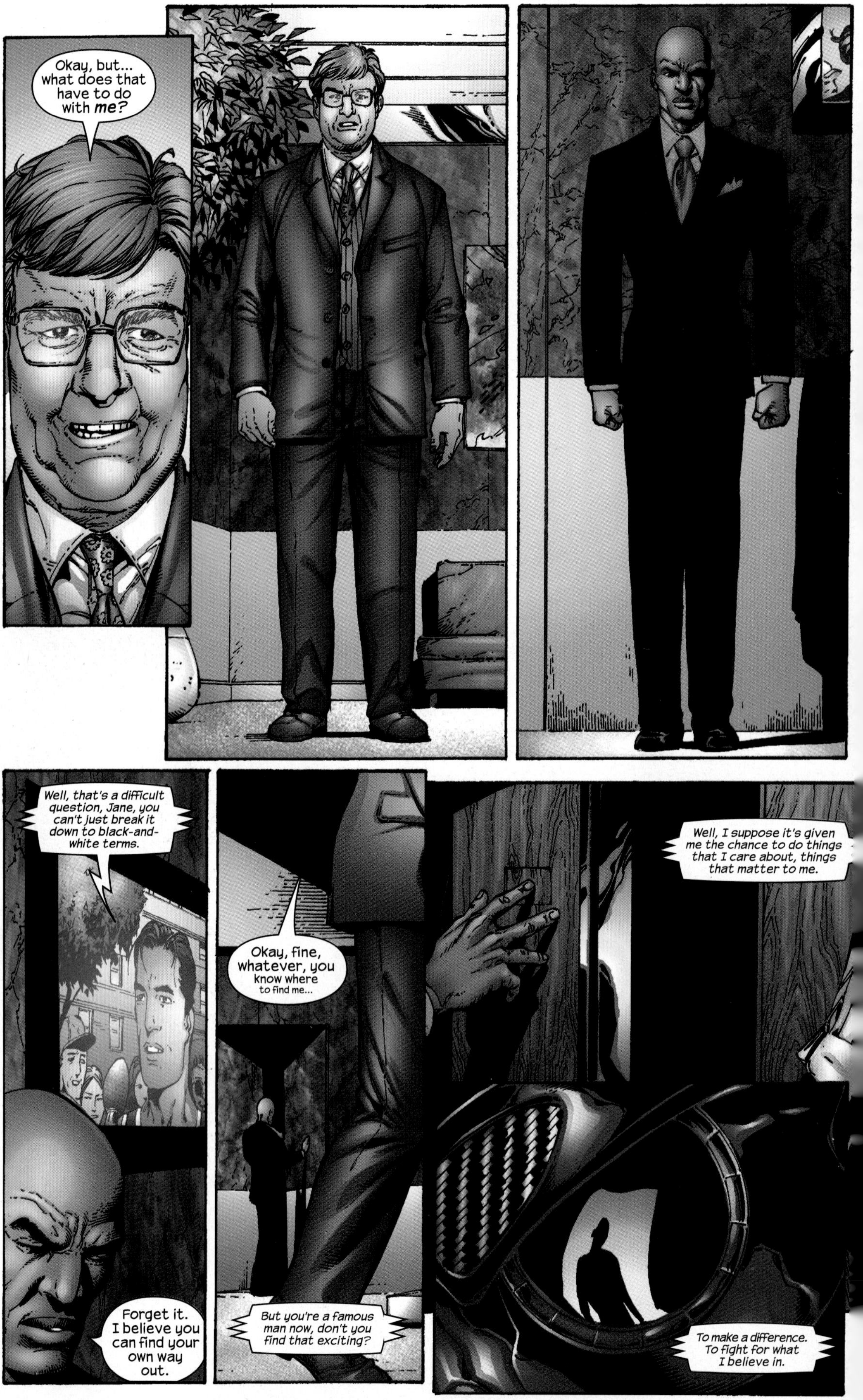
Okay, but... what does that have to do with *me*?
Well, that's a difficult question, Jane, you can't just break it down to black-and-white terms.
Okay, fine, whatever, you know where to find me...
Well, I suppose it's given me the chance to do things that I care about, things that matter to me.
Forget it. I believe you can find your own way out.
But you're a famous man now, don't you find that exciting?
To make a difference. To fight for what I believe in.

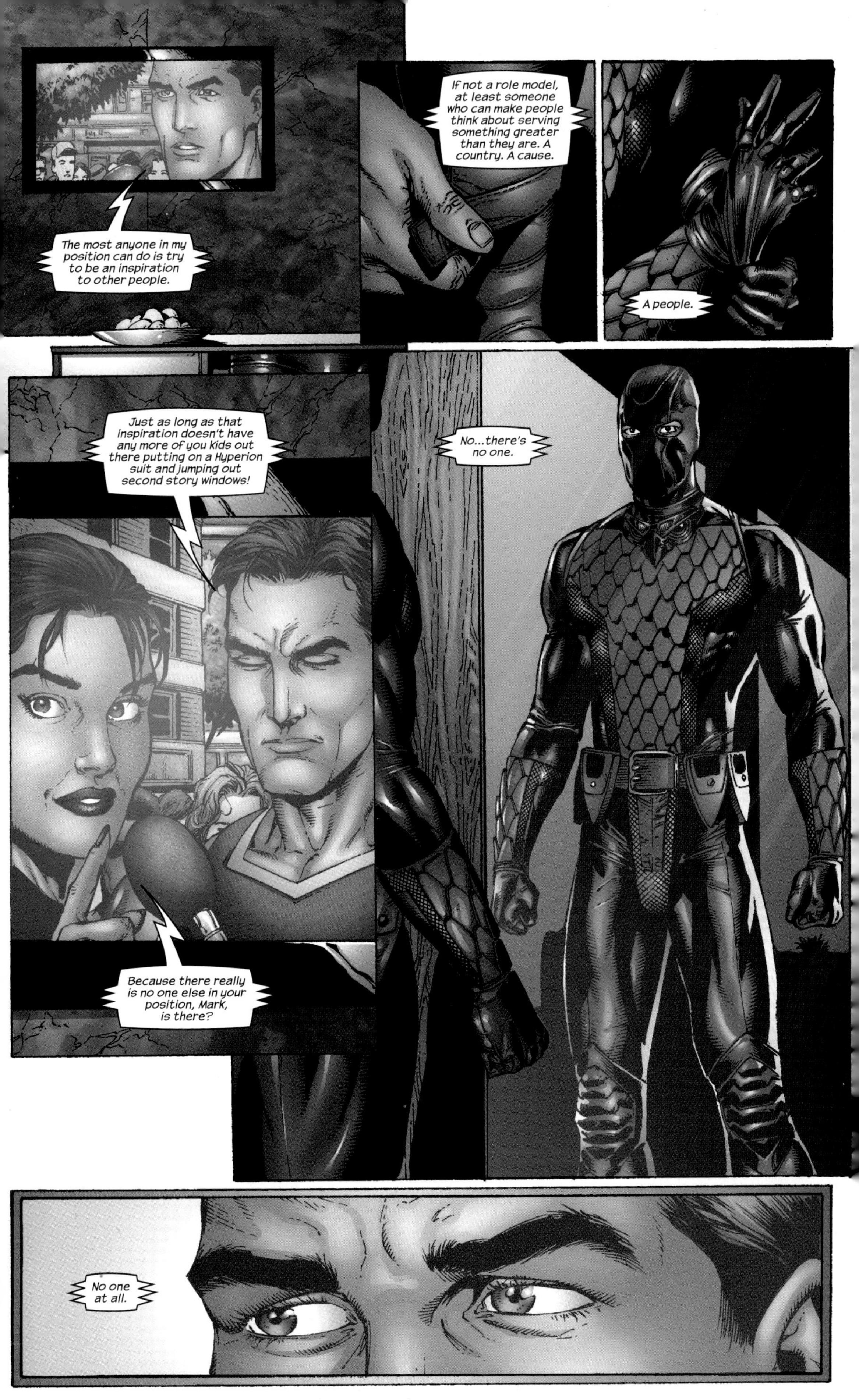

The most anyone in my position can do is try to be an inspiration to other people.
If not a role model, at least someone who can make people think about serving something greater than they are. A country. A cause.
A people.
Just as long as that inspiration doesn't have any more of you kids out there putting on a Hyperion suit and jumping out second story windows!
Because there really is no one else in your position, Mark, is there?
No...there's no one.
No one at all.

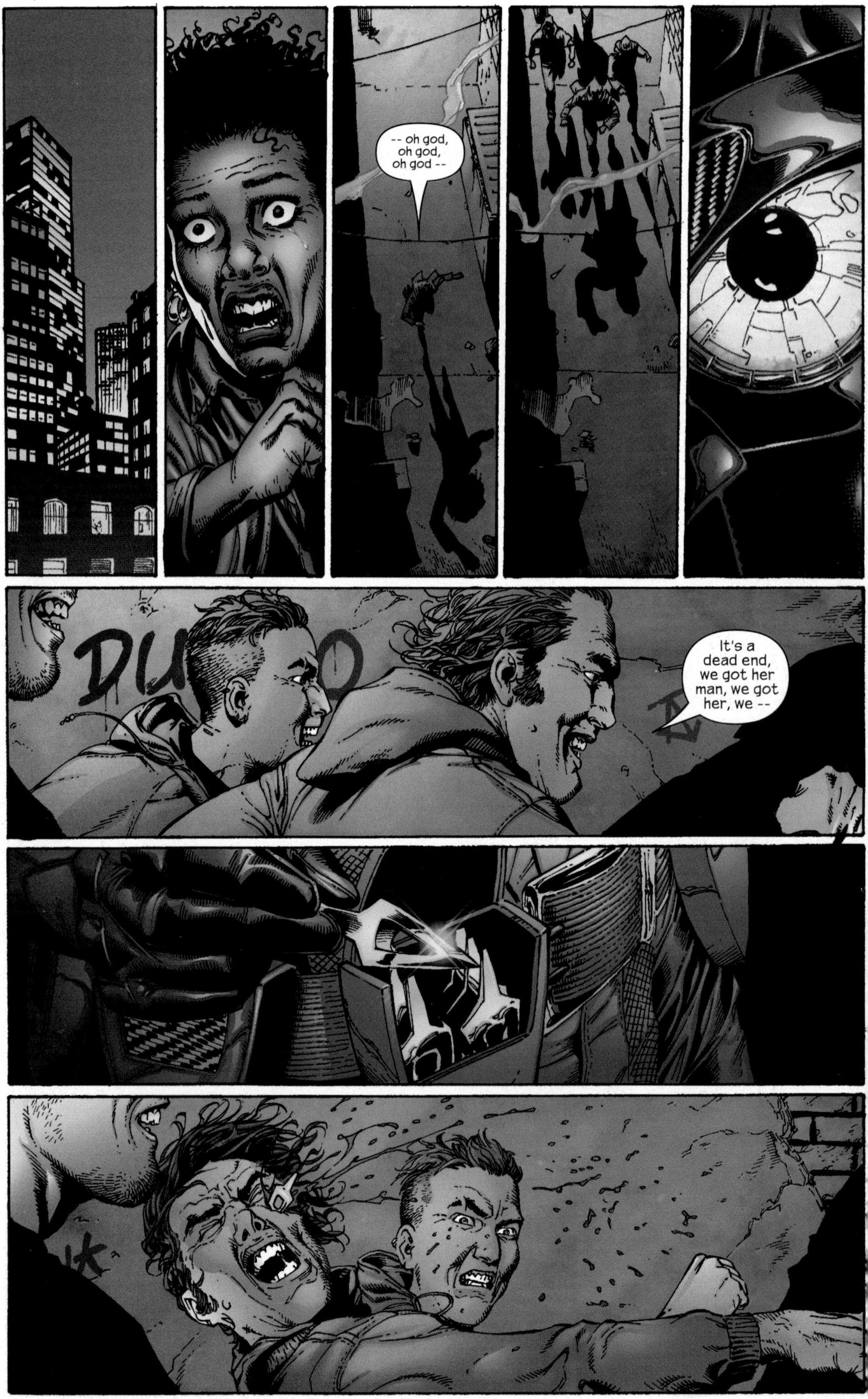
-- oh god,
oh god,
oh god --
It's a
dead end,
we got her
man, we got
her, we --

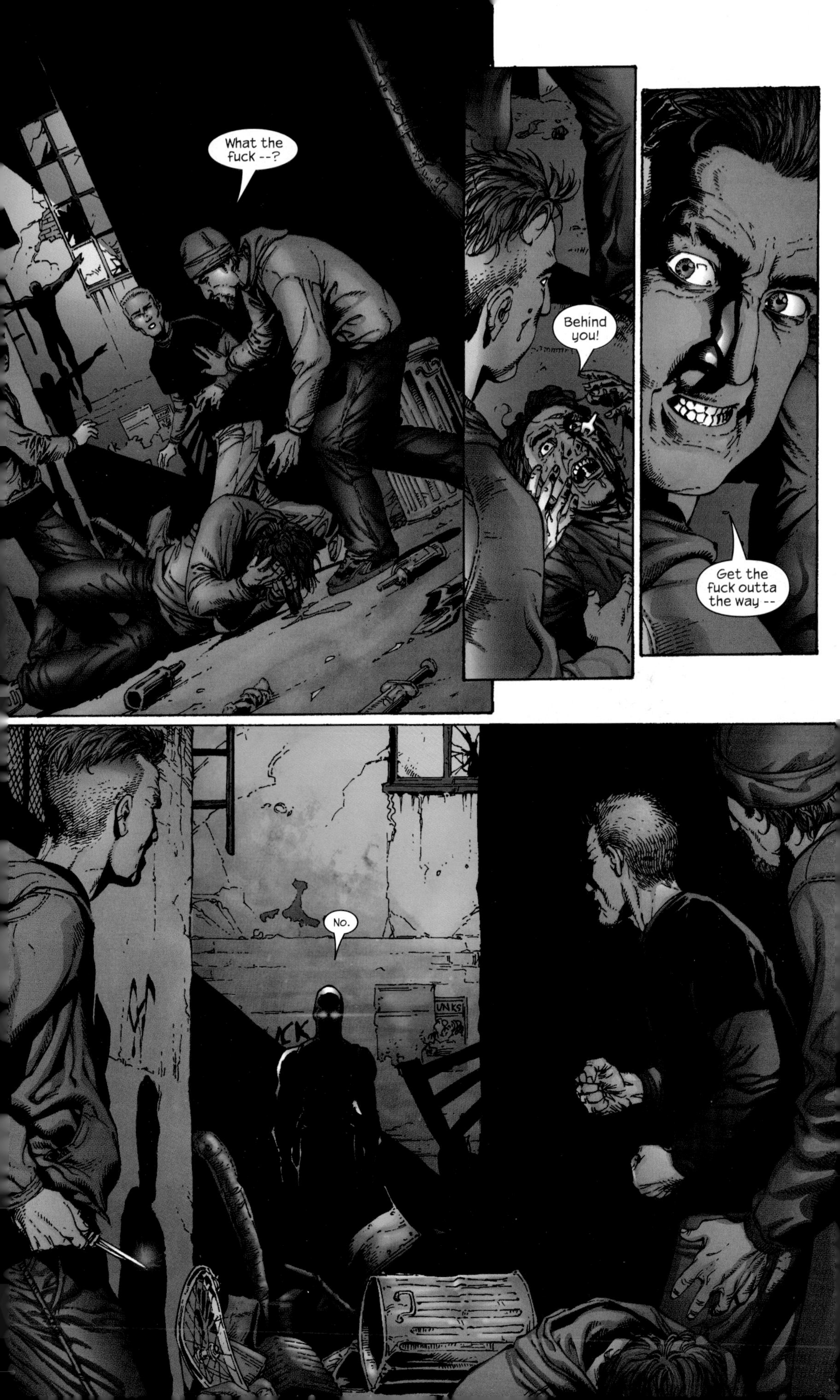
What the fuck --?
Behind you!
Get the fuck outta the way --
No.

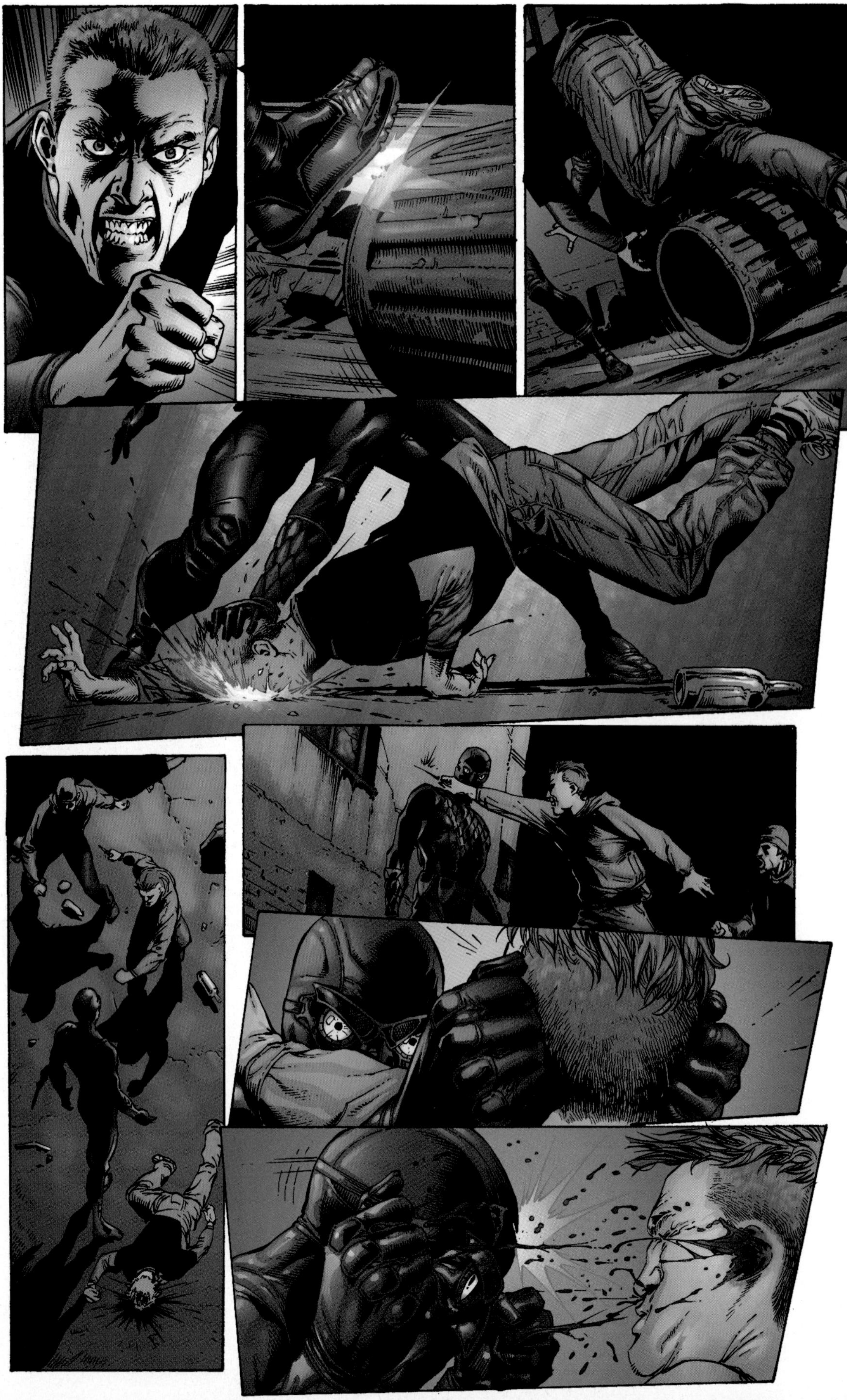

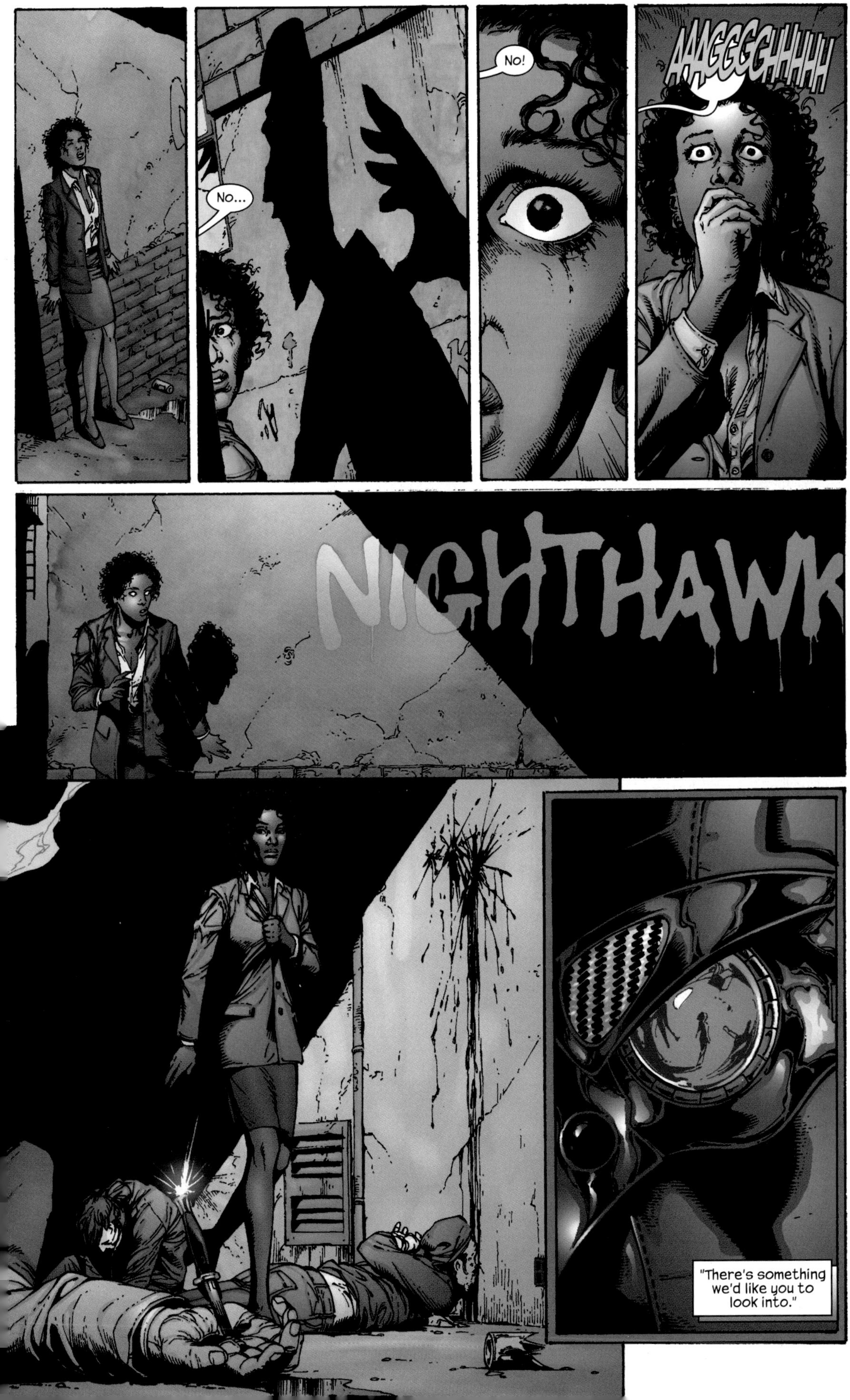

No...
No!
AAAGGGGHHHH
NIGHTHAWK
"There's something we'd like you to look into."

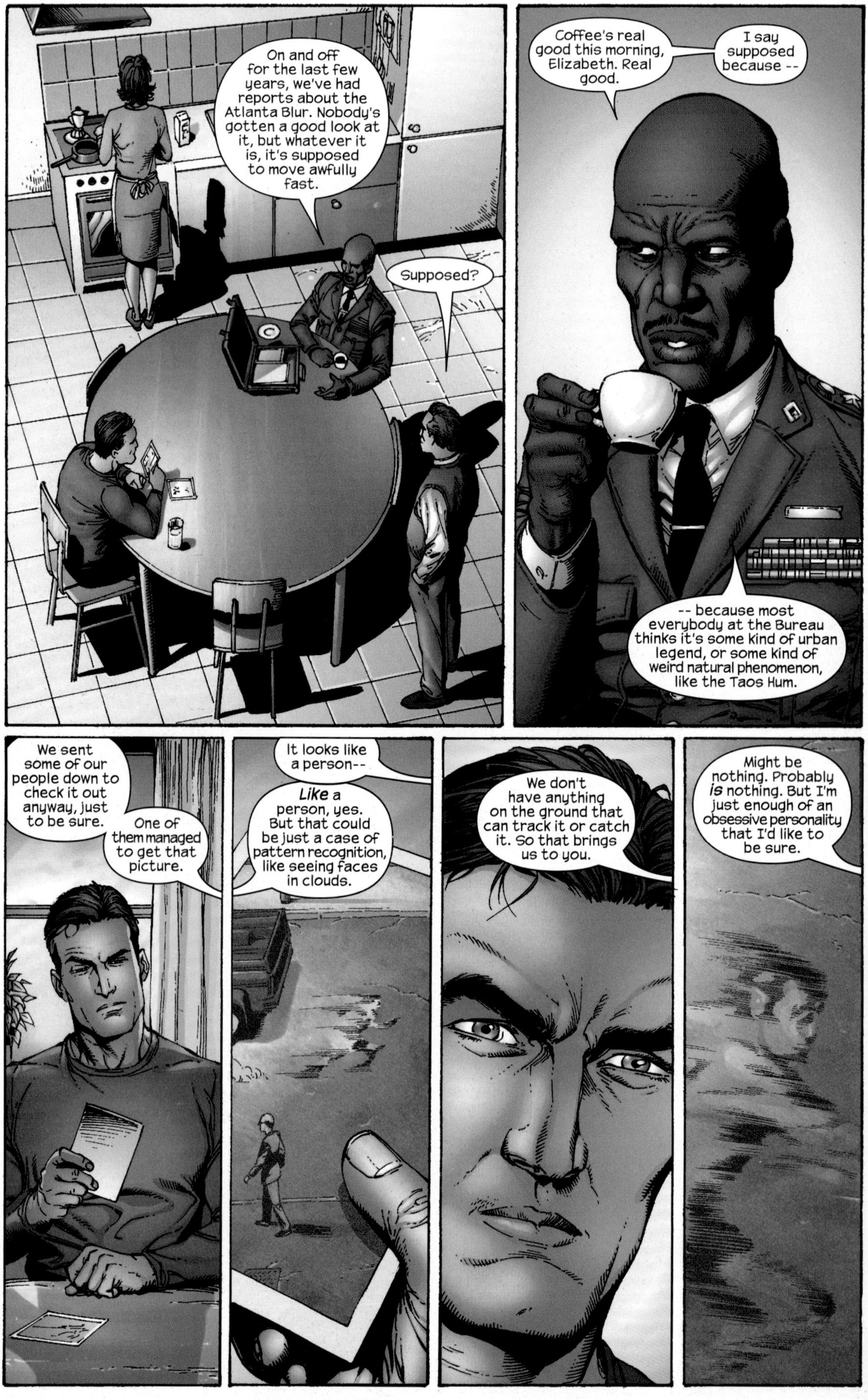

On and off for the last few years, we've had reports about the Atlanta Blur. Nobody's gotten a good look at it, but whatever it is, it's supposed to move awfully fast.
Supposed?
Coffee's real good this morning, Elizabeth. Real good.
I say supposed because --
-- because most everybody at the Bureau thinks it's some kind of urban legend, or some kind of weird natural phenomenon, like the Taos Hum.
We sent some of our people down to check it out anyway, just to be sure.
One of them managed to get that picture.
It looks like a person--
Like a person, yes. But that could be just a case of pattern recognition, like seeing faces in clouds.
We don't have anything on the ground that can track it or catch it. So that brings us to you.
Might be nothing. Probably *is* nothing. But I'm just enough of an obsessive personality that I'd like to be sure.

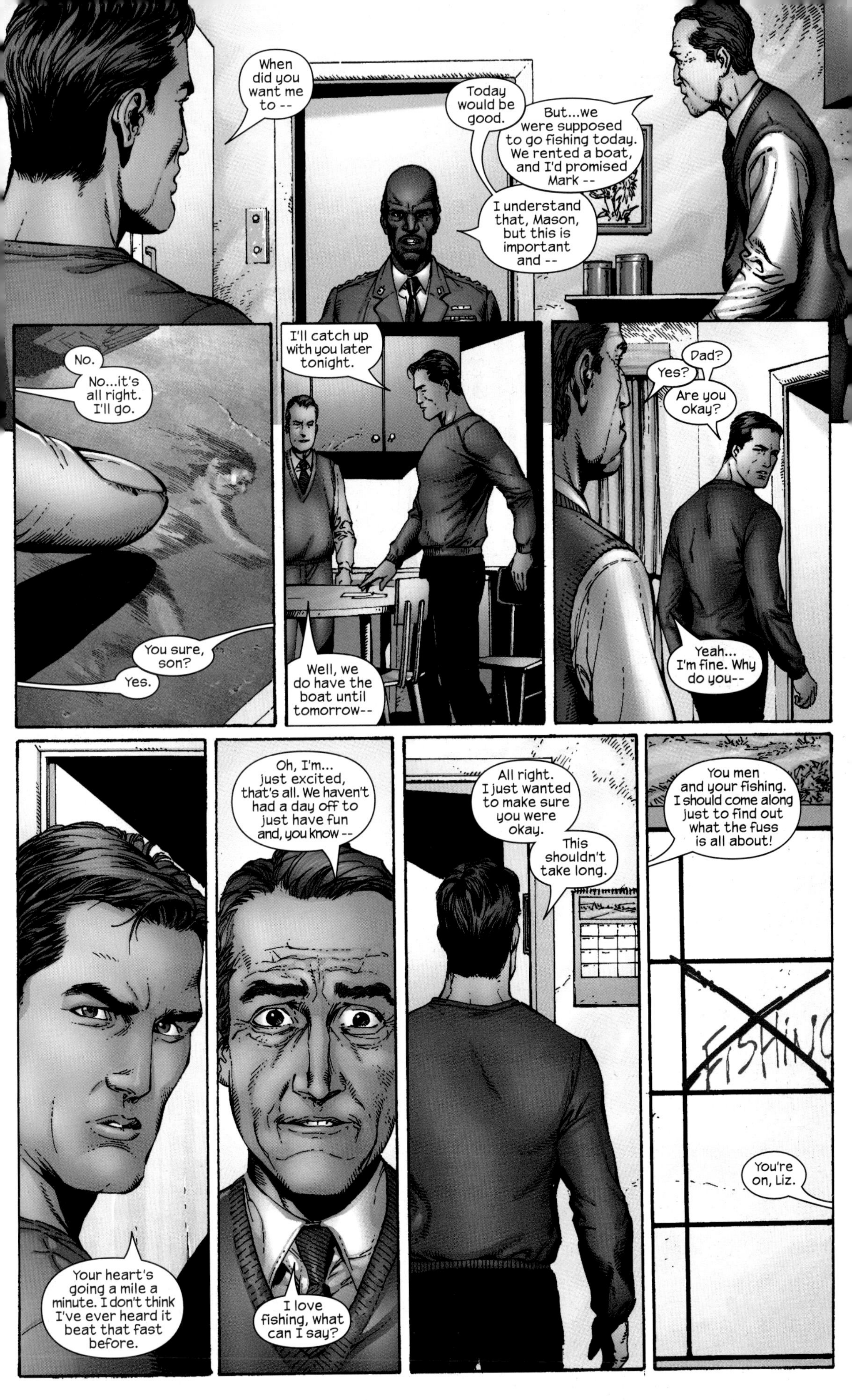
When did you want me to --
Today would be good.
But...we were supposed to go fishing today. We rented a boat, and I'd promised Mark --
I understand that, Mason, but this is important and --
No.
No...it's all right. I'll go.
You sure, son?
Yes.
I'll catch up with you later tonight.
Well, we do have the boat until tomorrow--
Dad?
Yes?
Are you okay?
Yeah... I'm fine. Why do you--
Your heart's going a mile a minute. I don't think I've ever heard it beat that fast before.
Oh, I'm... just excited, that's all. We haven't had a day off to just have fun and, you know --
I love fishing, what can I say?
All right. I just wanted to make sure you were okay.
This shouldn't take long.
You men and your fishing. I should come along just to find out what the fuss is all about!
FISHING
You're on, Liz.

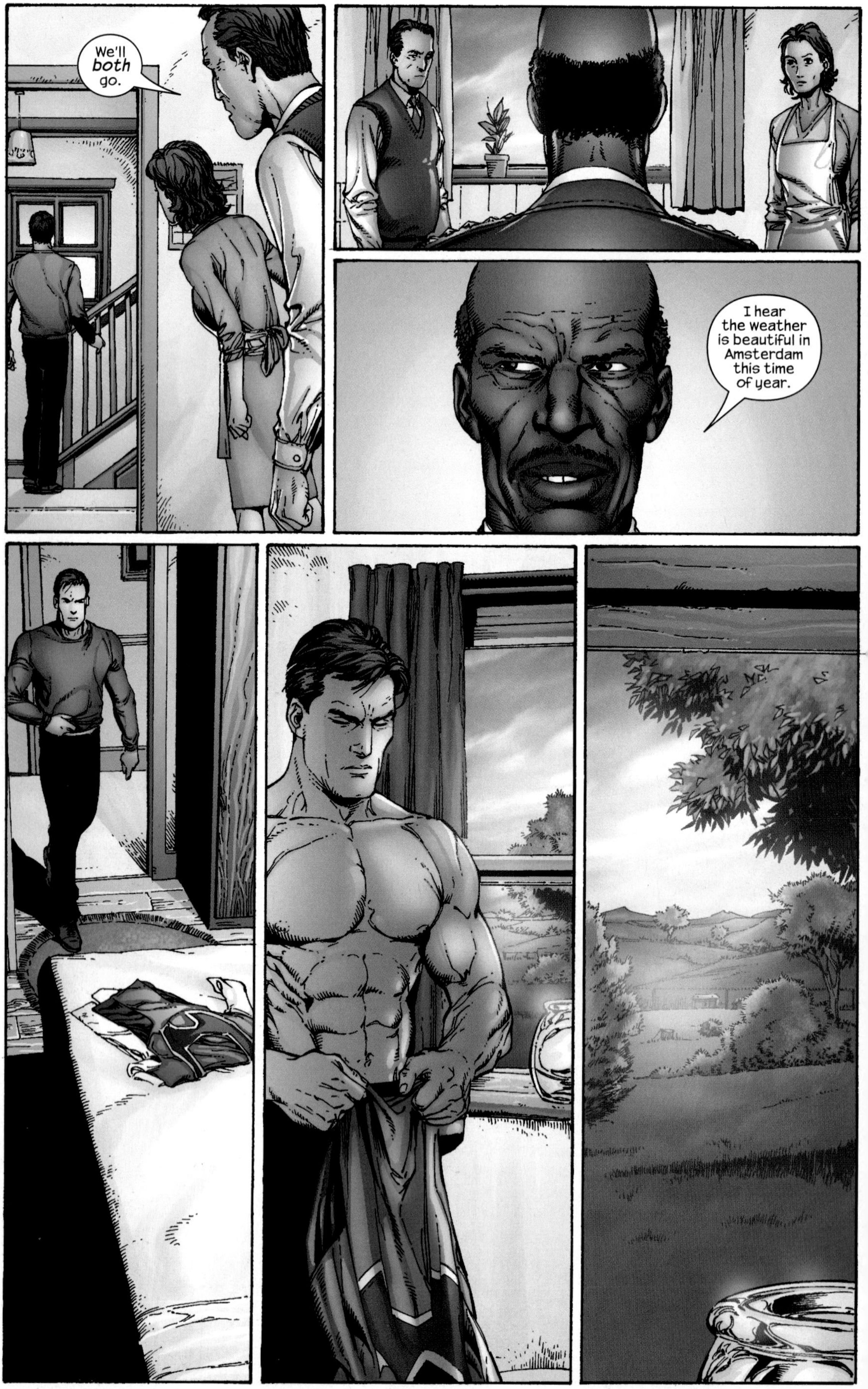
We'll both go.
I hear the weather is beautiful in Amsterdam this time of year.

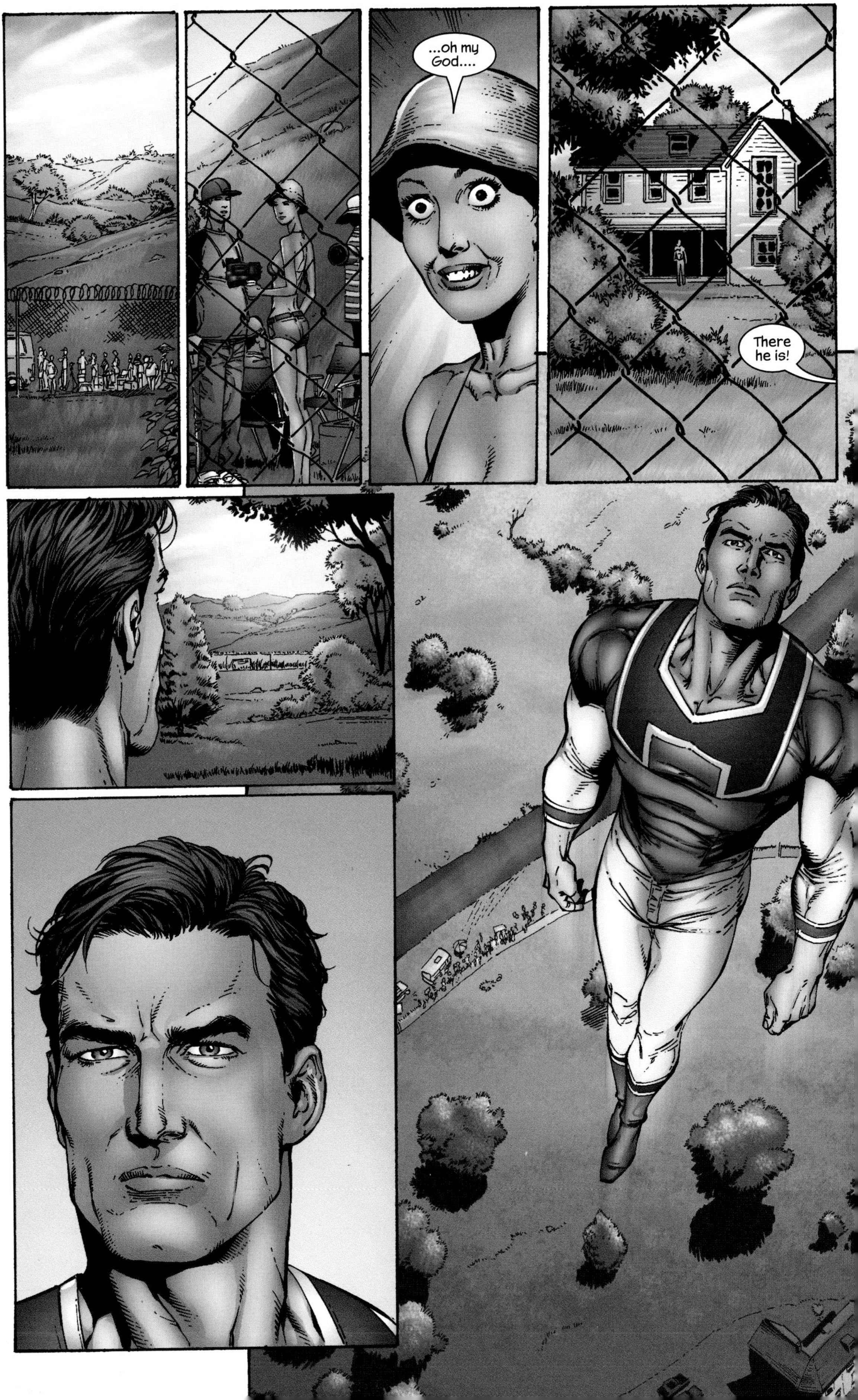
...oh my God....
There he is!

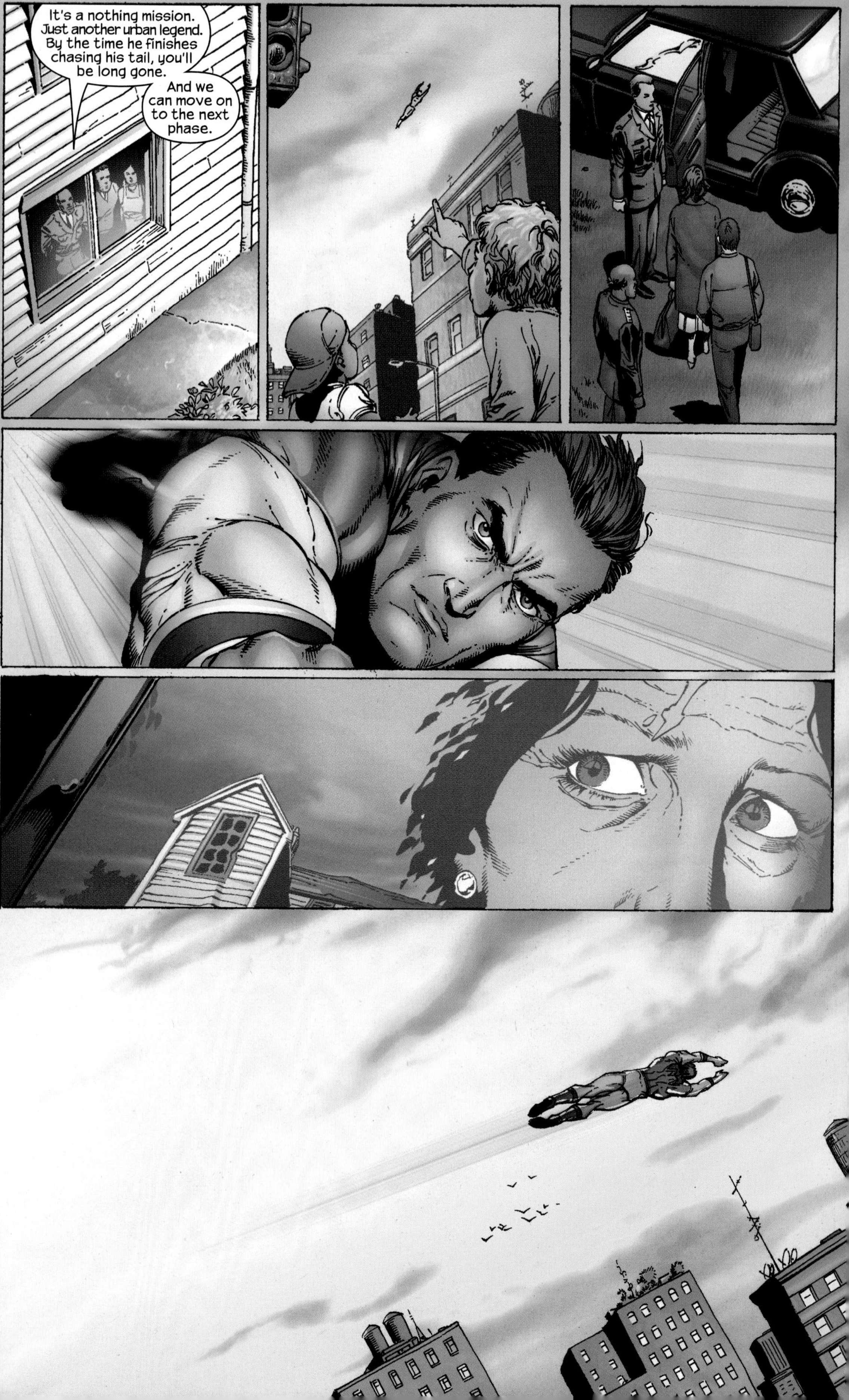
It's a nothing mission. Just another urban legend. By the time he finishes chasing his tail, you'll be long gone.
And we can move on to the next phase.

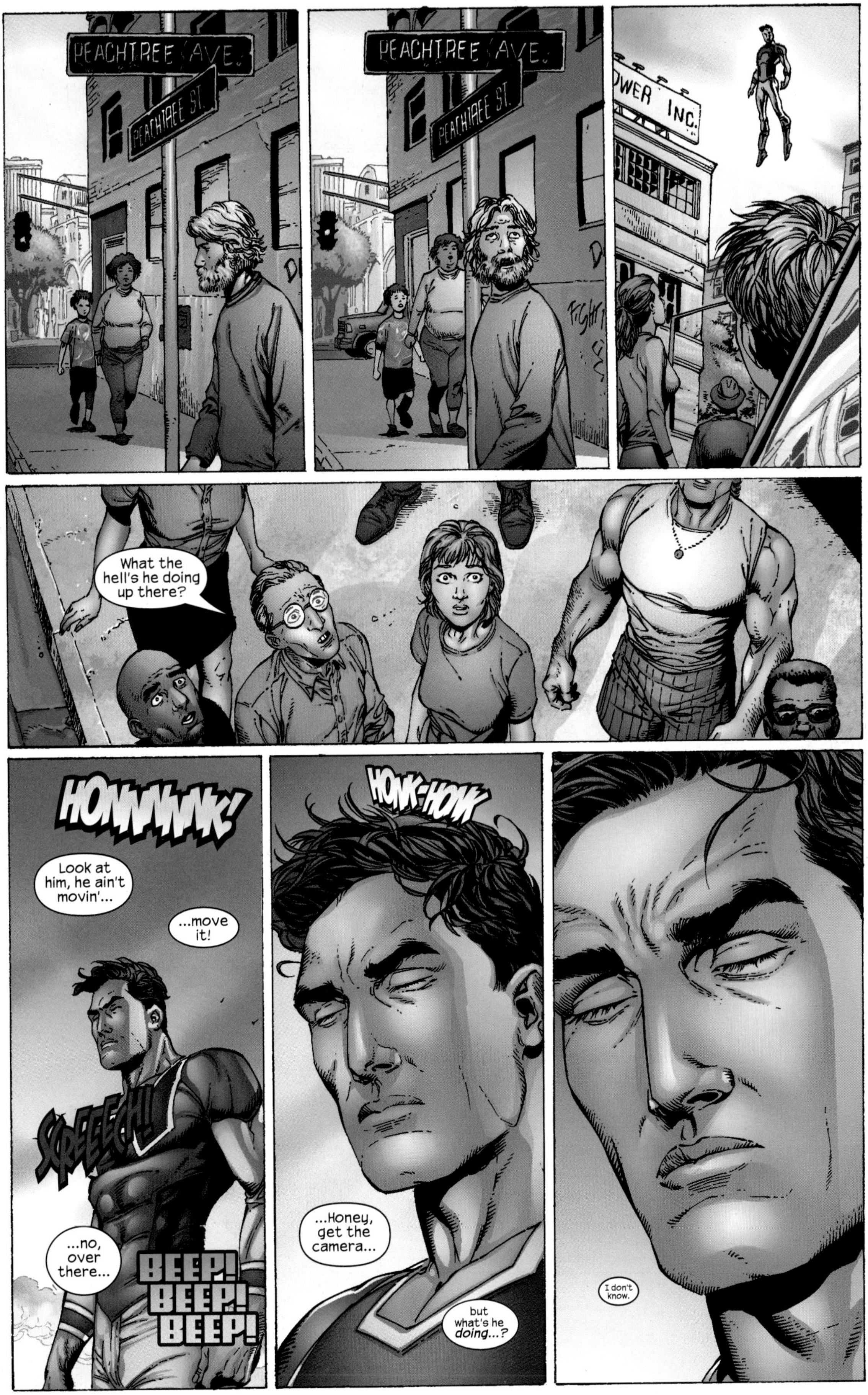
PEACHTREE AVE.
PEACHTREE ST.
WER INC.
What the hell's he doing up there?
HONNNNK!
Look at him, he ain't movin'...
...move it!
SCREEECH!
...no, over there...
BEEP! BEEP! BEEP!
HONK-HONK
...Honey, get the camera...
but what's he doing...?
I don't know.

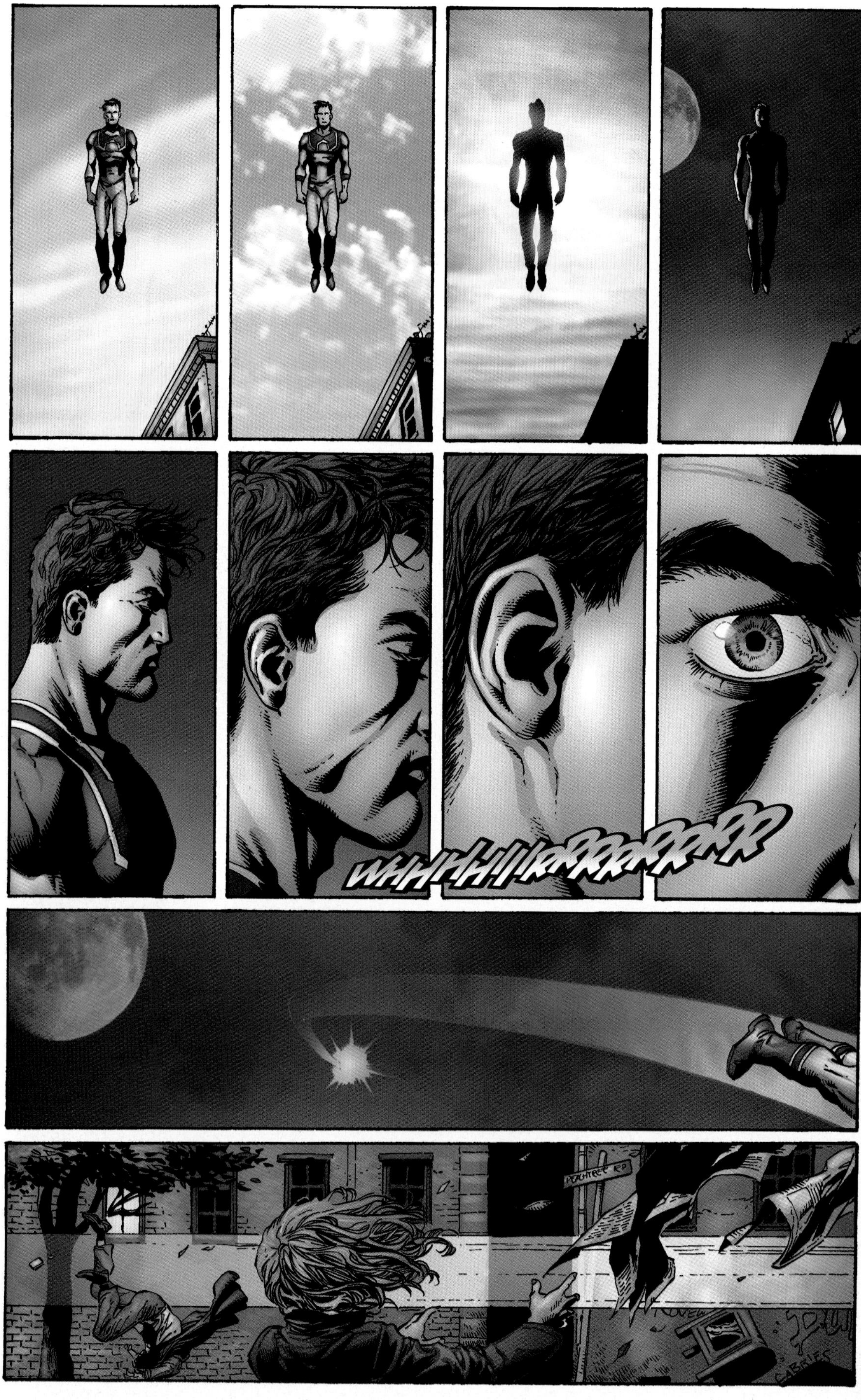
WHHHHIIRRRRRRRRR
PEACHTREE RD

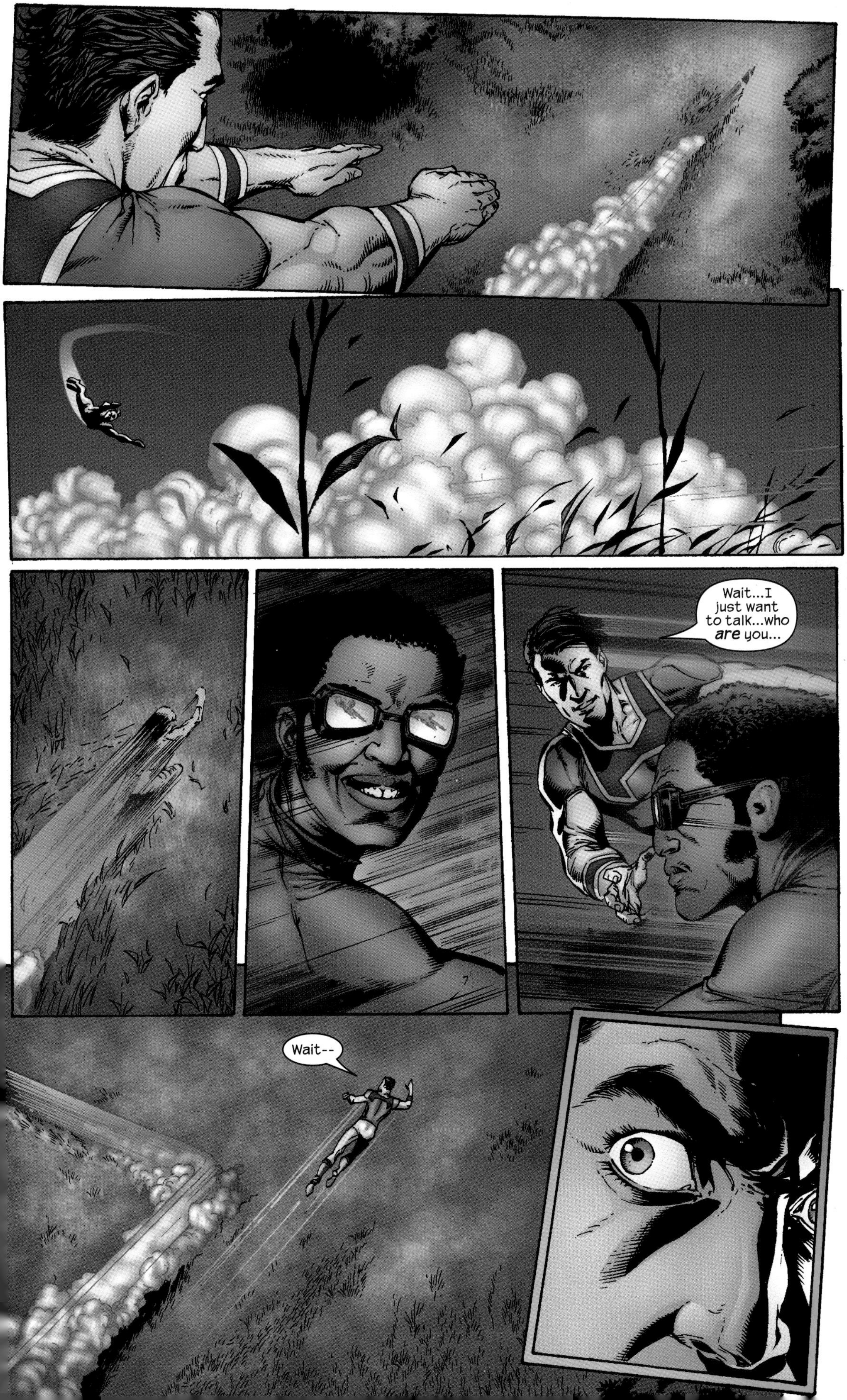

Wait...I just want to talk...who are you...
Wait--

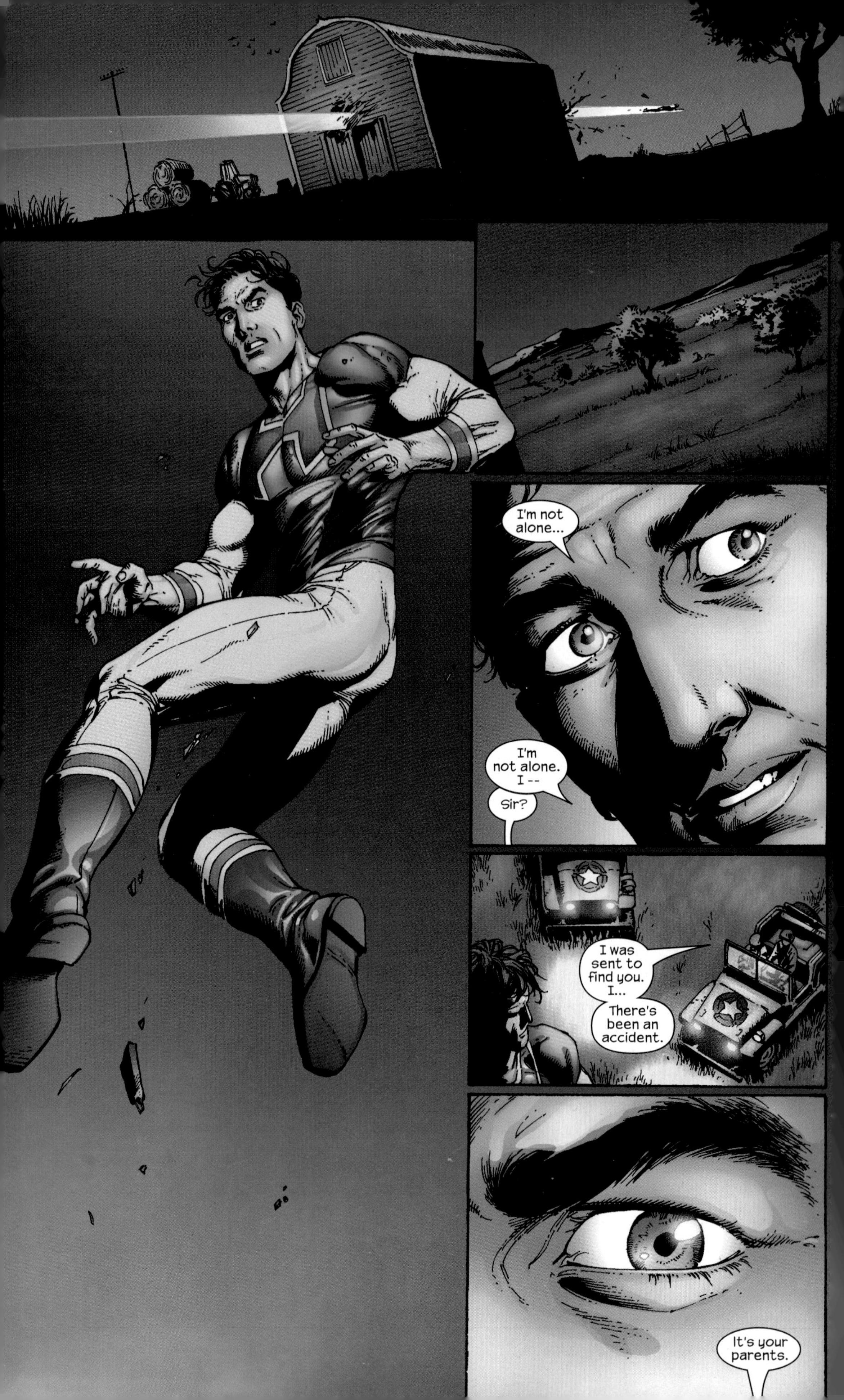

I'm not alone...
I'm not alone. I --
Sir?
I was sent to find you. I...
There's been an accident.
It's your parents.

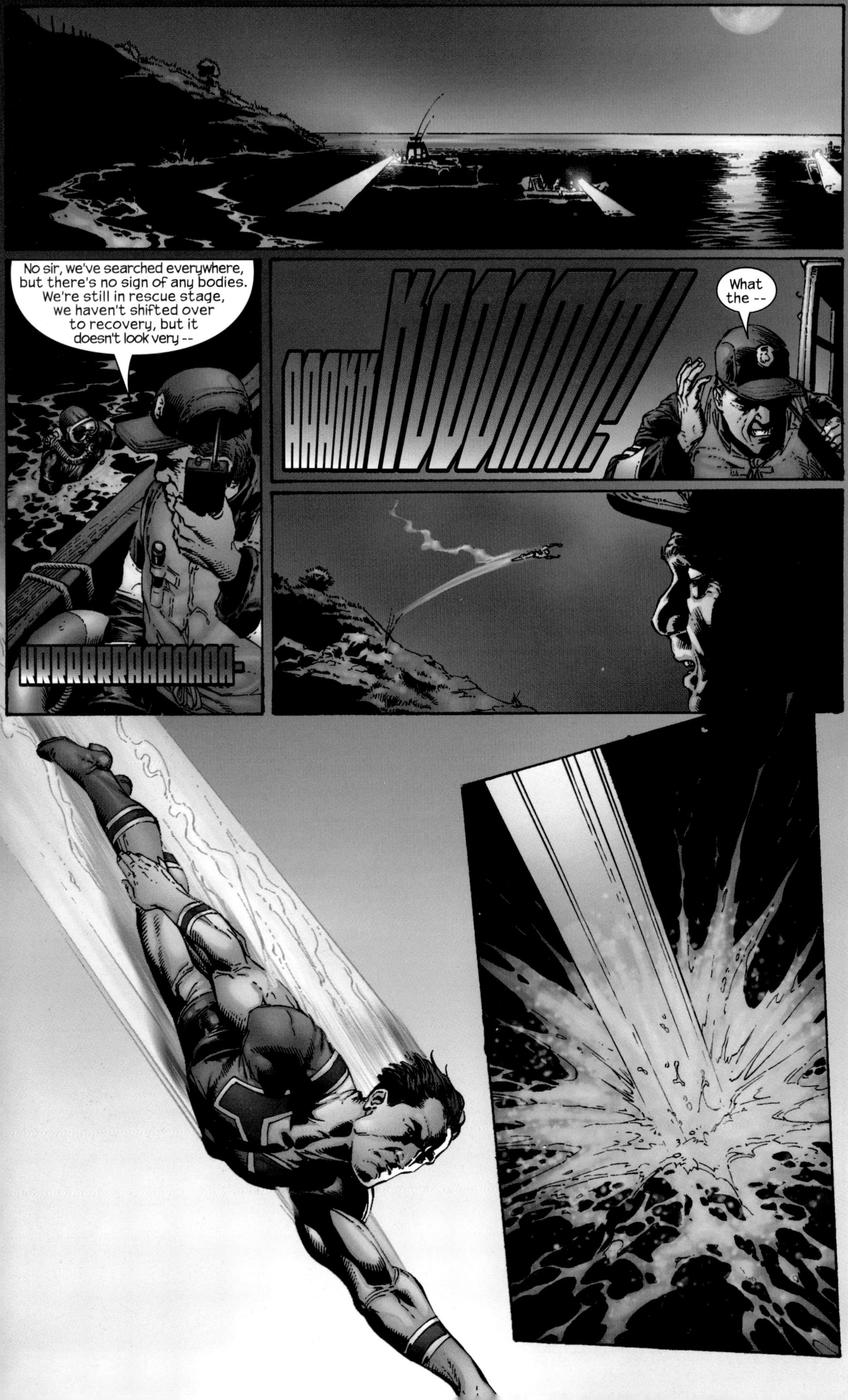

No sir, we've searched everywhere, but there's no sign of any bodies. We're still in rescue stage, we haven't shifted over to recovery, but it doesn't look very --
KRRRRRRAAAAAAA
AAAKKKOOOMM!
What the --

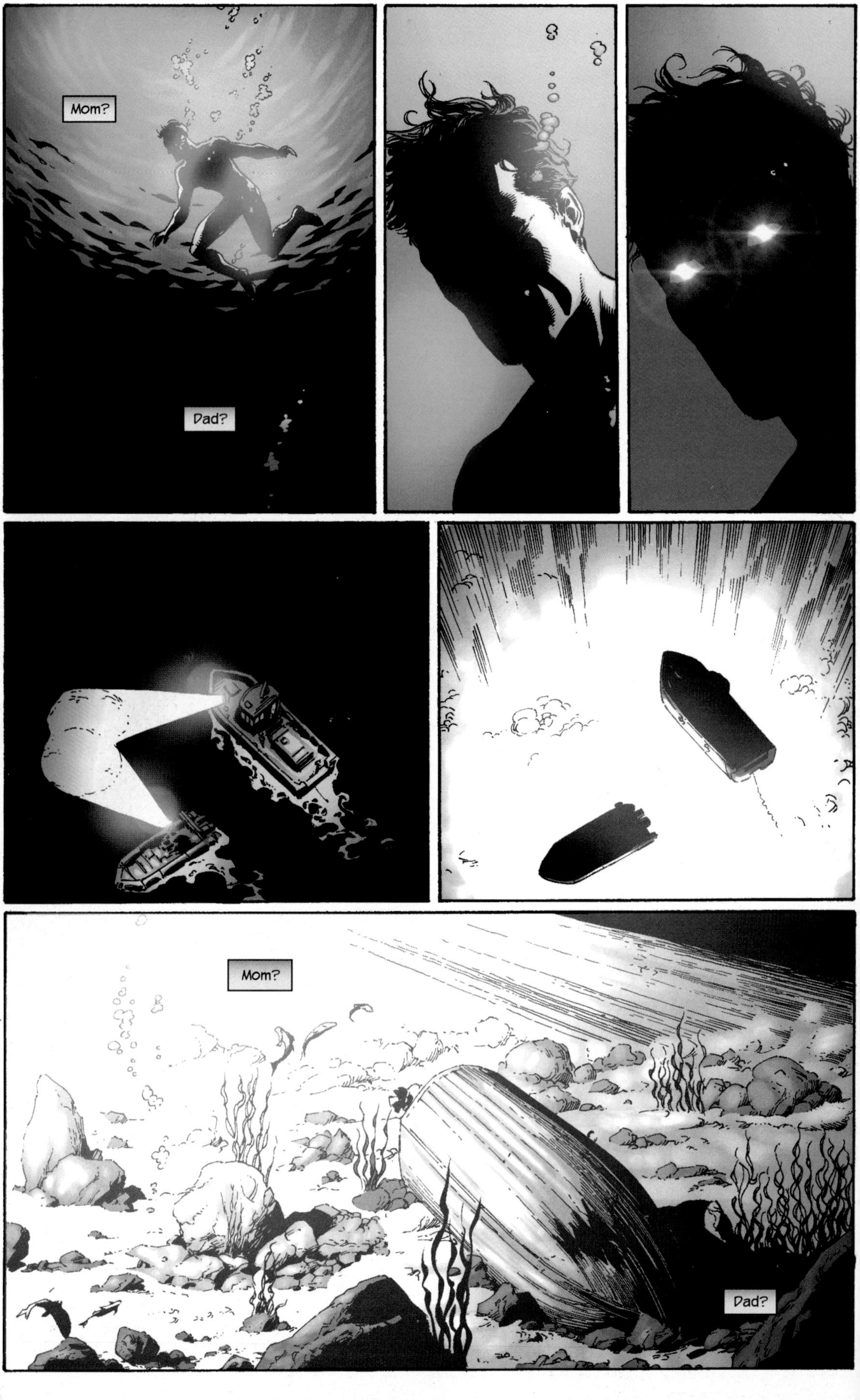
Mom?
Dad?
Mom?
Dad?

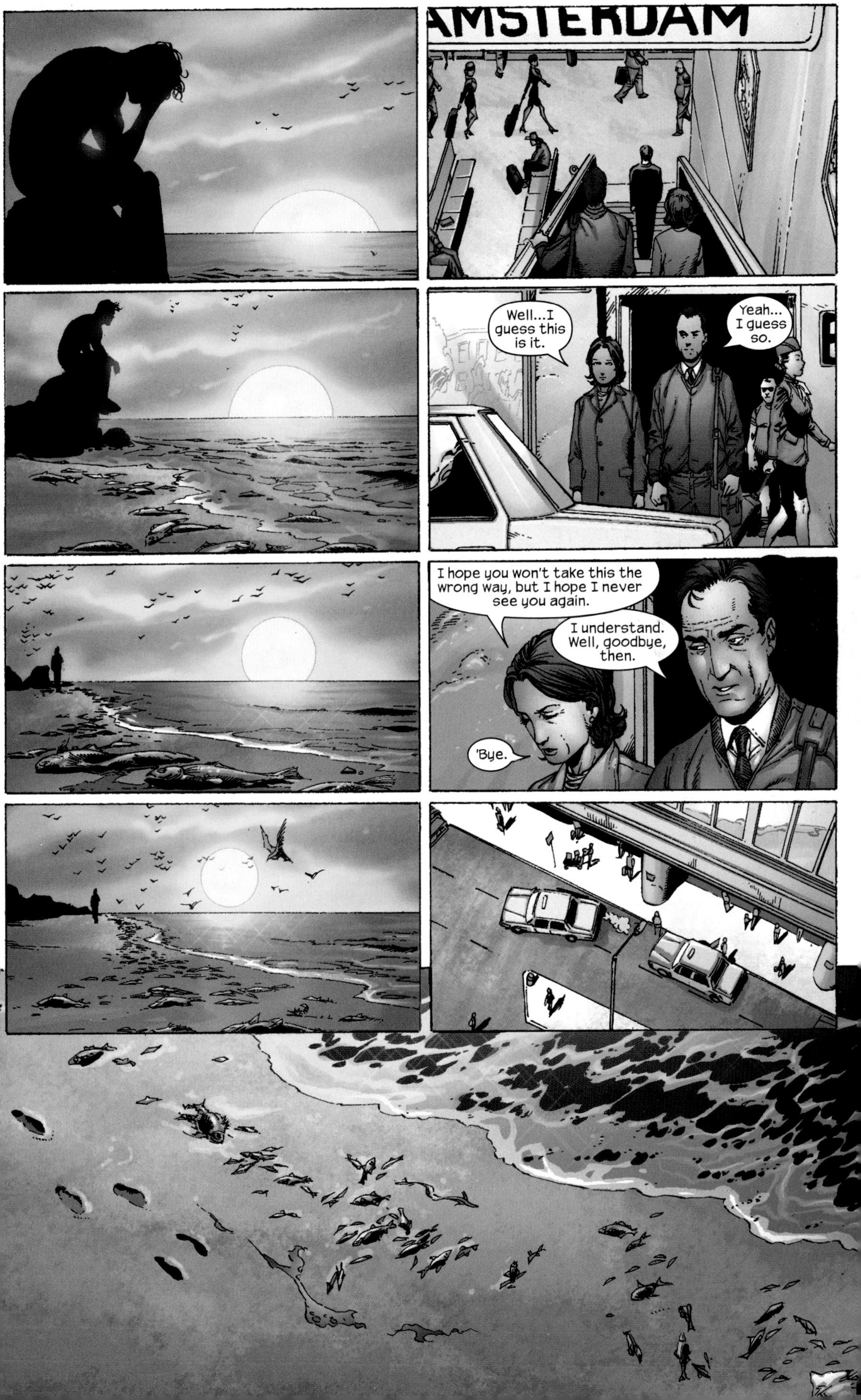
AMSTERDAM
Well...I guess this is it.
Yeah... I guess so.
I hope you won't take this the wrong way, but I hope I never see you again.
I understand. Well, goodbye, then.
'Bye.

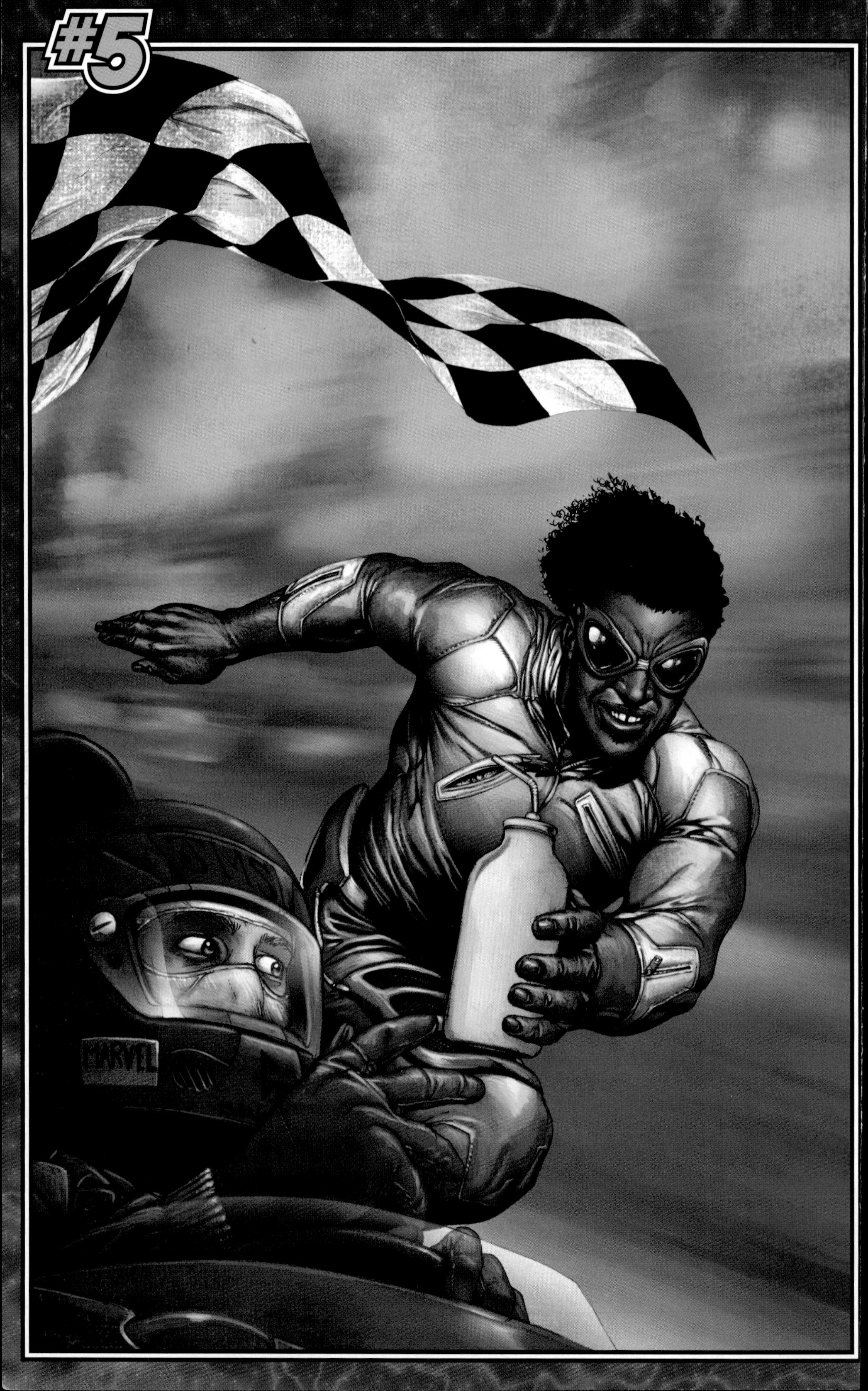
#5
MARVEL

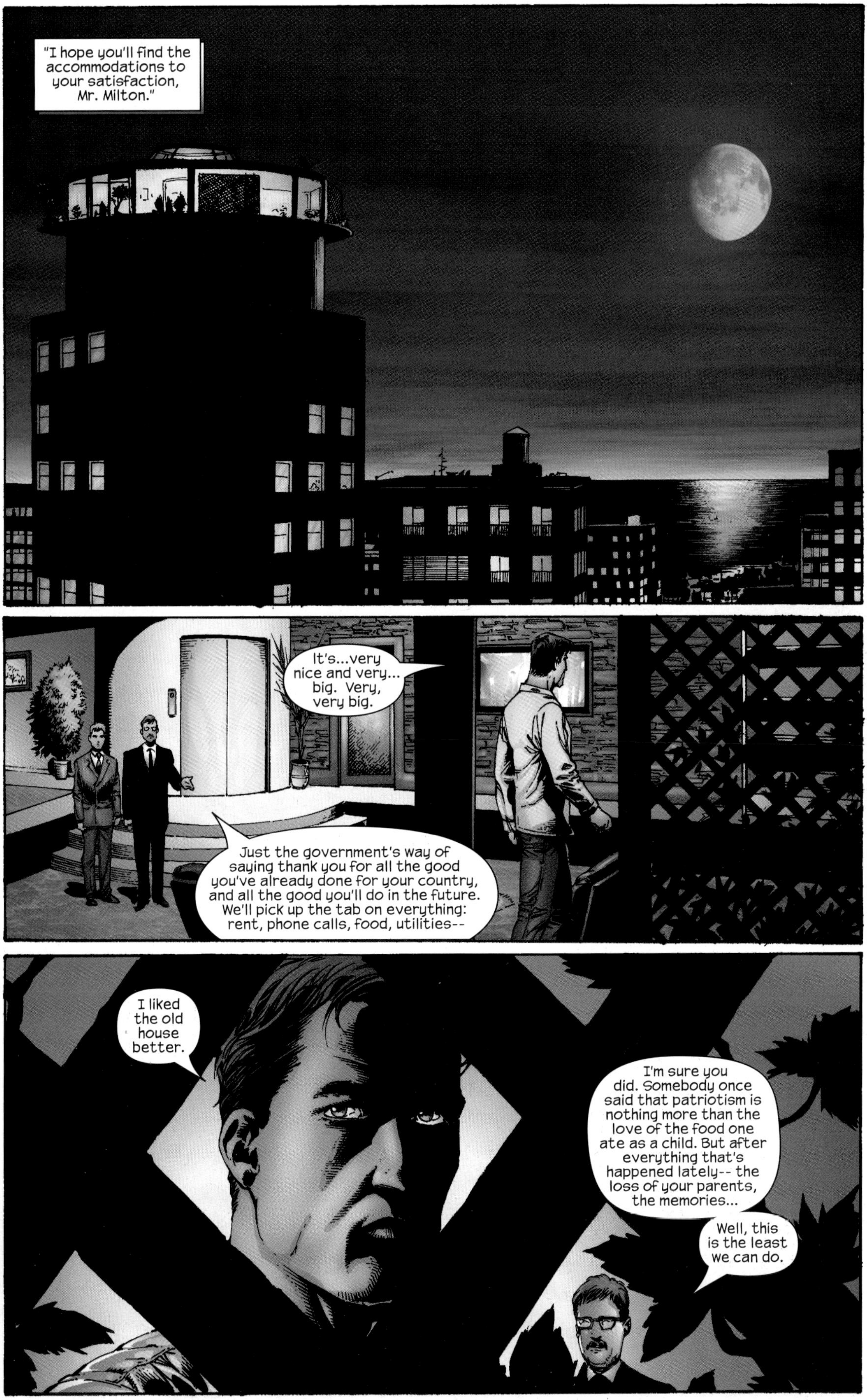
"I hope you'll find the accommodations to your satisfaction, Mr. Milton."
It's...very nice and very... big. Very, very big.
Just the government's way of saying thank you for all the good you've already done for your country, and all the good you'll do in the future. We'll pick up the tab on everything: rent, phone calls, food, utilities--
I liked the old house better.
I'm sure you did. Somebody once said that patriotism is nothing more than the love of the food one ate as a child. But after everything that's happened lately-- the loss of your parents, the memories...
Well, this is the least we can do.

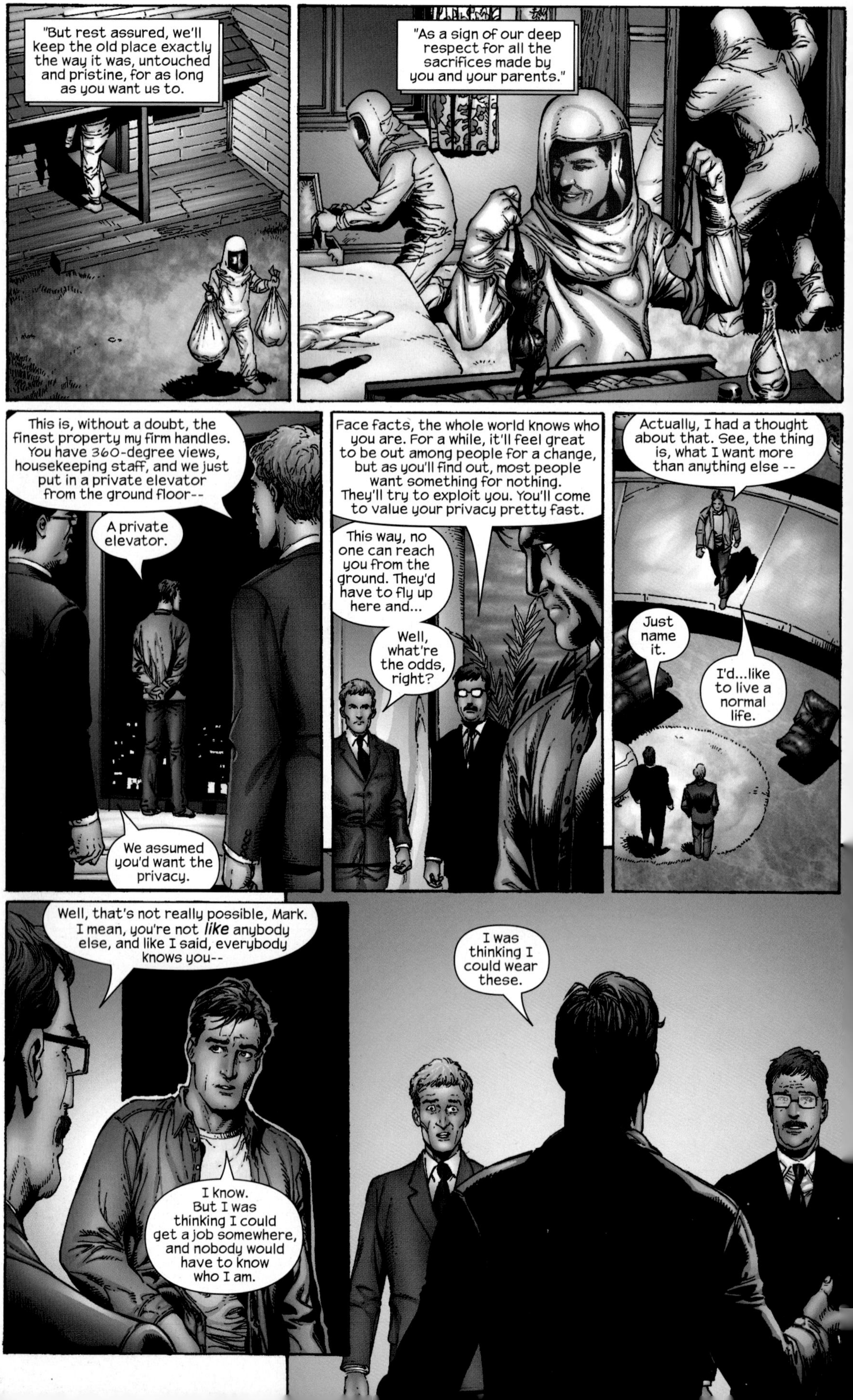
"But rest assured, we'll keep the old place exactly the way it was, untouched and pristine, for as long as you want us to.
"As a sign of our deep respect for all the sacrifices made by you and your parents."
This is, without a doubt, the finest property my firm handles. You have 360-degree views, housekeeping staff, and we just put in a private elevator from the ground floor--
A private elevator.
We assumed you'd want the privacy.
Face facts, the whole world knows who you are. For a while, it'll feel great to be out among people for a change, but as you'll find out, most people want something for nothing. They'll try to exploit you. You'll come to value your privacy pretty fast.
This way, no one can reach you from the ground. They'd have to fly up here and...
Well, what're the odds, right?
Actually, I had a thought about that. See, the thing is, what I want more than anything else --
Just name it.
I'd...like to live a normal life.
Well, that's not really possible, Mark. I mean, you're not *like* anybody else, and like I said, everybody knows you--
I know. But I was thinking I could get a job somewhere, and nobody would have to know who I am.
I was thinking I could wear these.

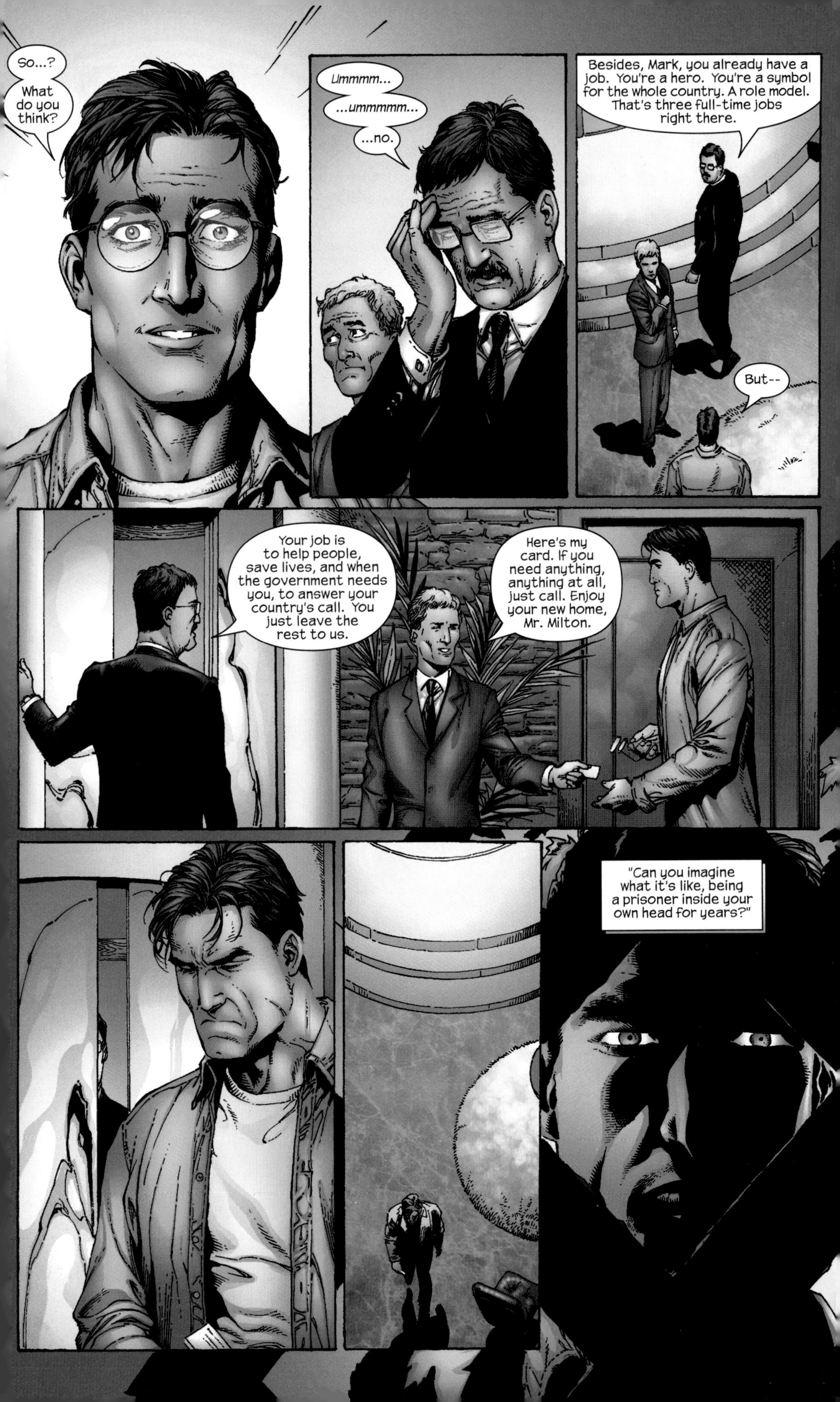

So...?
What do you think?
Ummmm...
...ummmmm...
...no.
Besides, Mark, you already have a job. You're a hero. You're a symbol for the whole country. A role model. That's three full-time jobs right there.
But--
Your job is to help people, save lives, and when the government needs you, to answer your country's call. You just leave the rest to us.
Here's my card. If you need anything, anything at all, just call. Enjoy your new home, Mr. Milton.
"Can you imagine what it's like, being a prisoner inside your own head for years?"

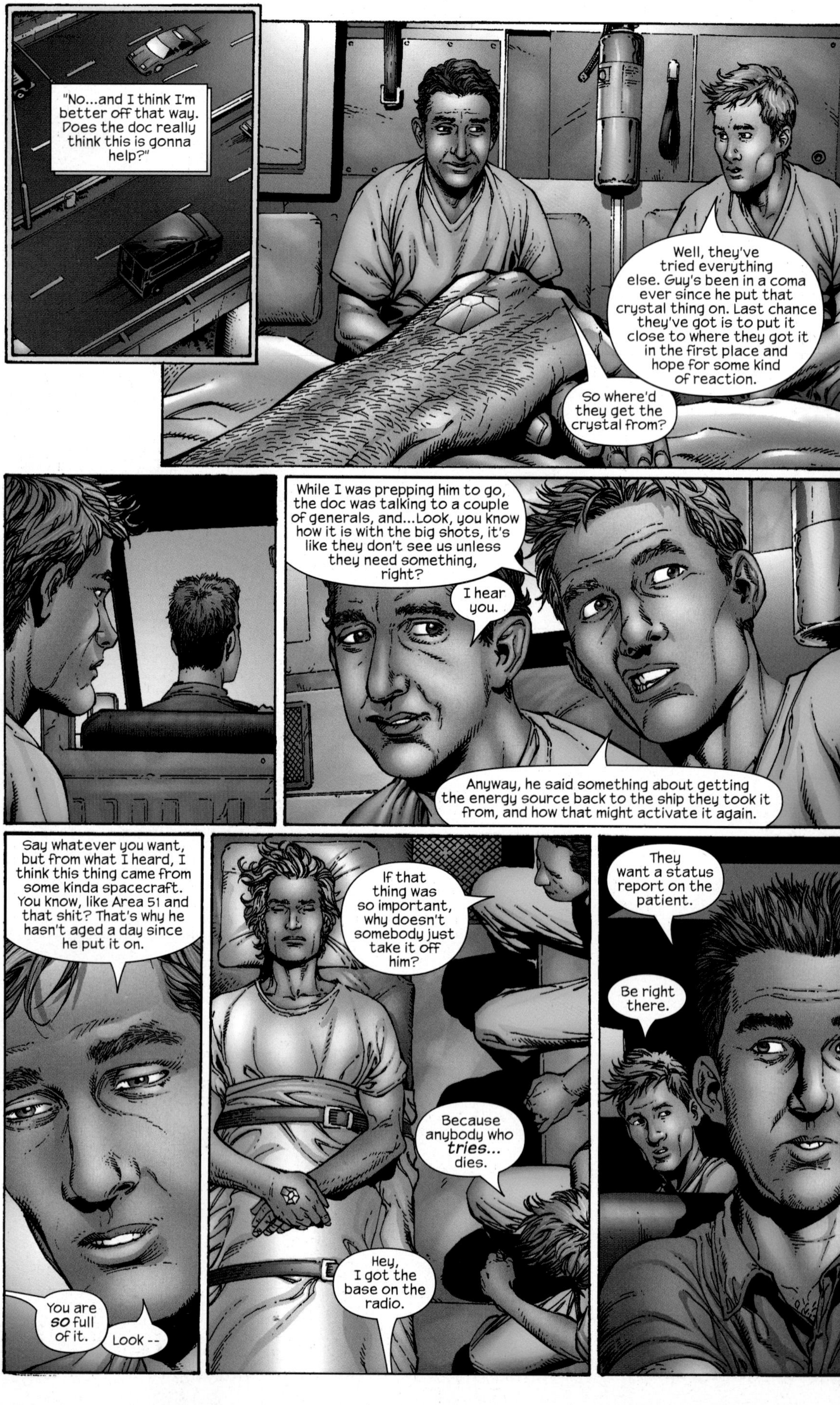
"No...and I think I'm better off that way. Does the doc really think this is gonna help?"
Well, they've tried everything else. Guy's been in a coma ever since he put that crystal thing on. Last chance they've got is to put it close to where they got it in the first place and hope for some kind of reaction.
So where'd they get the crystal from?
While I was prepping him to go, the doc was talking to a couple of generals, and...Look, you know how it is with the big shots, it's like they don't see us unless they need something, right?
I hear you.
Anyway, he said something about getting the energy source back to the ship they took it from, and how that might activate it again.
Say whatever you want, but from what I heard, I think this thing came from some kinda spacecraft. You know, like Area 51 and that shit? That's why he hasn't aged a day since he put it on.
You are *so* full of it.
Look --
If that thing was so important, why doesn't somebody just take it off him?
Because anybody who *tries*... dies.
Hey, I got the base on the radio.
They want a status report on the patient.
Be right there.

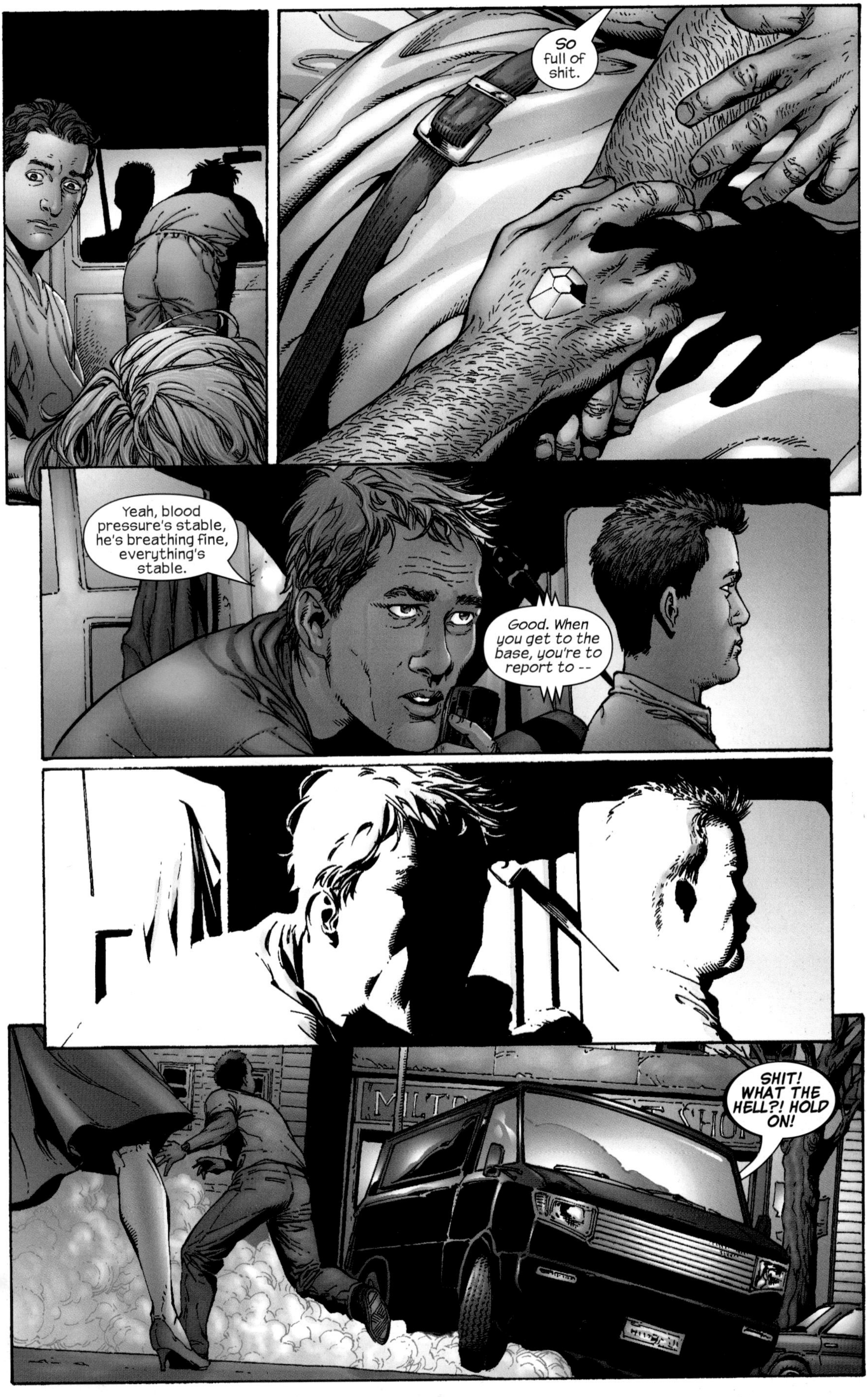
So full of shit.
Yeah, blood pressure's stable, he's breathing fine, everything's stable.
Good. When you get to the base, you're to report to --
SHIT! WHAT THE HELL?! HOLD ON!

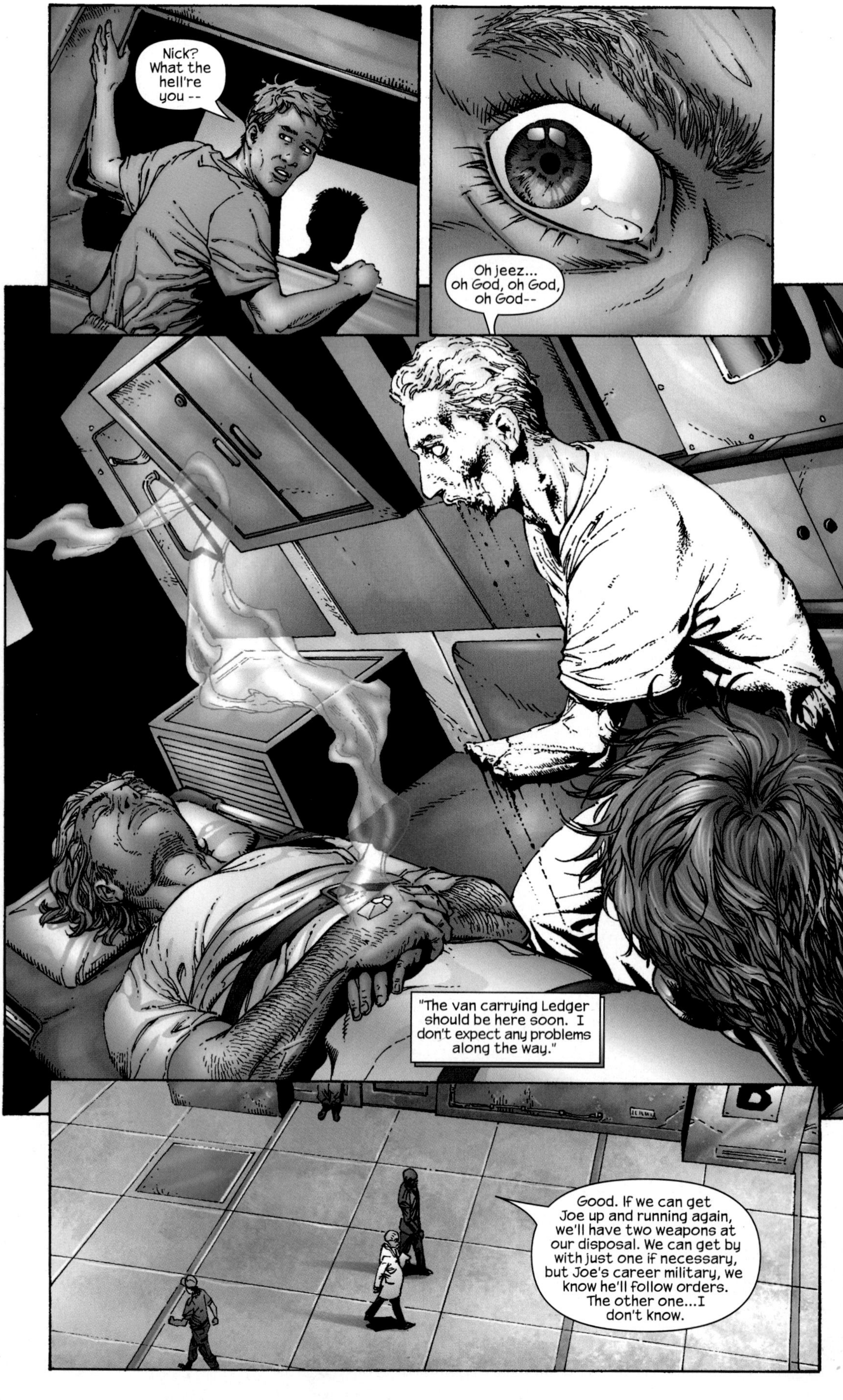

Nick? What the hell're you --
Oh jeez... oh God, oh God, oh God--
"The van carrying Ledger should be here soon. I don't expect any problems along the way."
Good. If we can get Joe up and running again, we'll have two weapons at our disposal. We can get by with just one if necessary, but Joe's career military, we know he'll follow orders. The other one...I don't know.

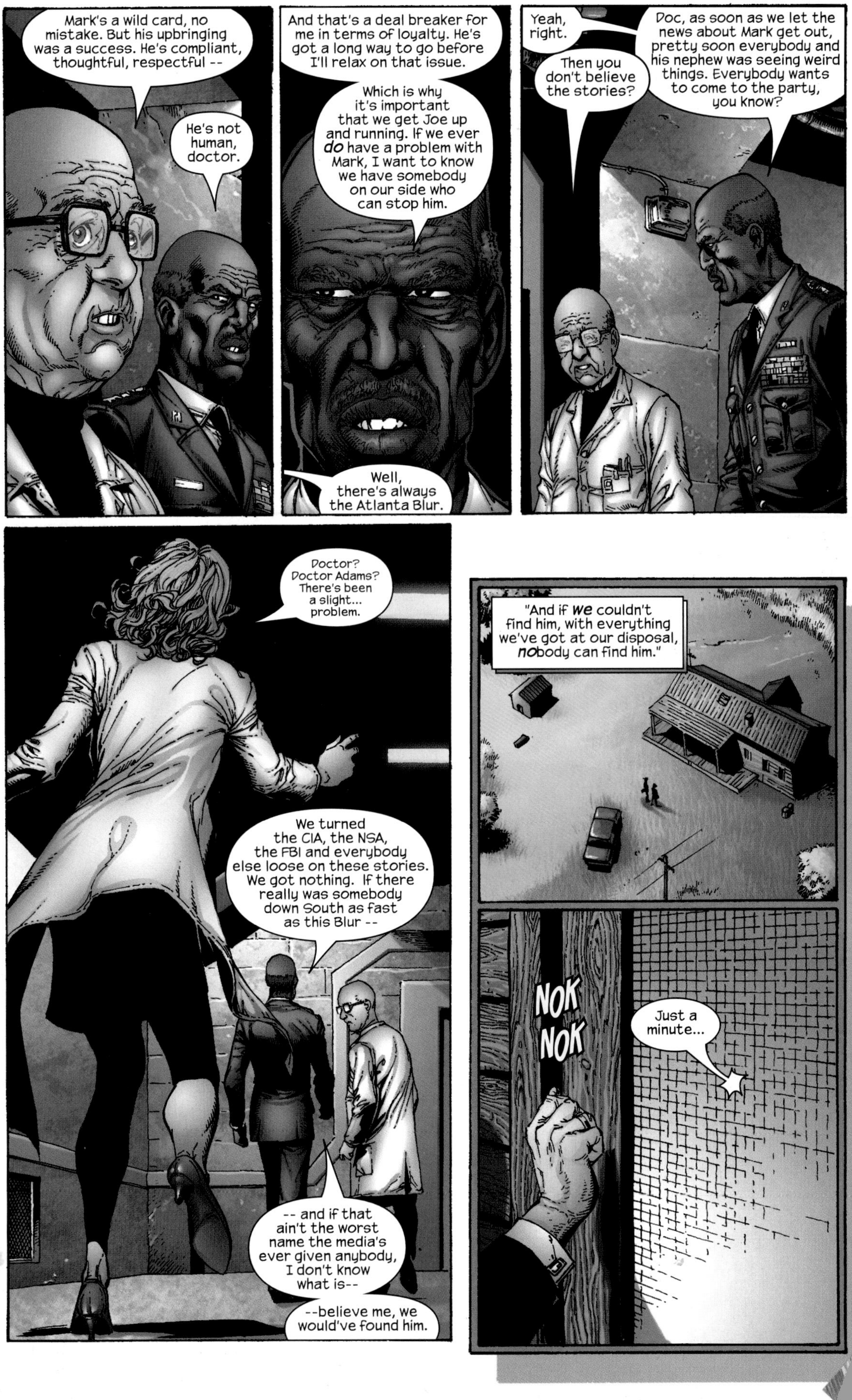
Mark's a wild card, no mistake. But his upbringing was a success. He's compliant, thoughtful, respectful --
He's not human, doctor.
And that's a deal breaker for me in terms of loyalty. He's got a long way to go before I'll relax on that issue.
Which is why it's important that we get Joe up and running. If we ever *do* have a problem with Mark, I want to know we have somebody on our side who can stop him.
Well, there's always the Atlanta Blur.
Yeah, right.
Then you don't believe the stories?
Doc, as soon as we let the news about Mark get out, pretty soon everybody and his nephew was seeing weird things. Everybody wants to come to the party, you know?
Doctor? Doctor Adams? There's been a slight... problem.
We turned the CIA, the NSA, the FBI and everybody else loose on these stories. We got nothing. If there really was somebody down South as fast as this Blur --
-- and if that ain't the worst name the media's ever given anybody, I don't know what is--
--believe me, we would've found him.
"And if *we* couldn't find him, with everything we've got at our disposal, *no*body can find him."
NOK NOK
Just a minute...

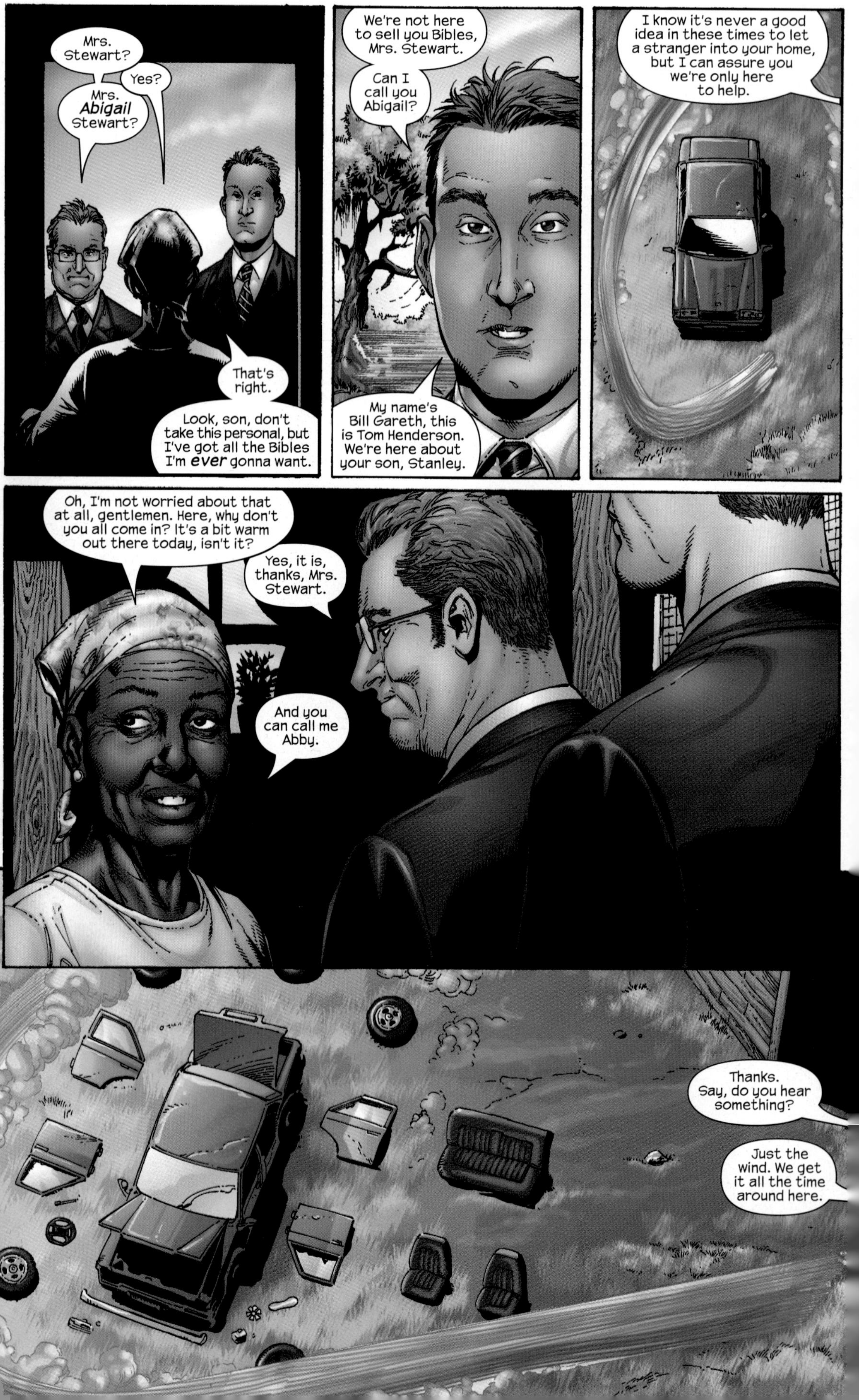
Mrs. Stewart?
Yes?
Mrs. Abigail Stewart?
That's right.
Look, son, don't take this personal, but I've got all the Bibles I'm ever gonna want.
We're not here to sell you Bibles, Mrs. Stewart.
Can I call you Abigail?
My name's Bill Gareth, this is Tom Henderson. We're here about your son, Stanley.
I know it's never a good idea in these times to let a stranger into your home, but I can assure you we're only here to help.
Oh, I'm not worried about that at all, gentlemen. Here, why don't you all come in? It's a bit warm out there today, isn't it?
Yes, it is, thanks, Mrs. Stewart.
And you can call me Abby.
Thanks. Say, do you hear something?
Just the wind. We get it all the time around here.

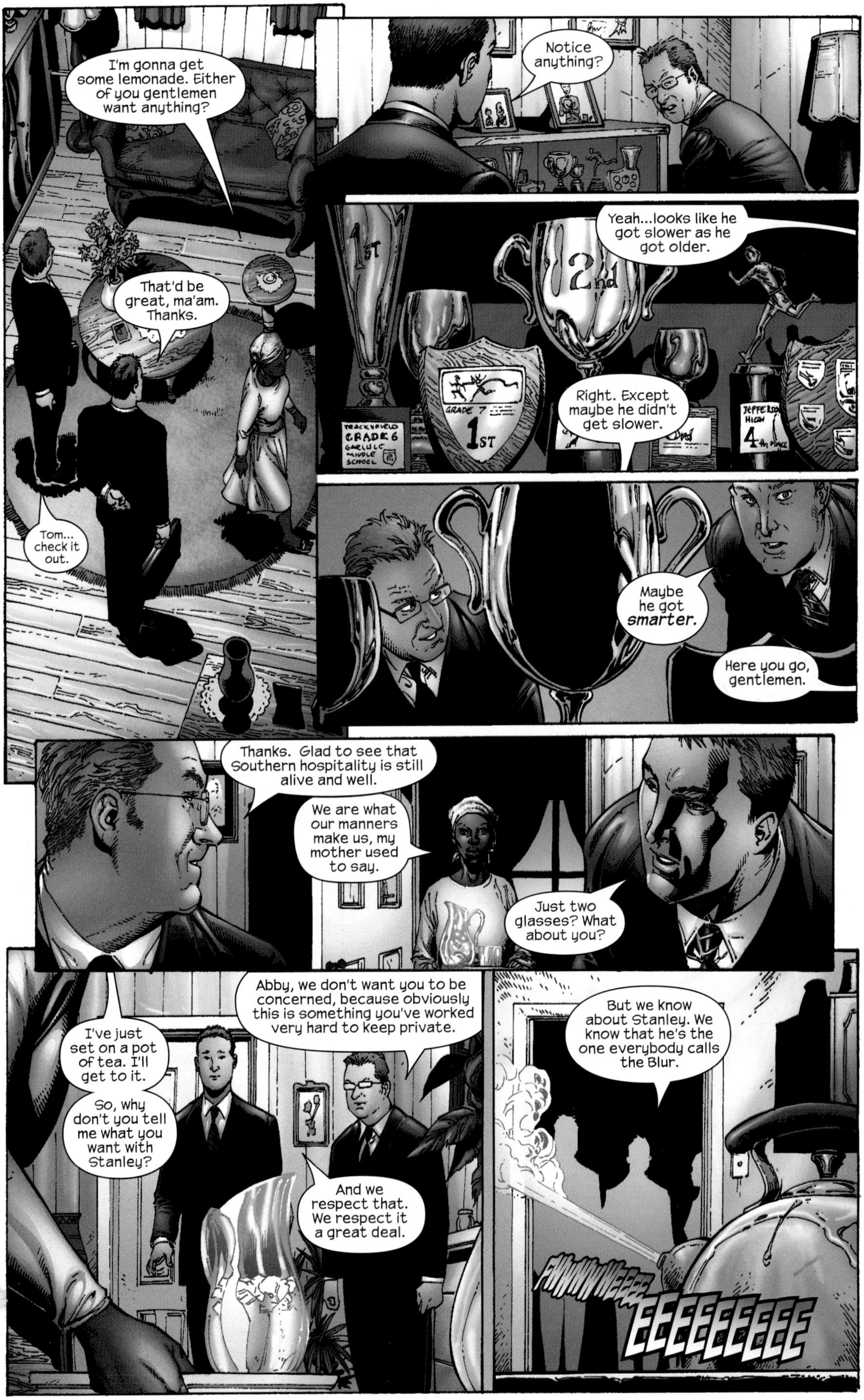

I'm gonna get some lemonade. Either of you gentlemen want anything?
That'd be great, ma'am. Thanks.
Tom... check it out.
Notice anything?
Yeah...looks like he got slower as he got older.
1ST
2nd
GRADE 7
1ST
TRACK+FIELD GRADE 6
JEFFERSON HIGH 4th PLACE
Right. Except maybe he didn't get slower.
Maybe he got *smarter*.
Here you go, gentlemen.
Thanks. Glad to see that Southern hospitality is still alive and well.
We are what our manners make us, my mother used to say.
Just two glasses? What about you?
I've just set on a pot of tea. I'll get to it.
So, why don't you tell me what you want with Stanley?
Abby, we don't want you to be concerned, because obviously this is something you've worked very hard to keep private.
And we respect that. We respect it a great deal.
But we know about Stanley. We know that he's the one everybody calls the Blur.
FWWWWWEEEE EEEEEEEEE

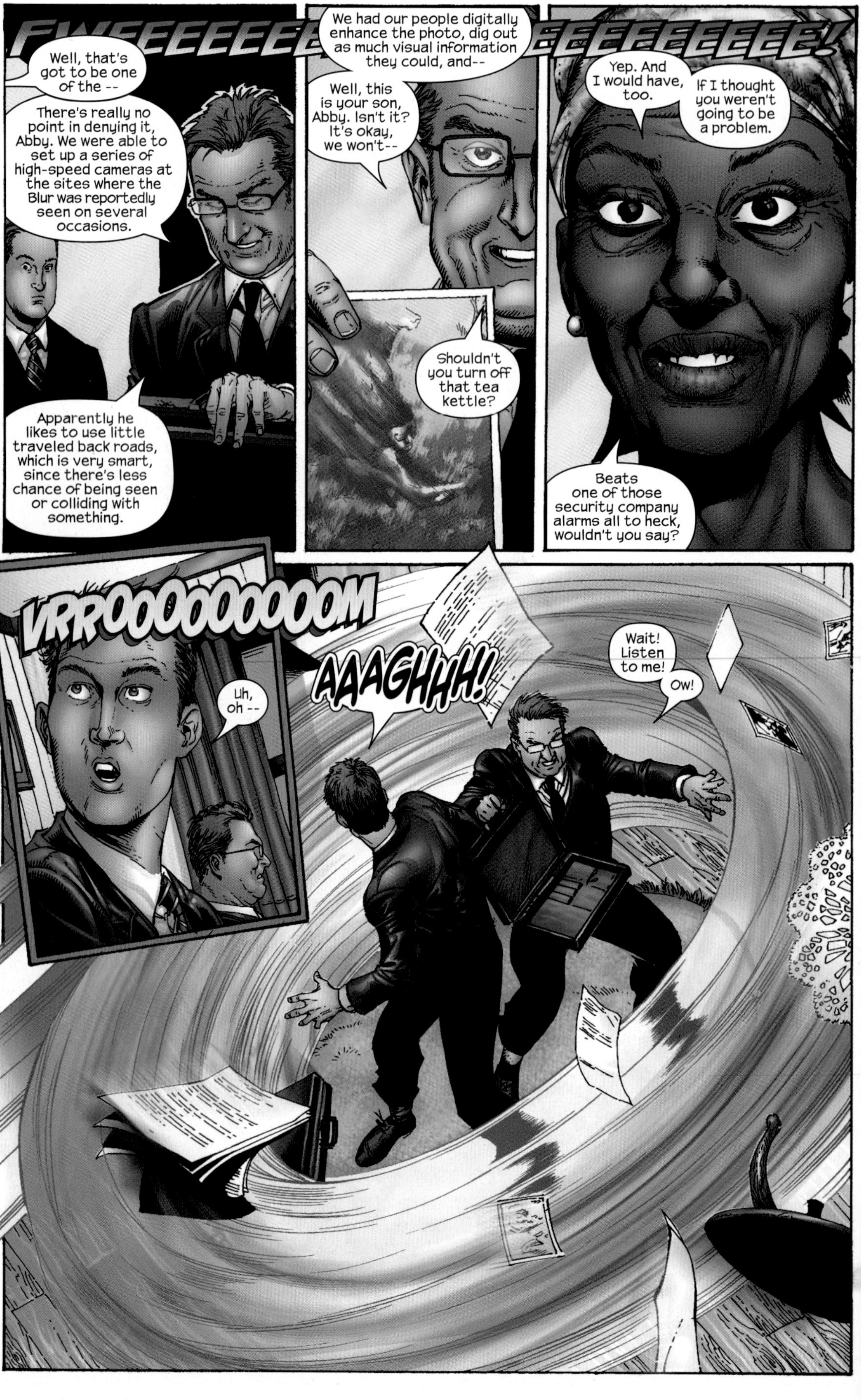
FWEEEEEEEEEEEEEEEEEEEEE!
Well, that's got to be one of the --
There's really no point in denying it, Abby. We were able to set up a series of high-speed cameras at the sites where the Blur was reportedly seen on several occasions.
Apparently he likes to use little traveled back roads, which is very smart, since there's less chance of being seen or colliding with something.
We had our people digitally enhance the photo, dig out as much visual information they could, and--
Well, this is your son, Abby. Isn't it? It's okay, we won't--
Shouldn't you turn off that tea kettle?
Yep. And I would have, too.
If I thought you weren't going to be a problem.
Beats one of those security company alarms all to heck, wouldn't you say?
VRROOOOOOOOOM
Uh, oh --
AAAGHHH!
Wait! Listen to me!
Ow!

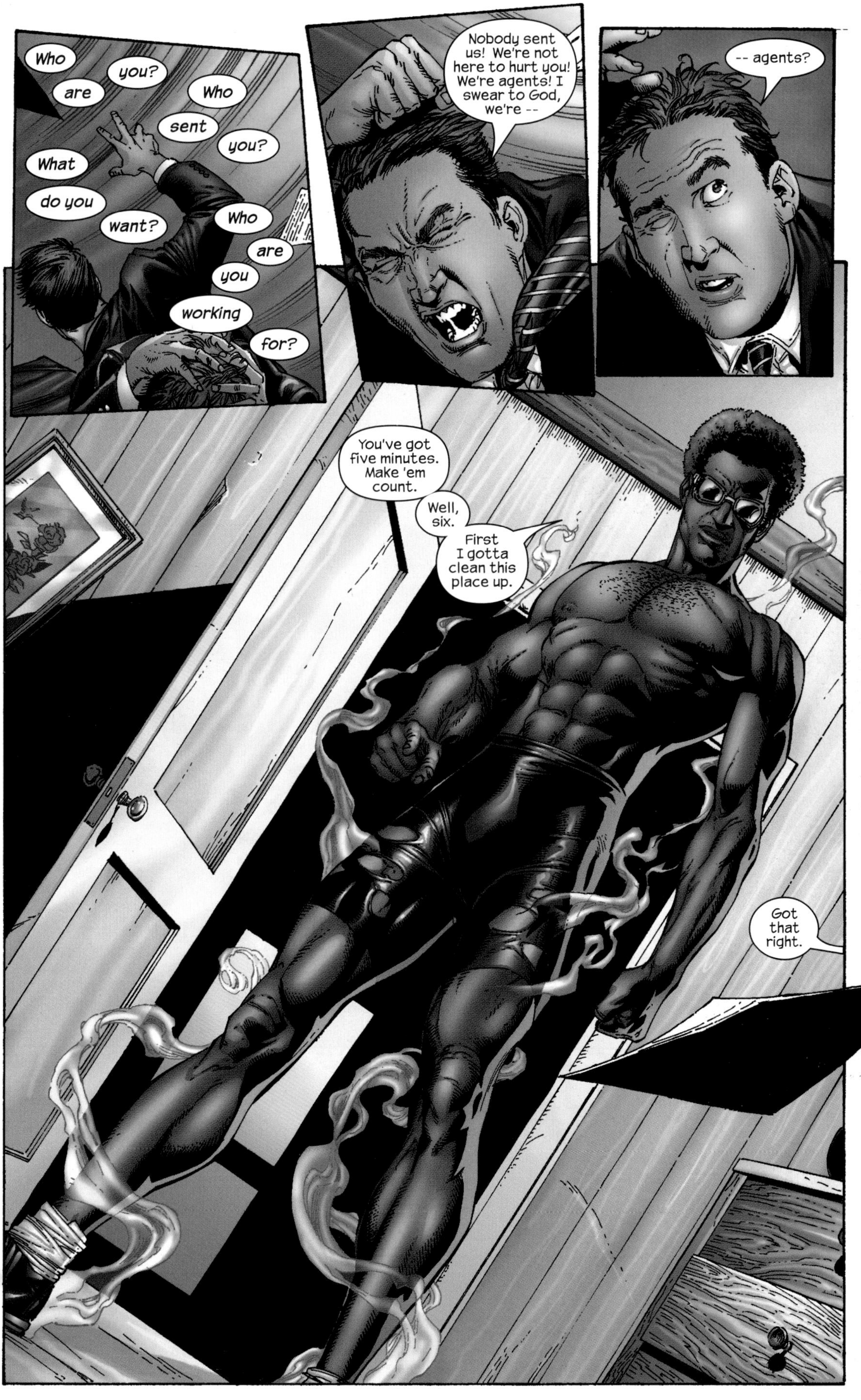
Who
are
you?
Who
sent
you?
What
do you
want?
Who
are
you
working
for?
Nobody sent us! We're not here to hurt you! We're agents! I swear to God, we're --
-- agents?
You've got five minutes. Make 'em count.
Well, six.
First I gotta clean this place up.
Got that right.

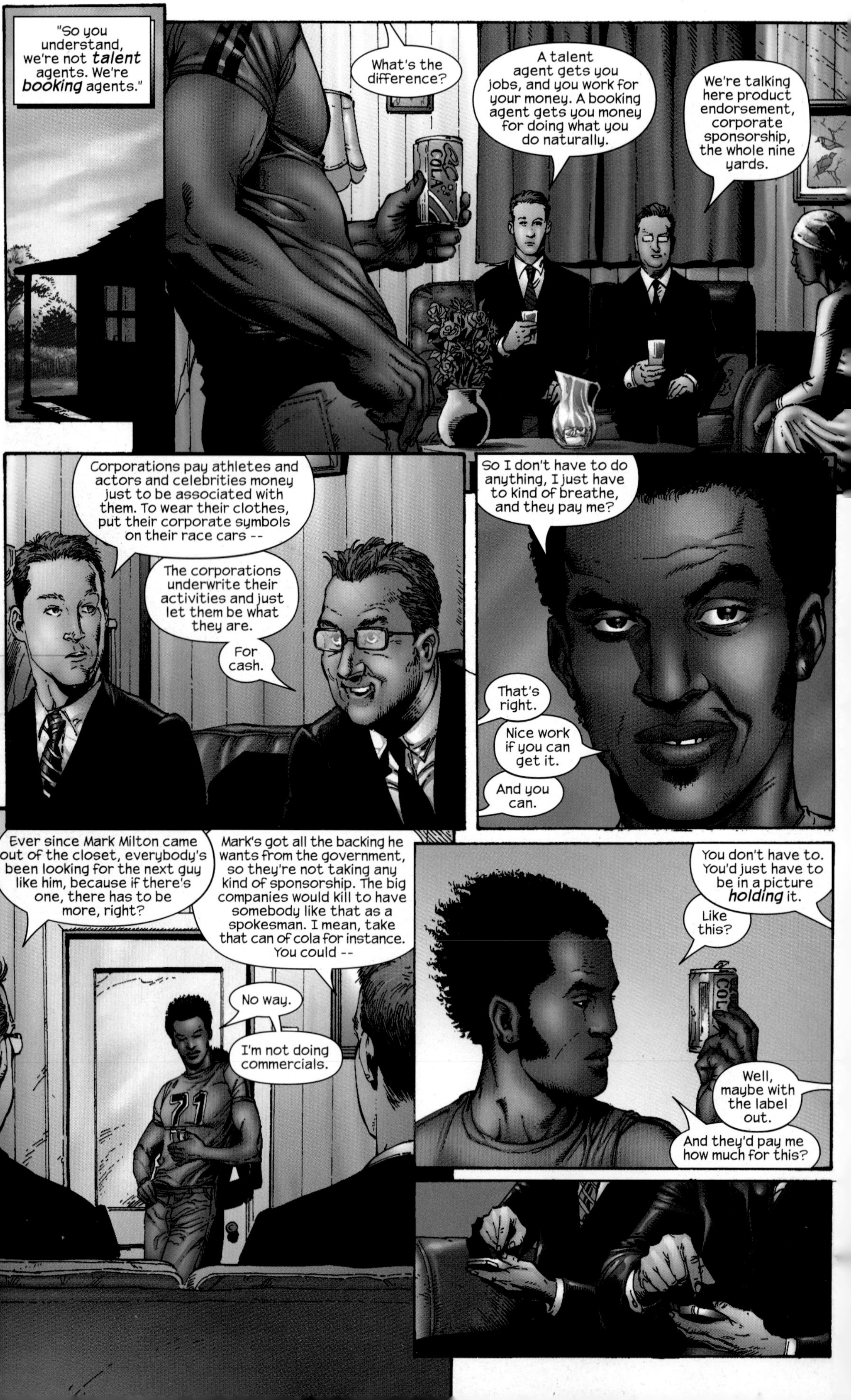
"So you understand, we're not *talent* agents. We're *booking* agents."
What's the difference?
A talent agent gets you jobs, and you work for your money. A booking agent gets you money for doing what you do naturally.
We're talking here product endorsement, corporate sponsorship, the whole nine yards.
Corporations pay athletes and actors and celebrities money just to be associated with them. To wear their clothes, put their corporate symbols on their race cars --
The corporations underwrite their activities and just let them be what they are.
For cash.
So I don't have to do anything, I just have to kind of breathe, and they pay me?
That's right.
Nice work if you can get it.
And you can.
Ever since Mark Milton came out of the closet, everybody's been looking for the next guy like him, because if there's one, there has to be more, right?
Mark's got all the backing he wants from the government, so they're not taking any kind of sponsorship. The big companies would kill to have somebody like that as a spokesman. I mean, take that can of cola for instance. You could --
No way.
I'm not doing commercials.
You don't have to. You'd just have to be in a picture *holding* it.
Like this?
Well, maybe with the label out.
And they'd pay me how much for this?

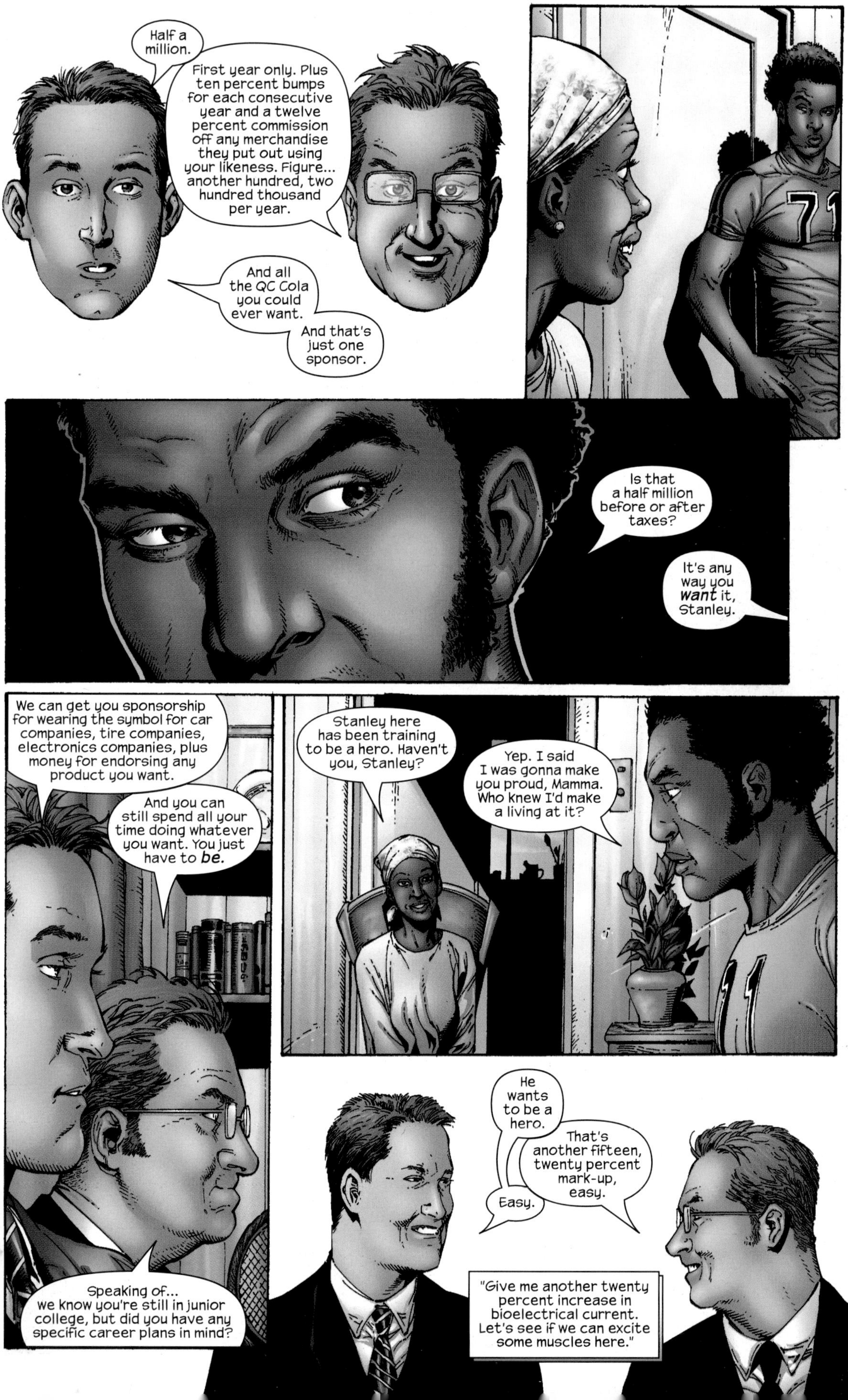
Half a million.
First year only. Plus ten percent bumps for each consecutive year and a twelve percent commission off any merchandise they put out using your likeness. Figure... another hundred, two hundred thousand per year.
And all the QC Cola you could ever want.
And that's just one sponsor.
Is that a half million before or after taxes?
It's any way you *want* it, Stanley.
We can get you sponsorship for wearing the symbol for car companies, tire companies, electronics companies, plus money for endorsing any product you want.
And you can still spend all your time doing whatever you want. You just have to *be.*
Stanley here has been training to be a hero. Haven't you, Stanley?
Yep. I said I was gonna make you proud, Mamma. Who knew I'd make a living at it?
Speaking of... we know you're still in junior college, but did you have any specific career plans in mind?
He wants to be a hero.
That's another fifteen, twenty percent mark-up, easy.
Easy.
"Give me another twenty percent increase in bioelectrical current. Let's see if we can excite some muscles here."

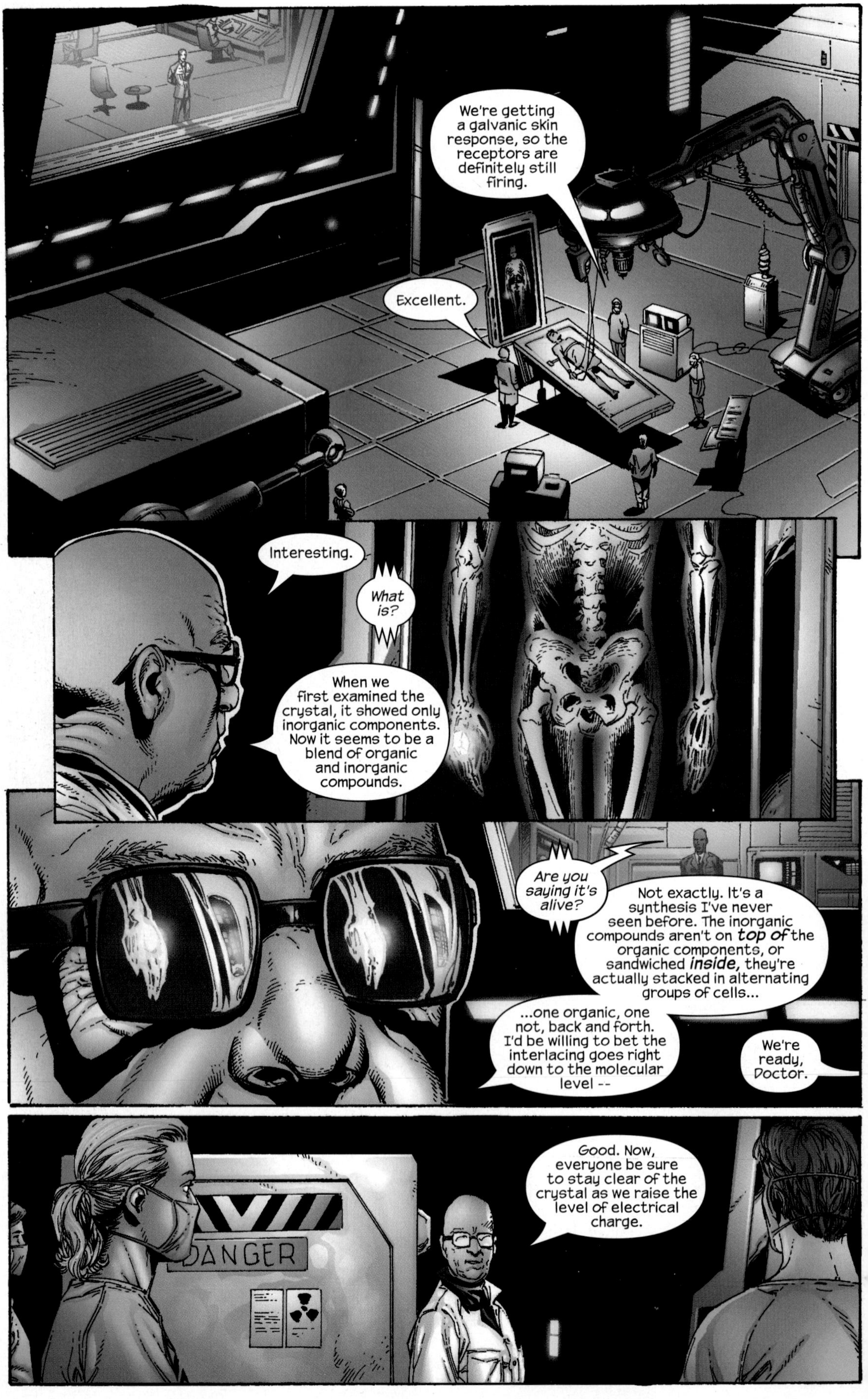

We're getting a galvanic skin response, so the receptors are definitely still firing.
Excellent.
Interesting.
What is?
When we first examined the crystal, it showed only inorganic components. Now it seems to be a blend of organic and inorganic compounds.
Are you saying it's alive?
Not exactly. It's a synthesis I've never seen before. The inorganic compounds aren't on *top of* the organic components, or sandwiched *inside,* they're actually stacked in alternating groups of cells...
...one organic, one not, back and forth. I'd be willing to bet the interlacing goes right down to the molecular level --
We're ready, Doctor.
DANGER
Good. Now, everyone be sure to stay clear of the crystal as we raise the level of electrical charge.

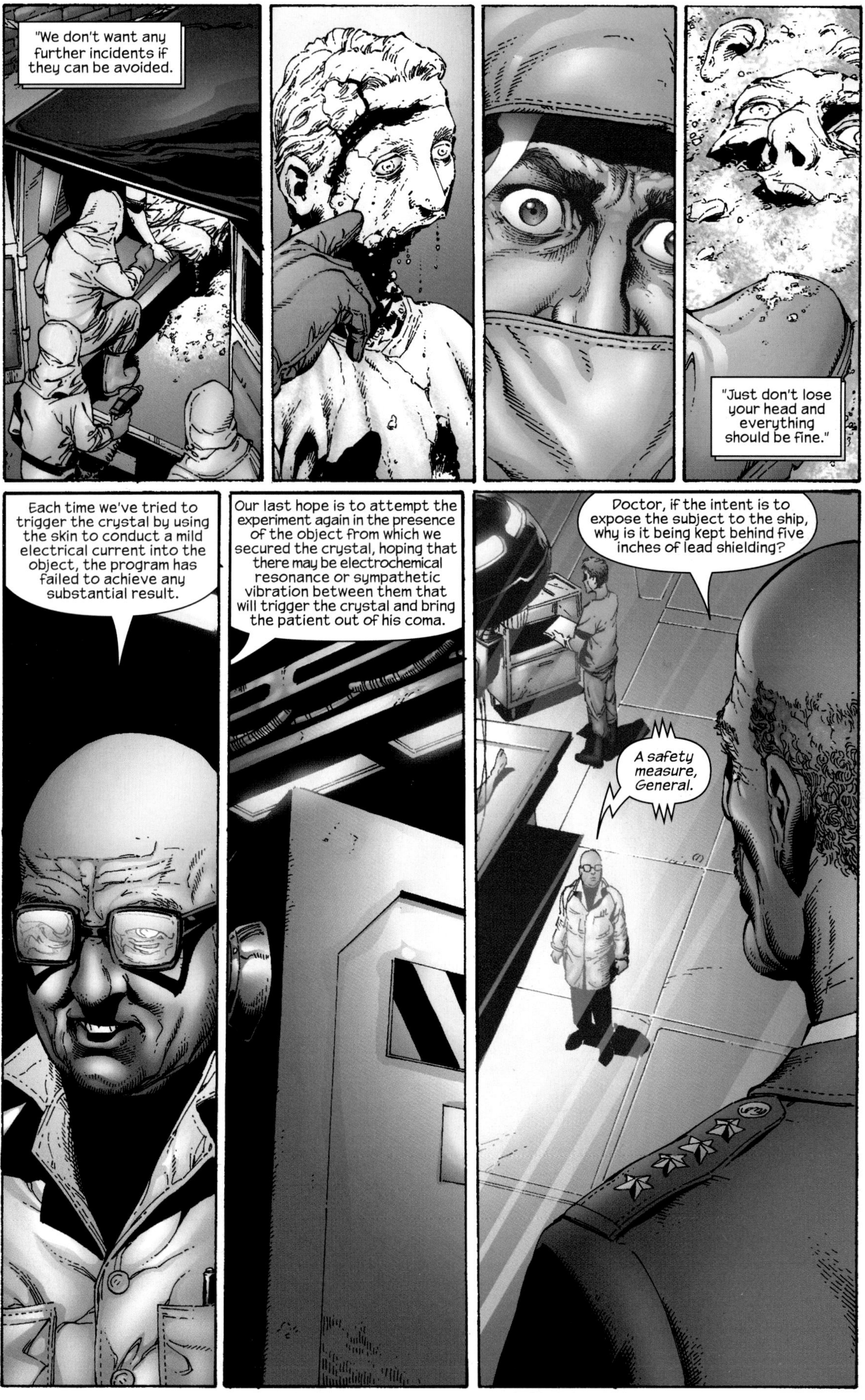
"We don't want any further incidents if they can be avoided.
"Just don't lose your head and everything should be fine."
Each time we've tried to trigger the crystal by using the skin to conduct a mild electrical current into the object, the program has failed to achieve any substantial result.
Our last hope is to attempt the experiment again in the presence of the object from which we secured the crystal, hoping that there may be electrochemical resonance or sympathetic vibration between them that will trigger the crystal and bring the patient out of his coma.
Doctor, if the intent is to expose the subject to the ship, why is it being kept behind five inches of lead shielding?
A safety measure, General.

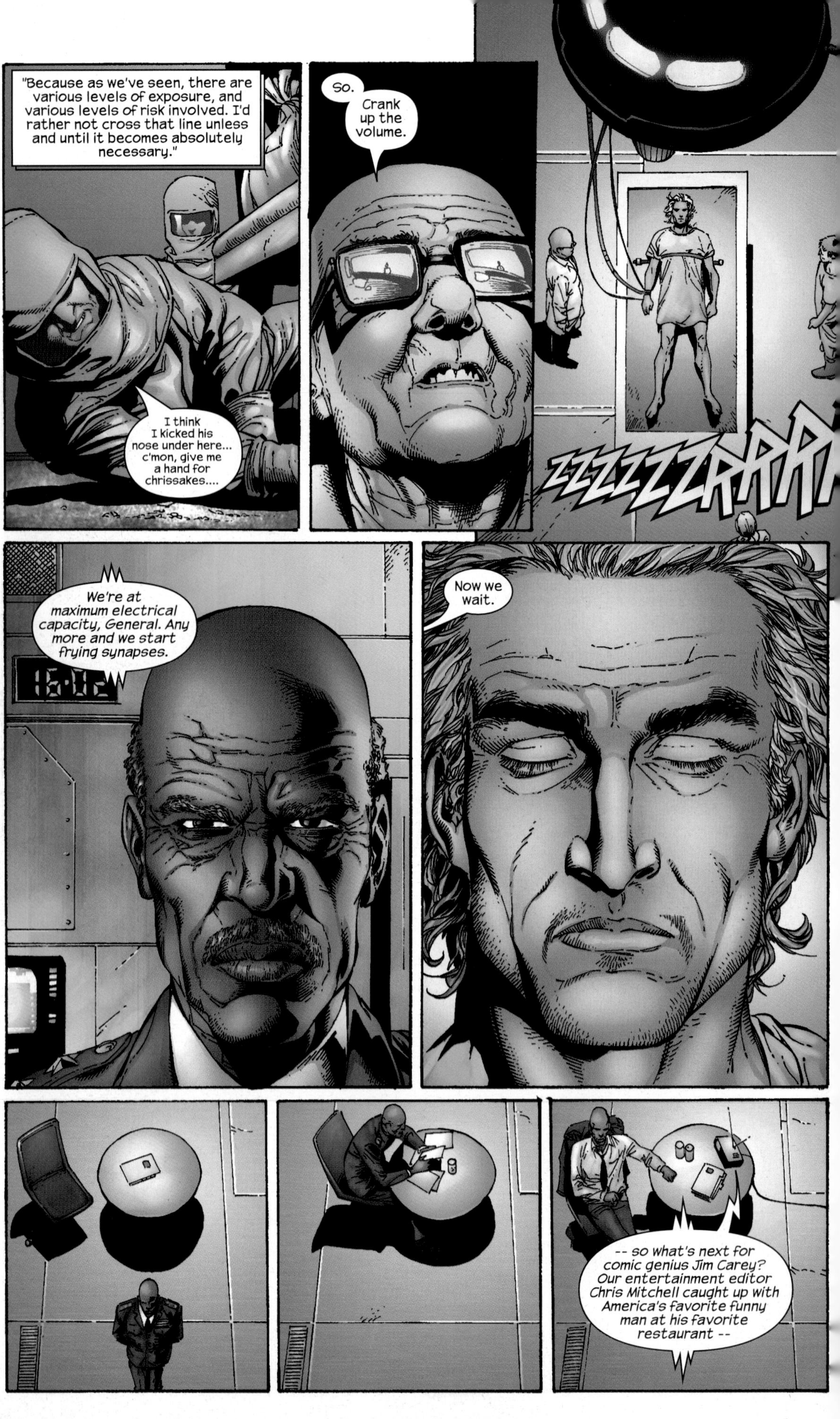

"Because as we've seen, there are various levels of exposure, and various levels of risk involved. I'd rather not cross that line unless and until it becomes absolutely necessary."
I think I kicked his nose under here... c'mon, give me a hand for chrissakes....
So.
Crank up the volume.
ZZZZZZRRRR
We're at maximum electrical capacity, General. Any more and we start frying synapses.
Now we wait.
-- so what's next for comic genius Jim Carey? Our entertainment editor Chris Mitchell caught up with America's favorite funny man at his favorite restaurant --

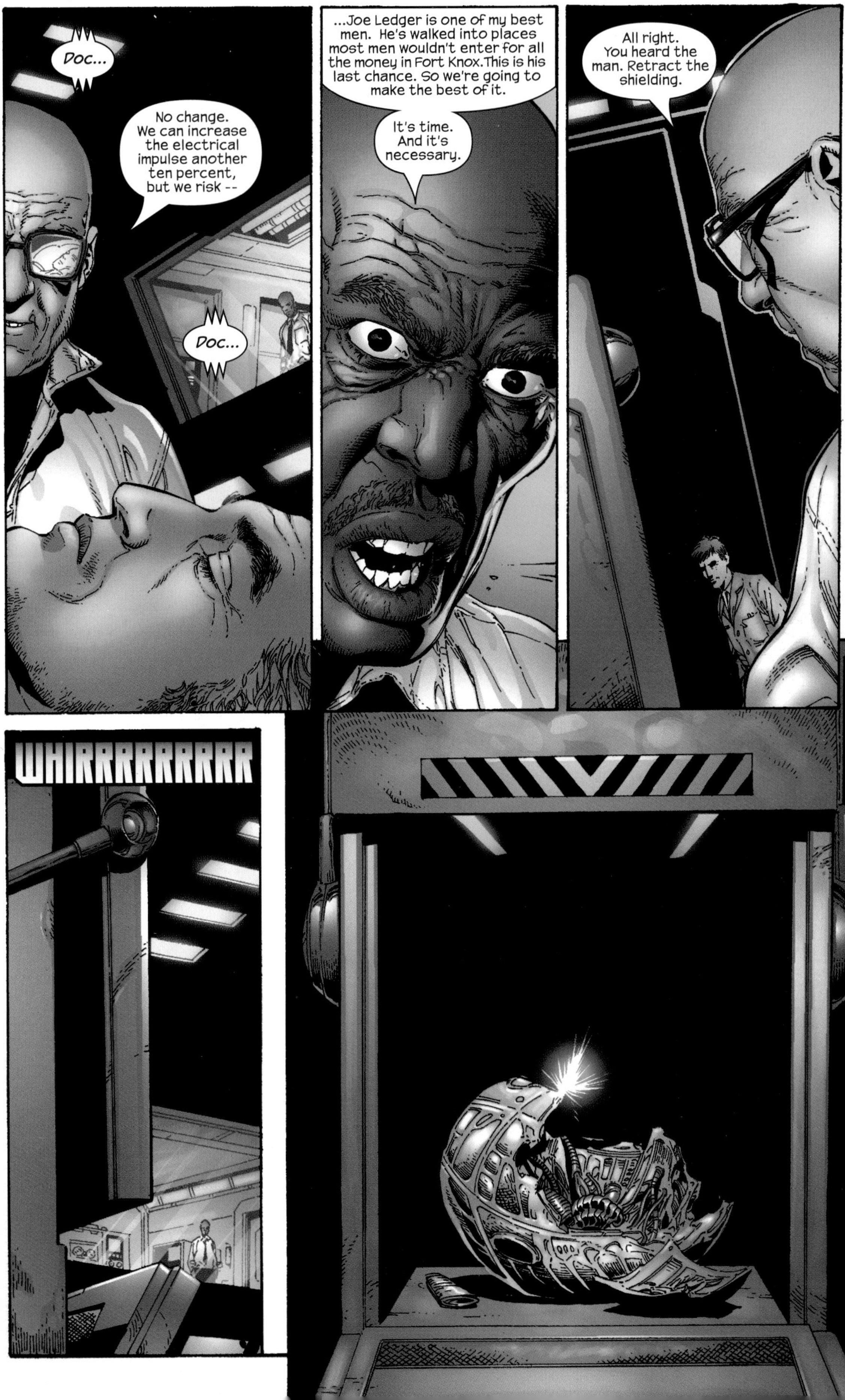

Doc...
No change. We can increase the electrical impulse another ten percent, but we risk --
Doc...
...Joe Ledger is one of my best men. He's walked into places most men wouldn't enter for all the money in Fort Knox. This is his last chance. So we're going to make the best of it.
It's time. And it's necessary.
All right. You heard the man. Retract the shielding.
WHIRRRRRRRRR

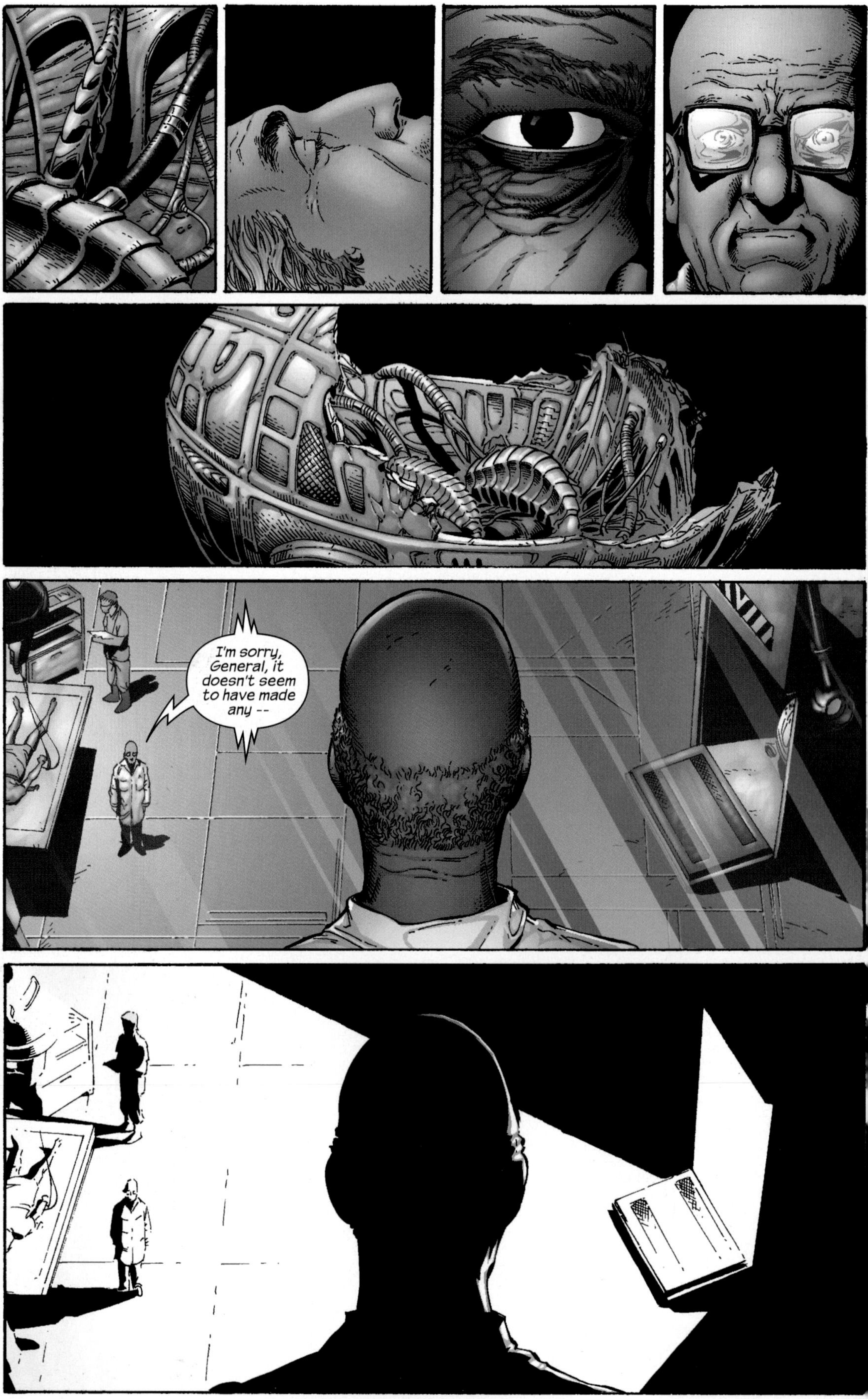
I'm sorry, General, it doesn't seem to have made any --

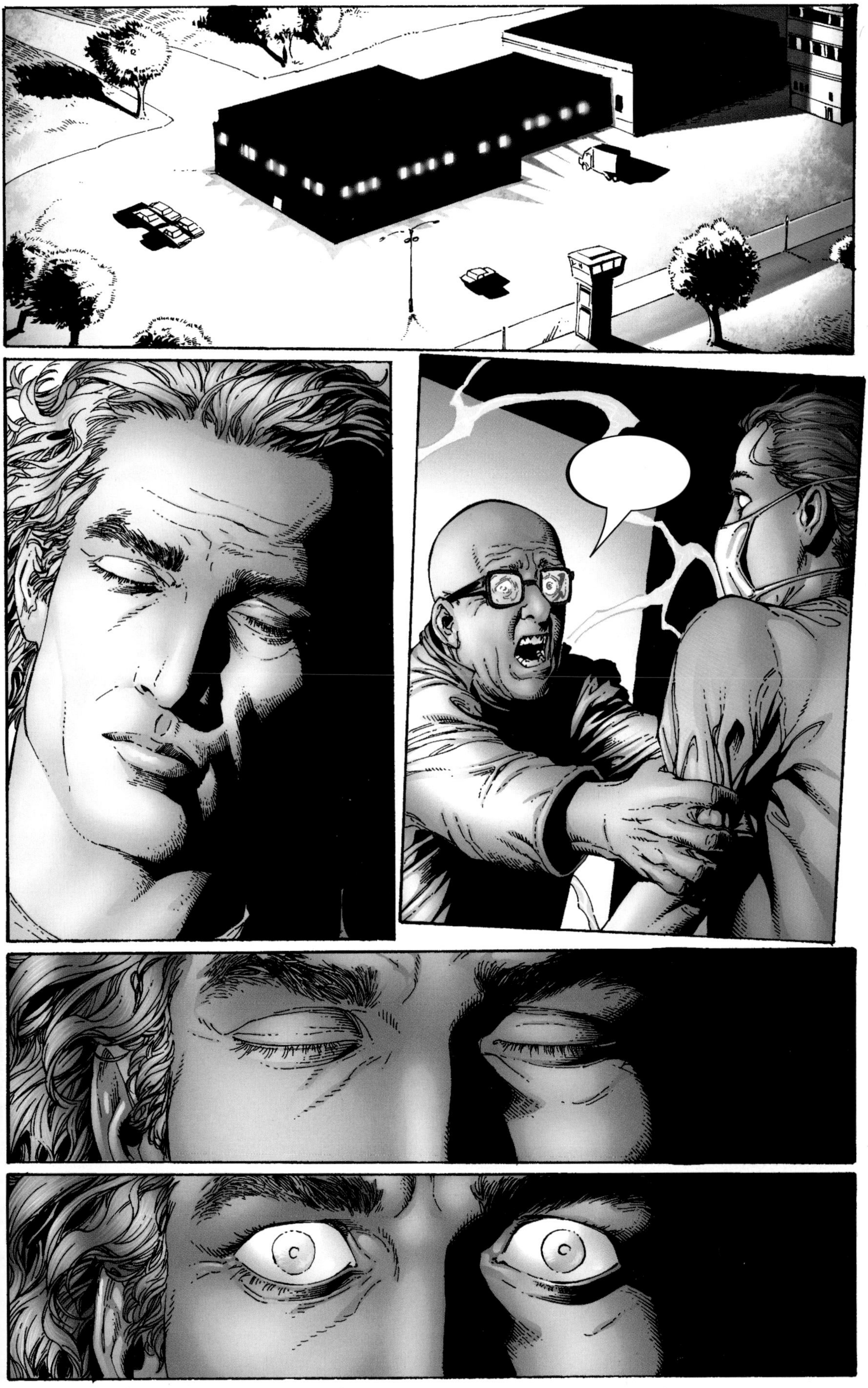

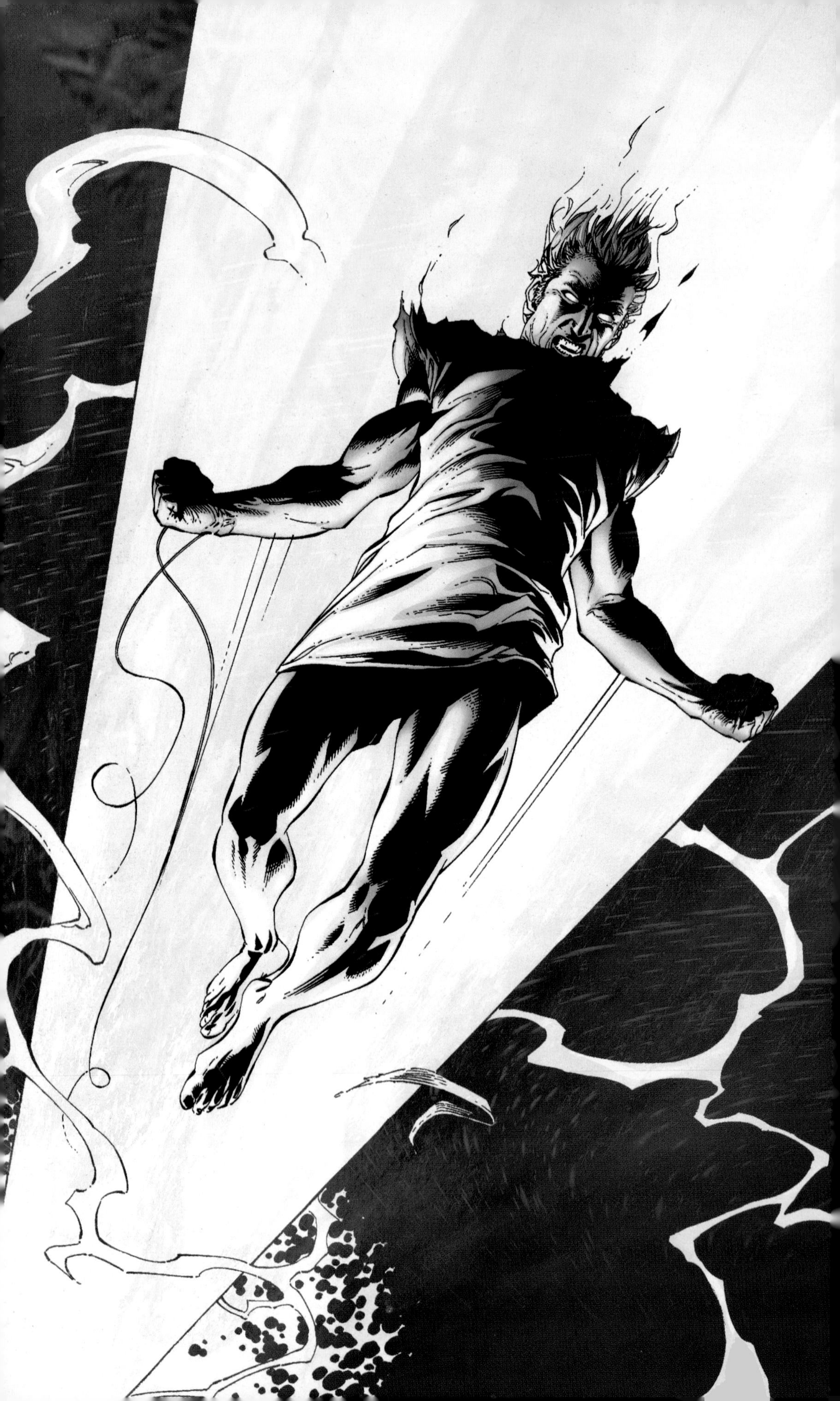

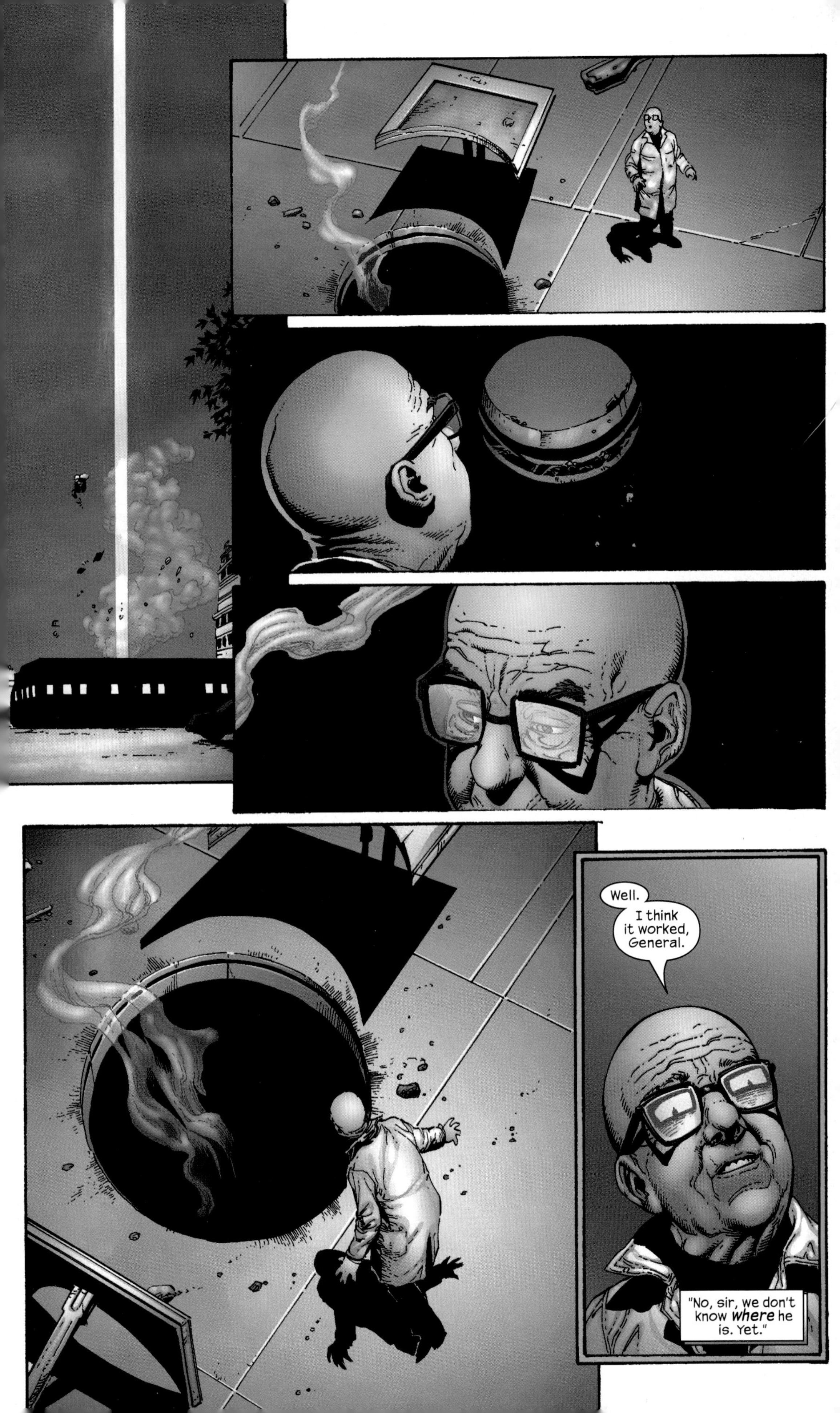
Well.
I think it worked, General.
"No, sir, we don't know *where* he is. Yet."

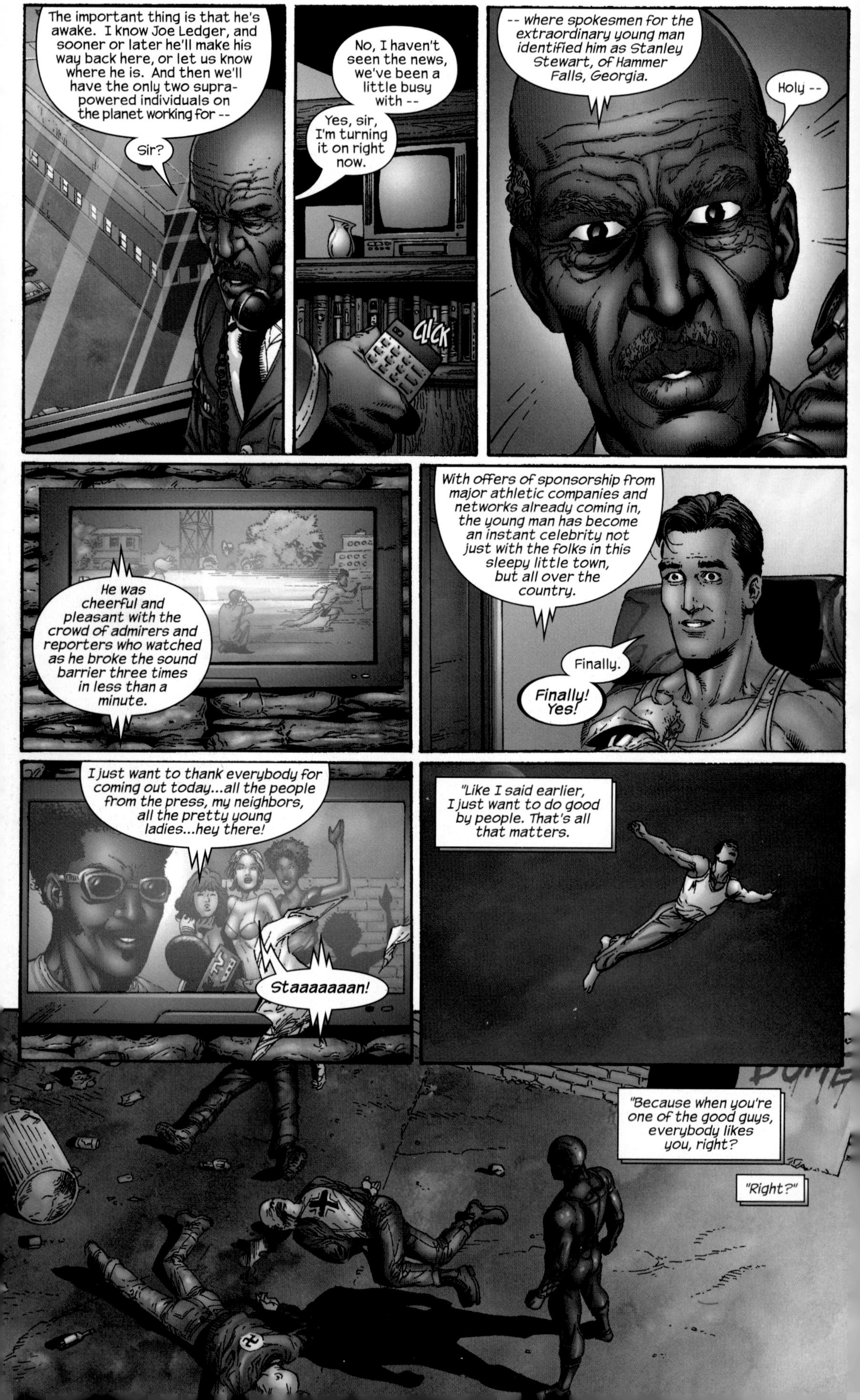
The important thing is that he's awake. I know Joe Ledger, and sooner or later he'll make his way back here, or let us know where he is. And then we'll have the only two supra-powered individuals on the planet working for --
Sir?
No, I haven't seen the news, we've been a little busy with --
Yes, sir, I'm turning it on right now.
CLICK
-- where spokesmen for the extraordinary young man identified him as Stanley Stewart, of Hammer Falls, Georgia.
Holy --
He was cheerful and pleasant with the crowd of admirers and reporters who watched as he broke the sound barrier three times in less than a minute.
With offers of sponsorship from major athletic companies and networks already coming in, the young man has become an instant celebrity not just with the folks in this sleepy little town, but all over the country.
Finally.
Finally! Yes!
I just want to thank everybody for coming out today...all the people from the press, my neighbors, all the pretty young ladies...hey there!
Staaaaaaan!
"Like I said earlier, I just want to do good by people. That's all that matters.
"Because when you're one of the good guys, everybody likes you, right?
"Right?"

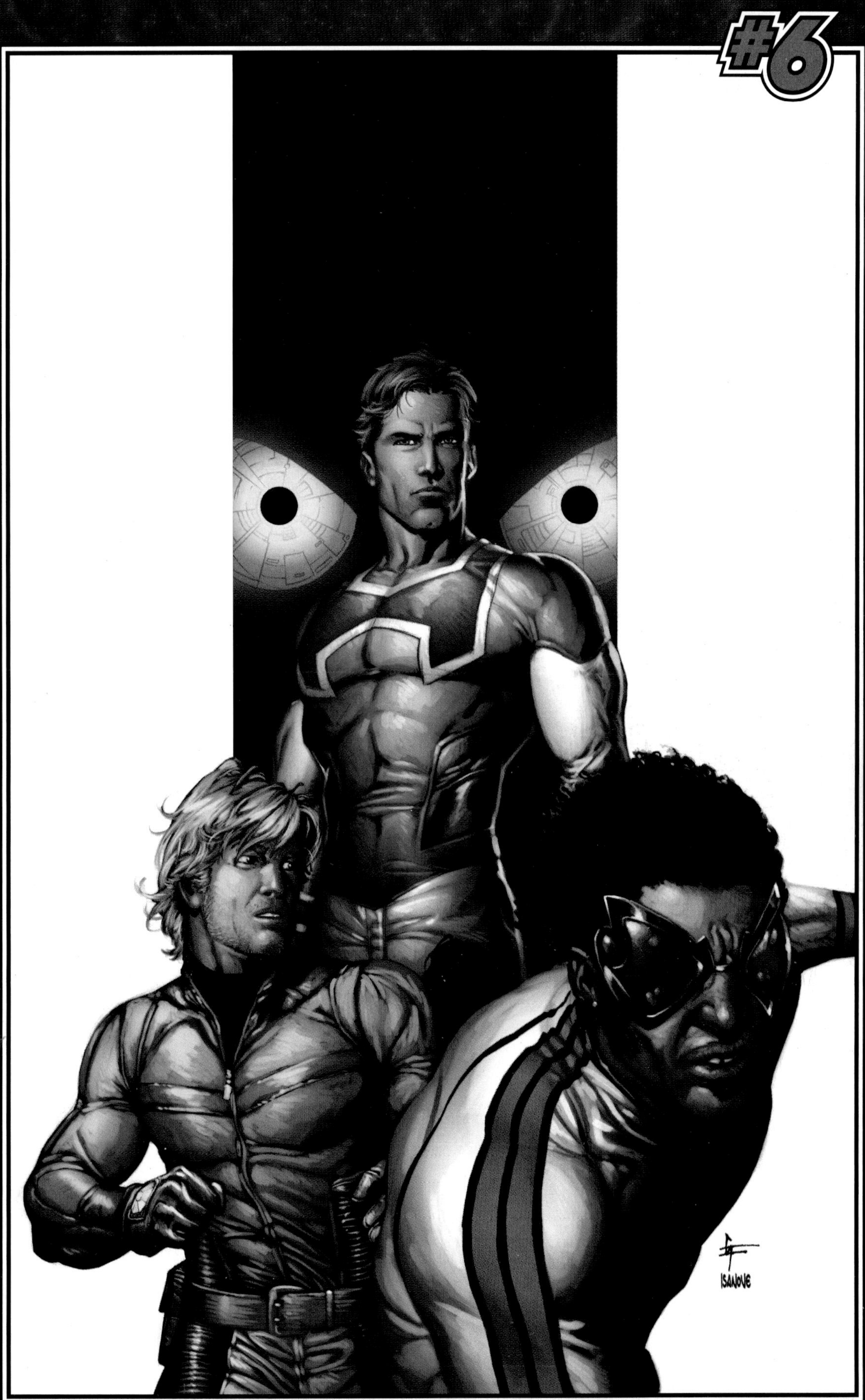
#6
ISANOVE

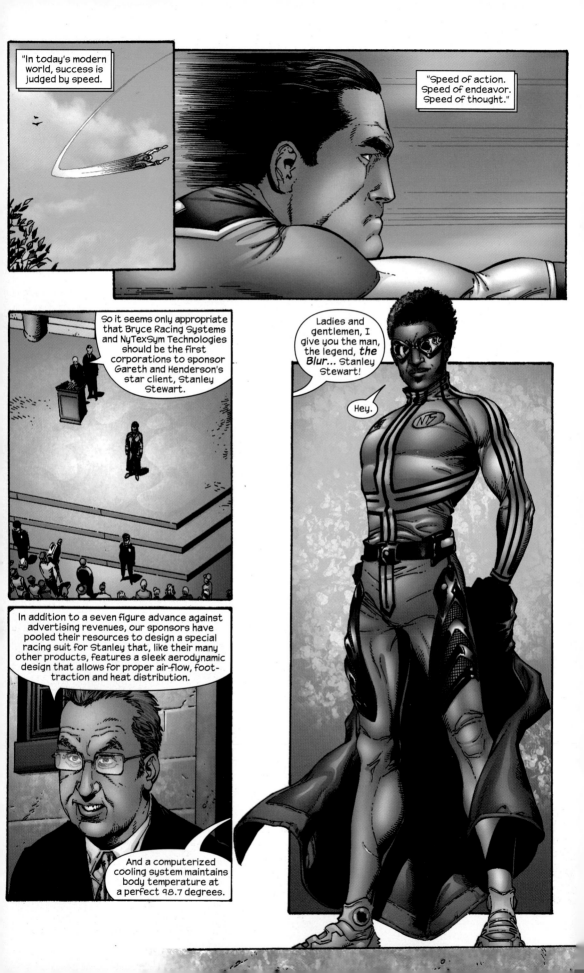

"In today's modern world, success is judged by speed.

"Speed of action. Speed of endeavor. Speed of thought."

So it seems only appropriate that Bryce Racing Systems and NyTexSym Technologies should be the first corporations to sponsor Gareth and Henderson's star client, Stanley Stewart.

Ladies and gentlemen, I give you the man, the legend, *the Blur...* Stanley Stewart!

Hey.

In addition to a seven figure advance against advertising revenues, our sponsors have pooled their resources to design a special racing suit for Stanley that, like their many other products, features a sleek aerodynamic design that allows for proper air-flow, foot-traction and heat distribution.

And a computerized cooling system maintains body temperature at a perfect 98.7 degrees.

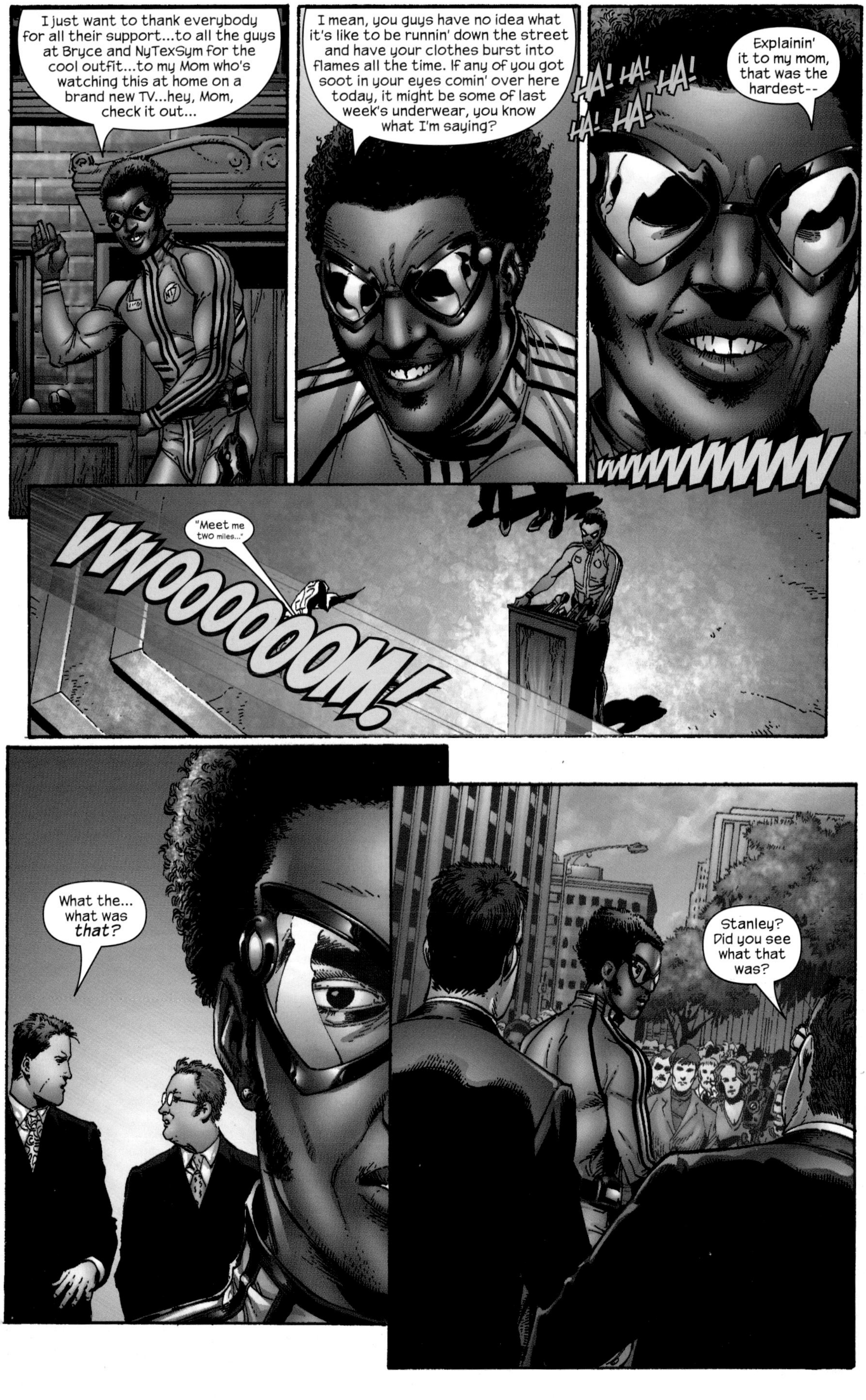

I just want to thank everybody for all their support...to all the guys at Bryce and NyTexSym for the cool outfit...to my Mom who's watching this at home on a brand new TV...hey, Mom, check it out...
I mean, you guys have no idea what it's like to be runnin' down the street and have your clothes burst into flames all the time. If any of you got soot in your eyes comin' over here today, it might be some of last week's underwear, you know what I'm saying?
HA! HA! HA! HA! HA!
Explainin' it to my mom, that was the hardest--
VVVVVVVVVV
VVVOOOOOOM!
"Meet me TWO miles..."
What the... what was *that*?
Stanley? Did you see what that was?

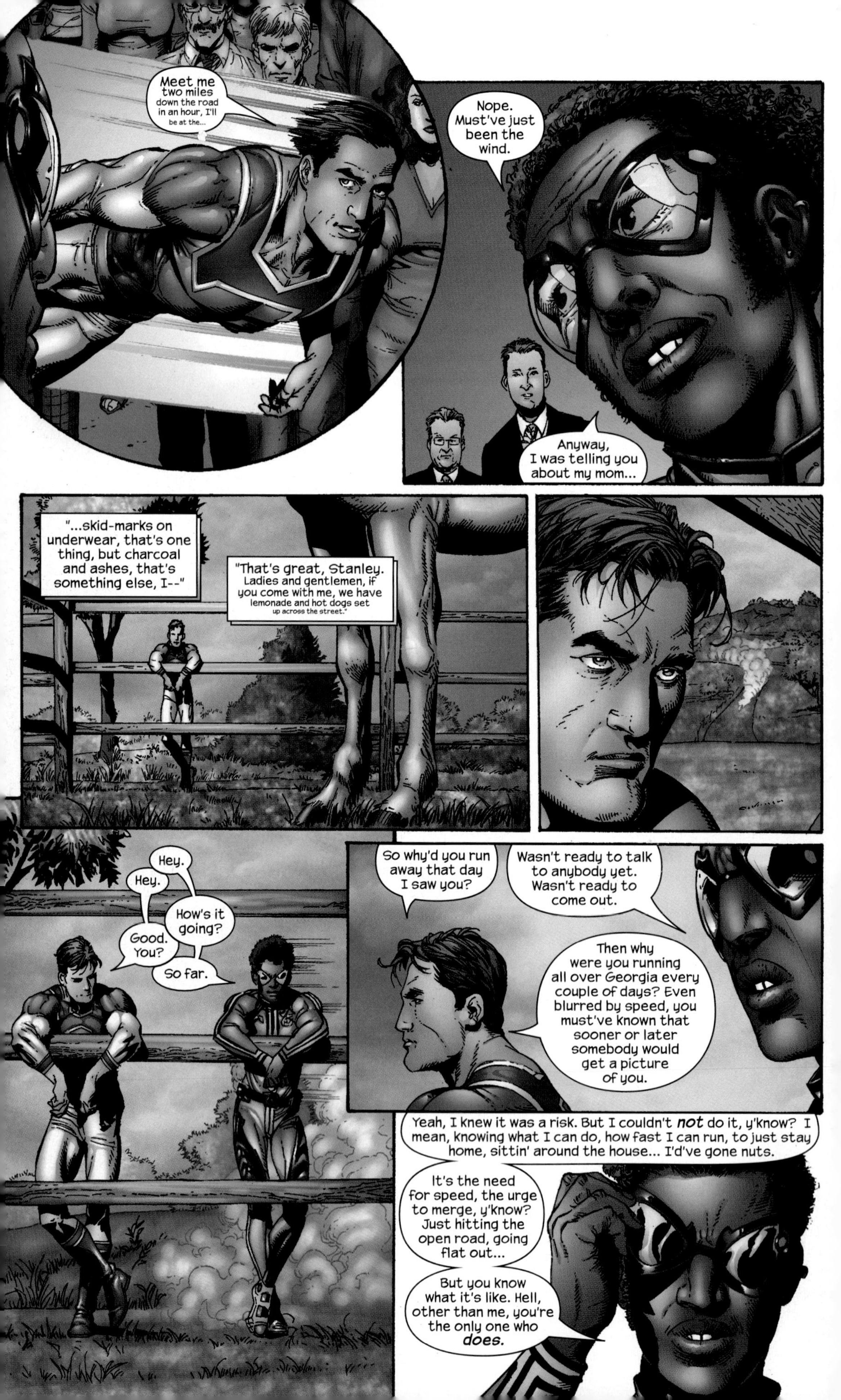

Meet me two miles down the road in an hour, I'll be at the...
Nope. Must've just been the wind.
Anyway, I was telling you about my mom...
"...skid-marks on underwear, that's one thing, but charcoal and ashes, that's something else, I--"
"That's great, Stanley. Ladies and gentlemen, if you come with me, we have lemonade and hot dogs set up across the street."
Hey.
Hey.
How's it going?
Good. You?
So far.
So why'd you run away that day I saw you?
Wasn't ready to talk to anybody yet. Wasn't ready to come out.
Then why were you running all over Georgia every couple of days? Even blurred by speed, you must've known that sooner or later somebody would get a picture of you.
Yeah, I knew it was a risk. But I couldn't *not* do it, y'know? I mean, knowing what I can do, how fast I can run, to just stay home, sittin' around the house... I'd've gone nuts.
It's the need for speed, the urge to merge, y'know? Just hitting the open road, going flat out...
But you know what it's like. Hell, other than me, you're the only one who *does.*

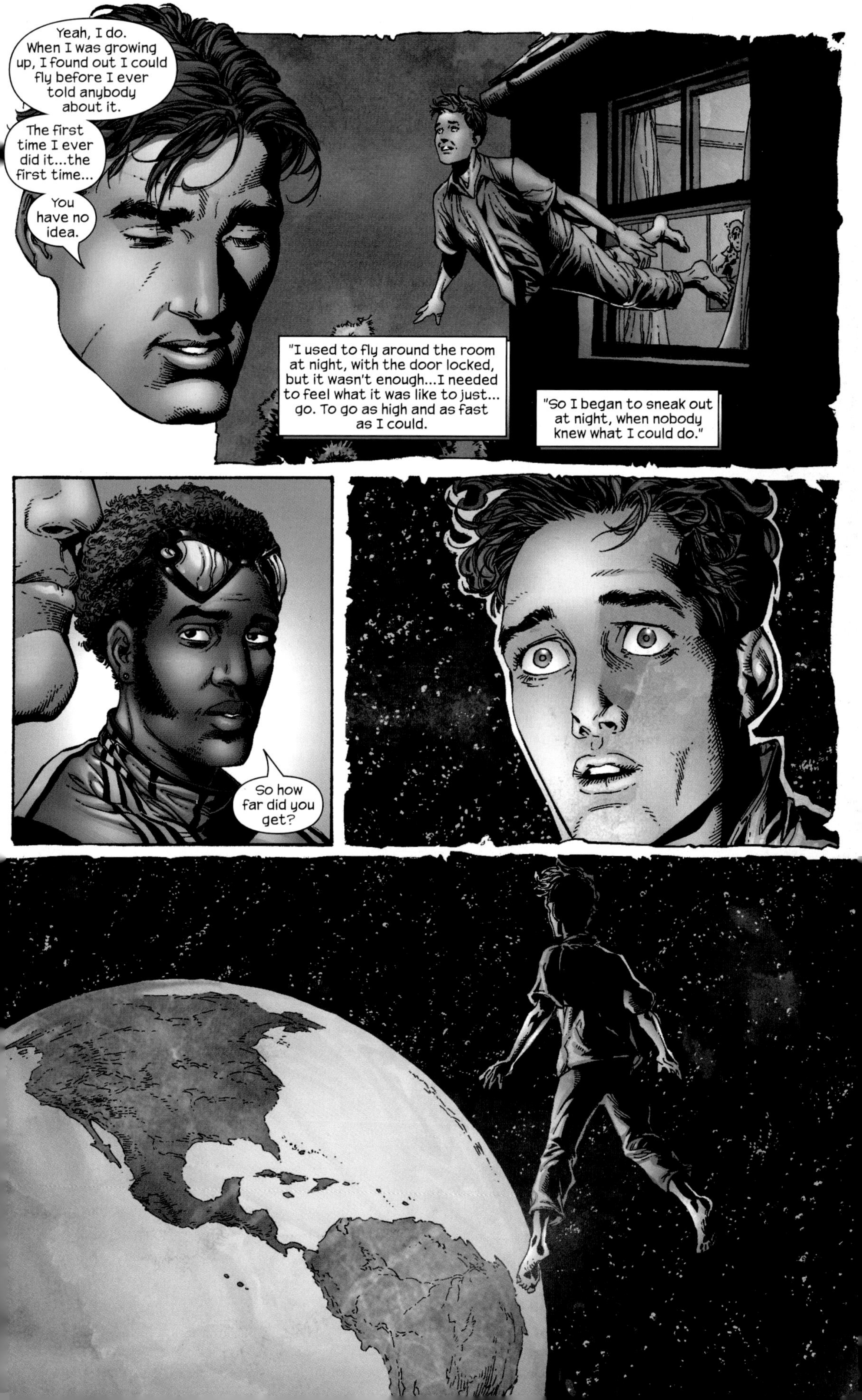

Yeah, I do. When I was growing up, I found out I could fly before I ever told anybody about it.
The first time I ever did it...the first time...
You have no idea.
"I used to fly around the room at night, with the door locked, but it wasn't enough...I needed to feel what it was like to just... go. To go as high and as fast as I could.
"So I began to sneak out at night, when nobody knew what I could do."
So how far did you get?

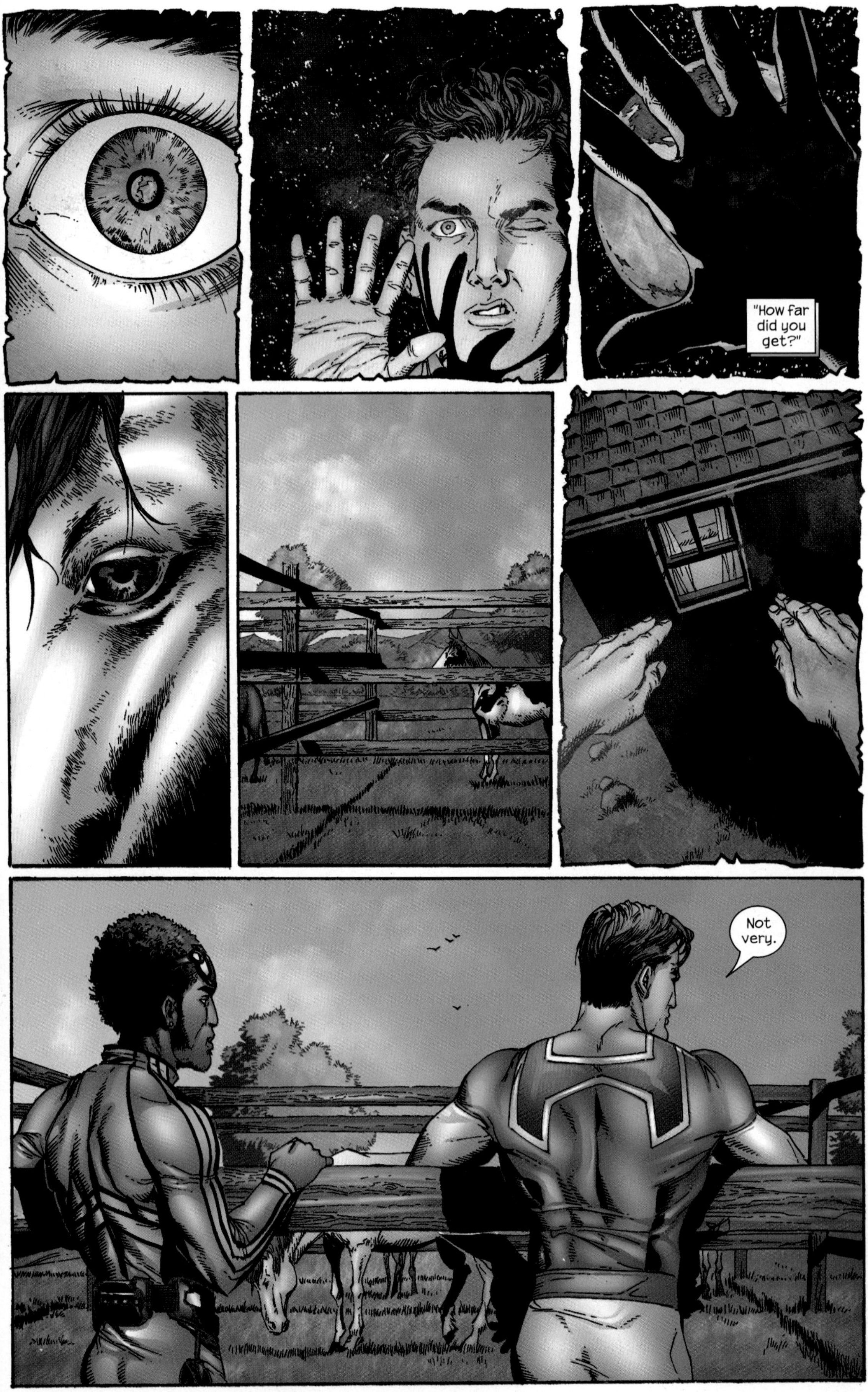
"How far did you get?"
Not very.

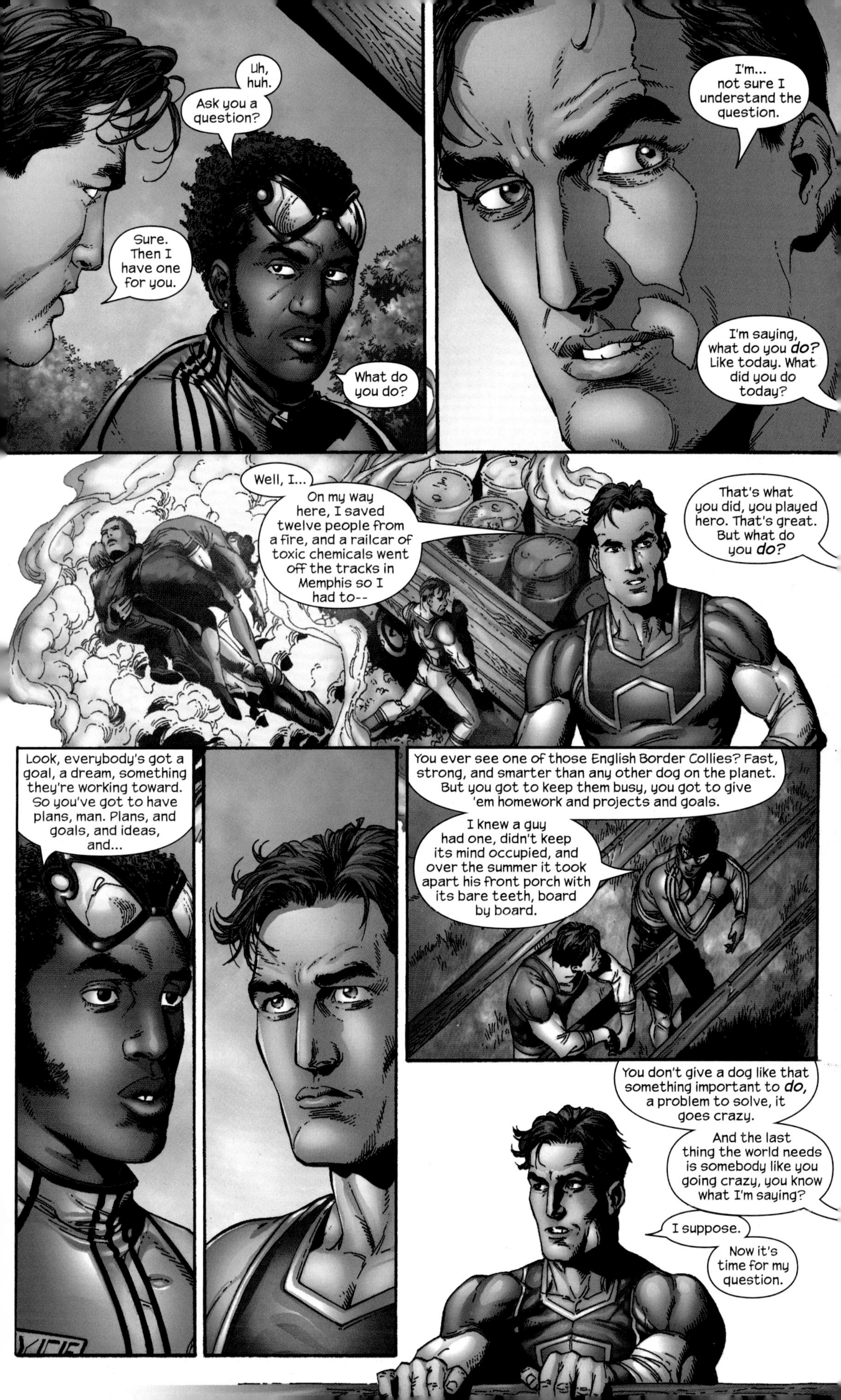
Uh, huh.
Ask you a question?
Sure. Then I have one for you.
What do you do?
I'm... not sure I understand the question.
I'm saying, what do you do? Like today. What did you do today?
Well, I...
On my way here, I saved twelve people from a fire, and a railcar of toxic chemicals went off the tracks in Memphis so I had to--
That's what you did, you played hero. That's great. But what do you do?
Look, everybody's got a goal, a dream, something they're working toward. So you've got to have plans, man. Plans, and goals, and ideas, and...
You ever see one of those English Border Collies? Fast, strong, and smarter than any other dog on the planet. But you got to keep them busy, you got to give 'em homework and projects and goals.
I knew a guy had one, didn't keep its mind occupied, and over the summer it took apart his front porch with its bare teeth, board by board.
You don't give a dog like that something important to do, a problem to solve, it goes crazy.
And the last thing the world needs is somebody like you going crazy, you know what I'm saying?
I suppose.
Now it's time for my question.

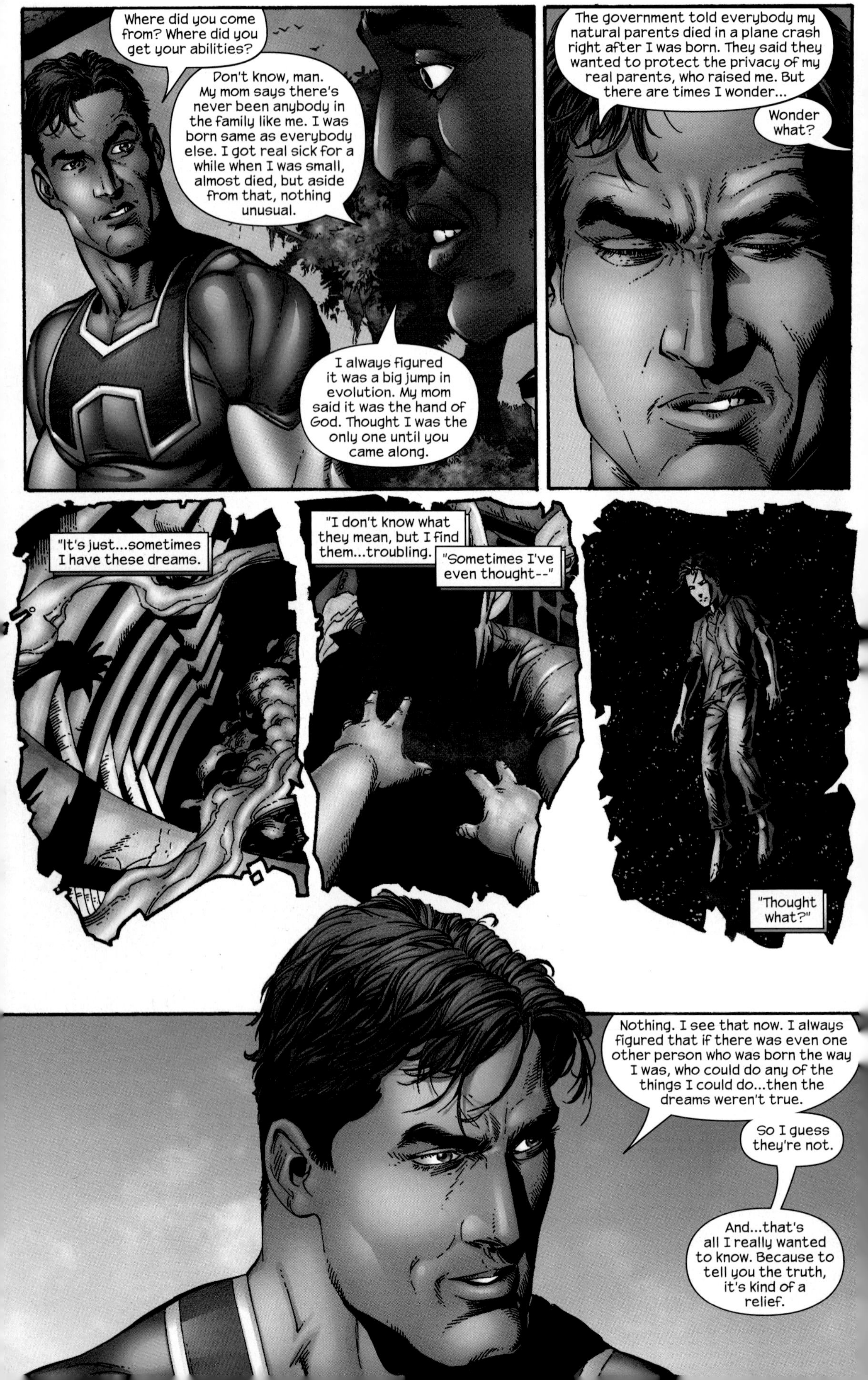

Where did you come from? Where did you get your abilities?
Don't know, man. My mom says there's never been anybody in the family like me. I was born same as everybody else. I got real sick for a while when I was small, almost died, but aside from that, nothing unusual.
I always figured it was a big jump in evolution. My mom said it was the hand of God. Thought I was the only one until you came along.
The government told everybody my natural parents died in a plane crash right after I was born. They said they wanted to protect the privacy of my real parents, who raised me. But there are times I wonder...
Wonder what?
"It's just...sometimes I have these dreams.
"I don't know what they mean, but I find them...troubling.
"Sometimes I've even thought--"
"Thought what?"
Nothing. I see that now. I always figured that if there was even one other person who was born the way I was, who could do any of the things I could do...then the dreams weren't true.
So I guess they're not.
And...that's all I really wanted to know. Because to tell you the truth, it's kind of a relief.

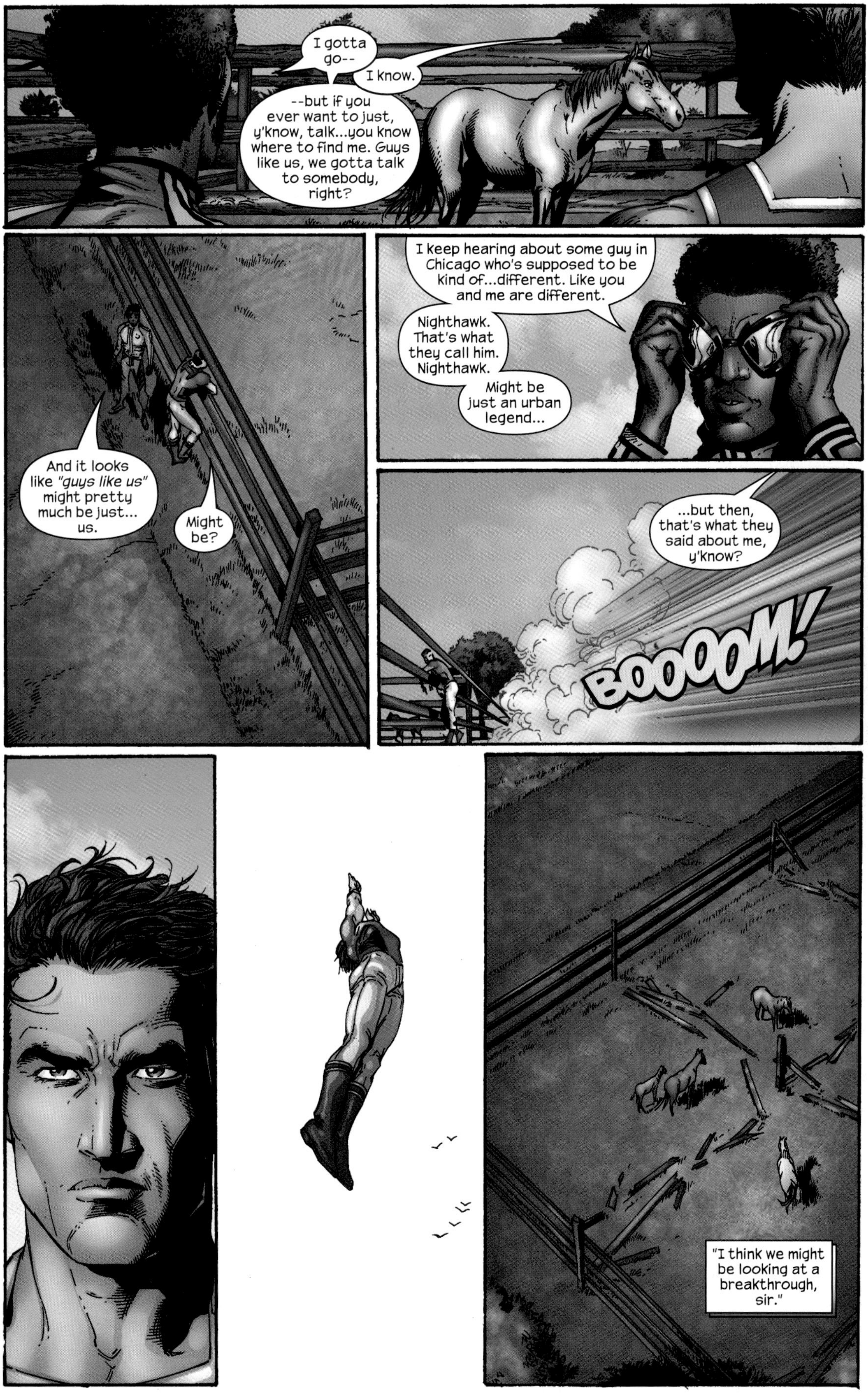
I gotta go--
I know.
--but if you ever want to just, y'know, talk...you know where to find me. Guys like us, we gotta talk to somebody, right?
And it looks like *"guys like us"* might pretty much be just... us.
Might be?
I keep hearing about some guy in Chicago who's supposed to be kind of...different. Like you and me are different.
Nighthawk. That's what they call him. Nighthawk.
Might be just an urban legend...
...but then, that's what they said about me, y'know?
BOOOOM!
"I think we might be looking at a breakthrough, sir."

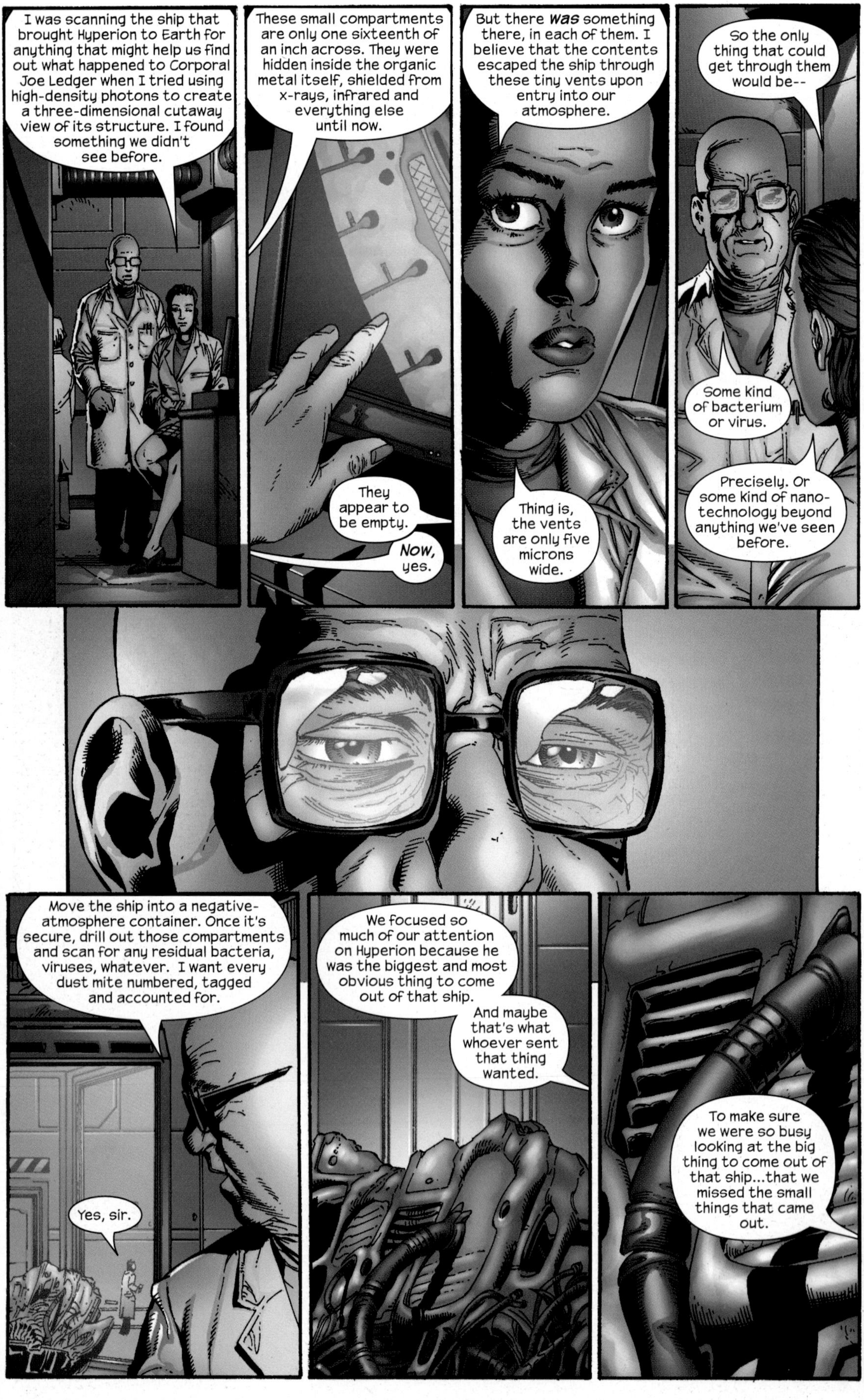
I was scanning the ship that brought Hyperion to Earth for anything that might help us find out what happened to Corporal Joe Ledger when I tried using high-density photons to create a three-dimensional cutaway view of its structure. I found something we didn't see before.
These small compartments are only one sixteenth of an inch across. They were hidden inside the organic metal itself, shielded from x-rays, infrared and everything else until now.
They appear to be empty.
NOW, yes.
But there ***was*** something there, in each of them. I believe that the contents escaped the ship through these tiny vents upon entry into our atmosphere.
Thing is, the vents are only five microns wide.
So the only thing that could get through them would be--
Some kind of bacterium or virus.
Precisely. Or some kind of nano-technology beyond anything we've seen before.
Move the ship into a negative-atmosphere container. Once it's secure, drill out those compartments and scan for any residual bacteria, viruses, whatever. I want every dust mite numbered, tagged and accounted for.
Yes, sir.
We focused so much of our attention on Hyperion because he was the biggest and most obvious thing to come out of that ship.
And maybe that's what whoever sent that thing wanted.
To make sure we were so busy looking at the big thing to come out of that ship...that we missed the small things that came out.

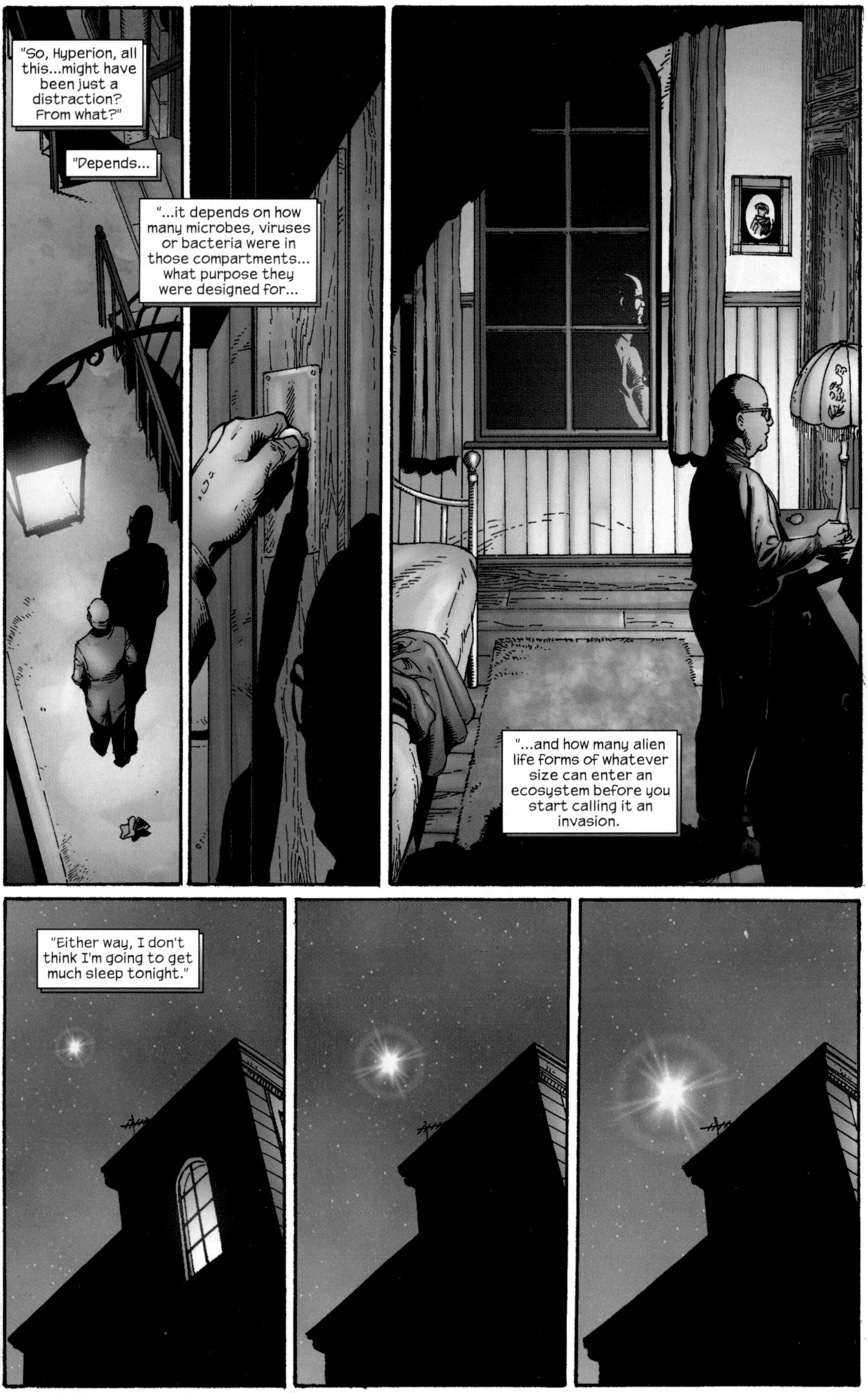
"So, Hyperion, all this...might have been just a distraction? From what?"
"Depends...
"...it depends on how many microbes, viruses or bacteria were in those compartments... what purpose they were designed for...
"...and how many alien life forms of whatever size can enter an ecosystem before you start calling it an invasion.
"Either way, I don't think I'm going to get much sleep tonight."

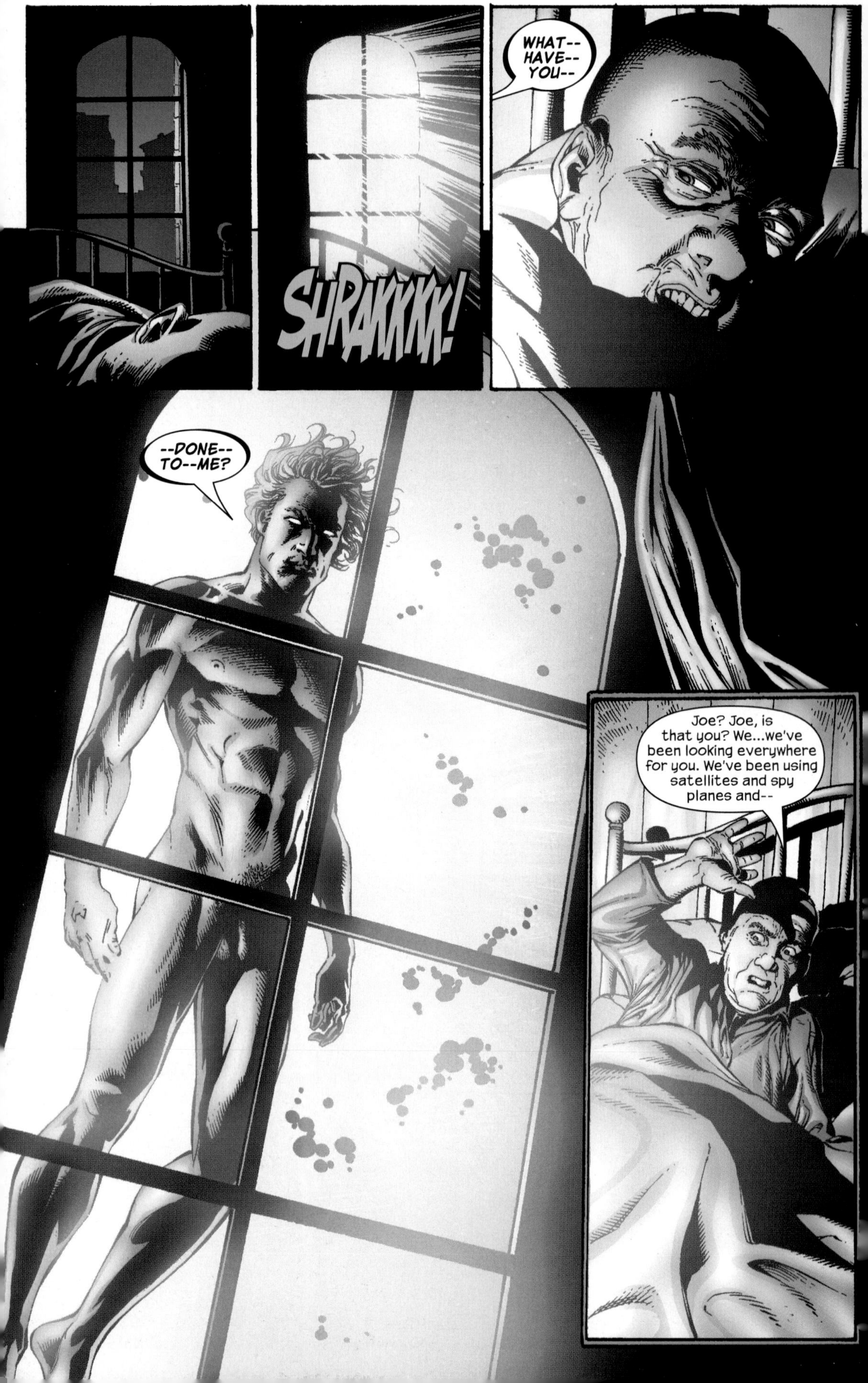
SHRAKKKK!
WHAT--
HAVE--
YOU--
--DONE--
TO--ME?
Joe? Joe, is that you? We...we've been looking everywhere for you. We've been using satellites and spy planes and--

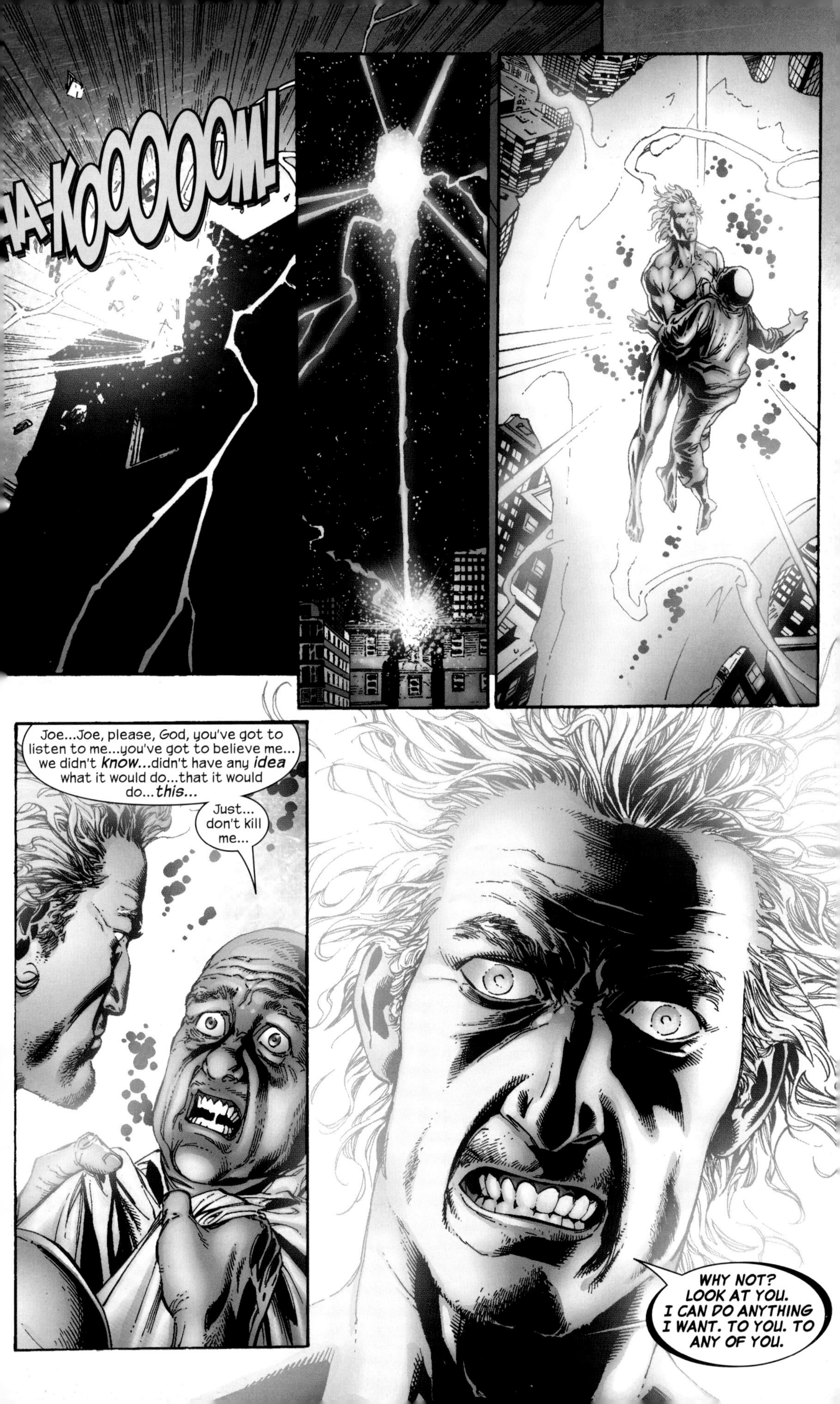
HA-KOOOOOM!
Joe...Joe, please, God, you've got to listen to me...you've got to believe me... we didn't *know*...didn't have any *idea* what it would do...that it would do...*this*...
Just... don't kill me...
WHY NOT? LOOK AT YOU. I CAN DO ANYTHING I WANT. TO YOU. TO ANY OF YOU.

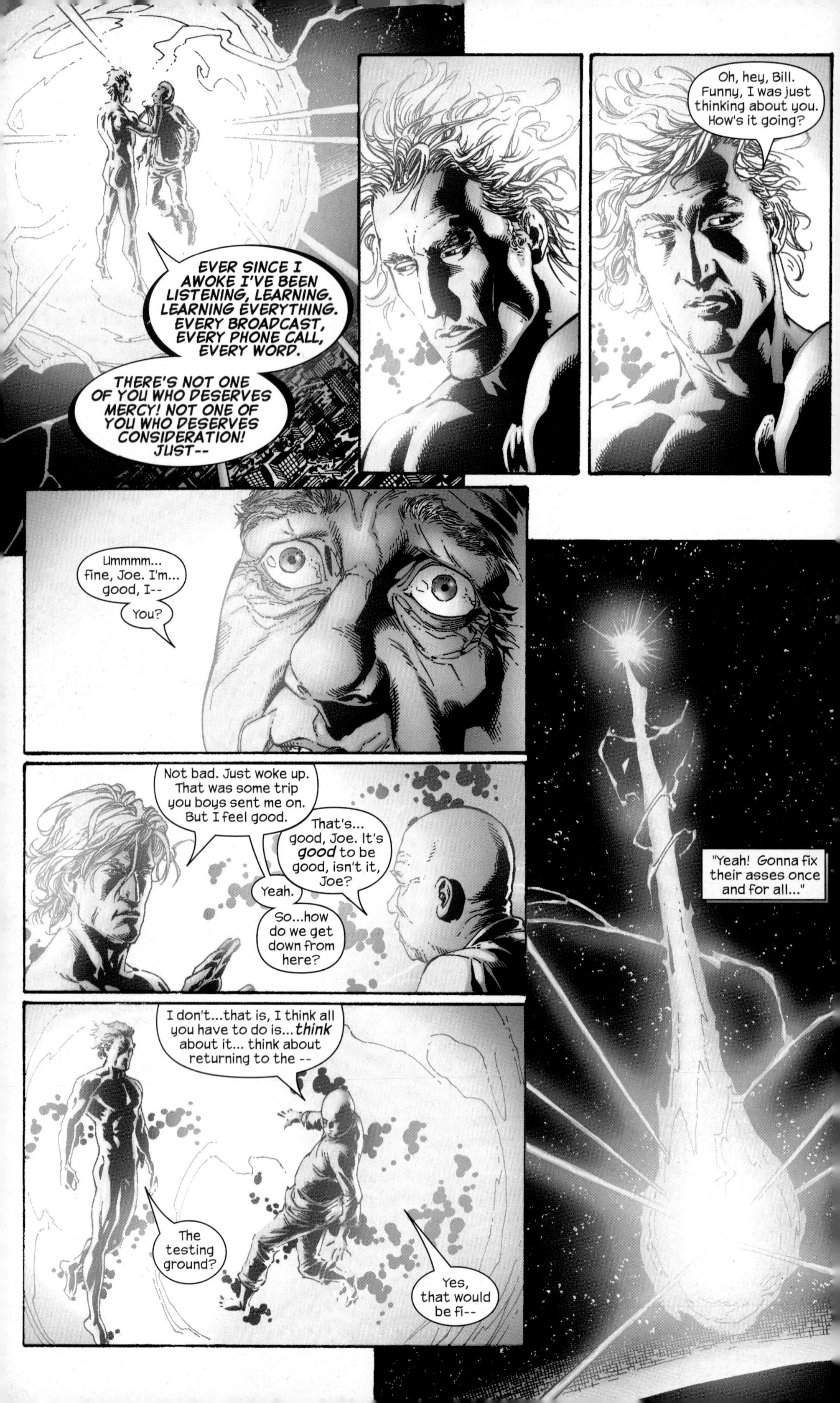
EVER SINCE I AWOKE I'VE BEEN LISTENING, LEARNING. LEARNING EVERYTHING. EVERY BROADCAST, EVERY PHONE CALL, EVERY WORD.
THERE'S NOT ONE OF YOU WHO DESERVES MERCY! NOT ONE OF YOU WHO DESERVES CONSIDERATION! JUST--
Oh, hey, Bill. Funny, I was just thinking about you. How's it going?
Ummmm... fine, Joe. I'm... good, I--
You?
Not bad. Just woke up. That was some trip you boys sent me on. But I feel good.
That's... good, Joe. It's *good* to be good, isn't it, Joe?
Yeah.
So...how do we get down from here?
I don't...that is, I think all you have to do is...*think* about it... think about returning to the --
The testing ground?
Yes, that would be fi--
"Yeah! Gonna fix their asses once and for all..."

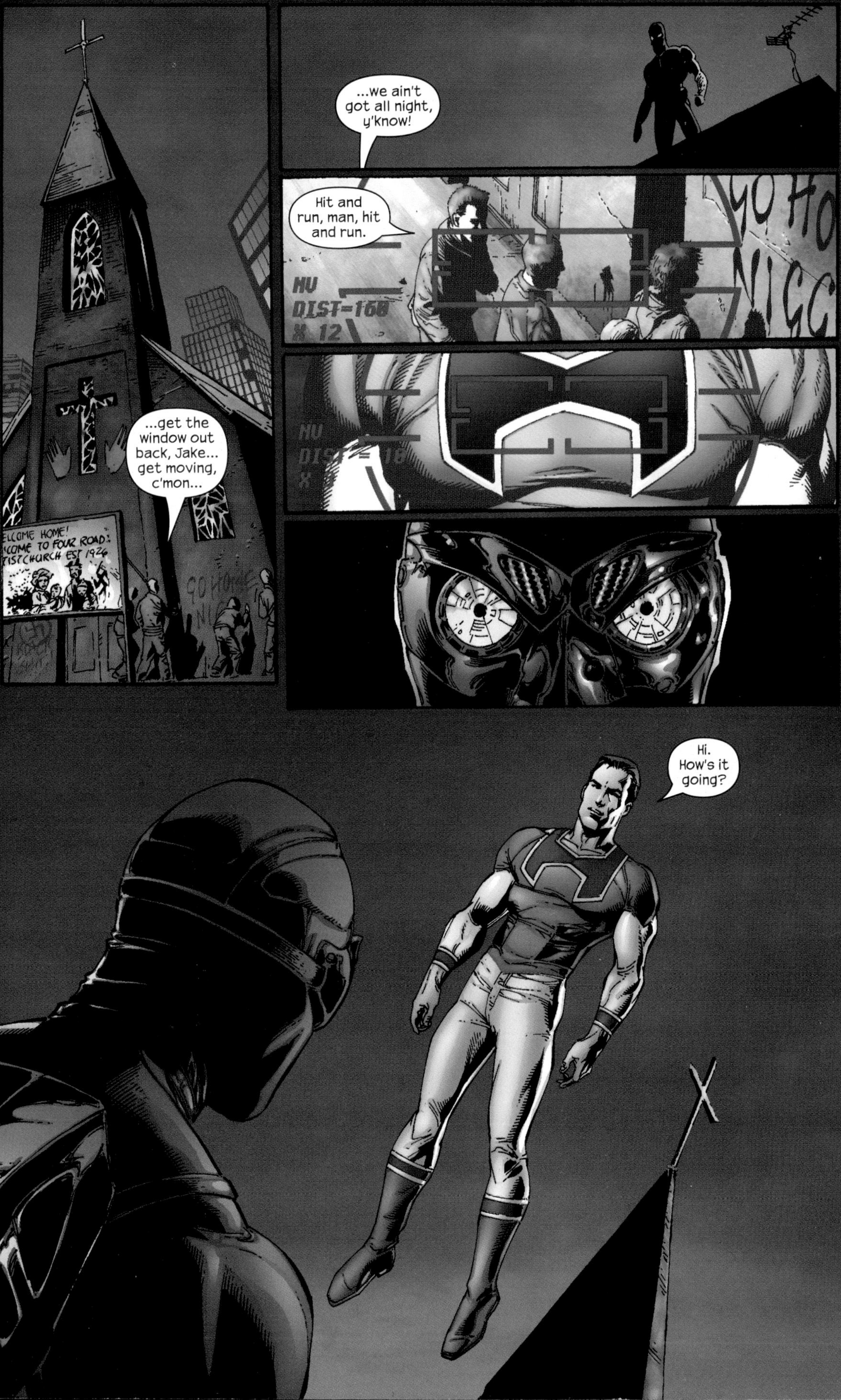

...get the window out back, Jake... get moving, c'mon...
ELCOME HOME!
COME TO FOUR ROAD
TIST CHURCH EST 1926
...we ain't got all night, y'know!
Hit and run, man, hit and run.
HU
DIST=168
X 12
Hi. How's it going?

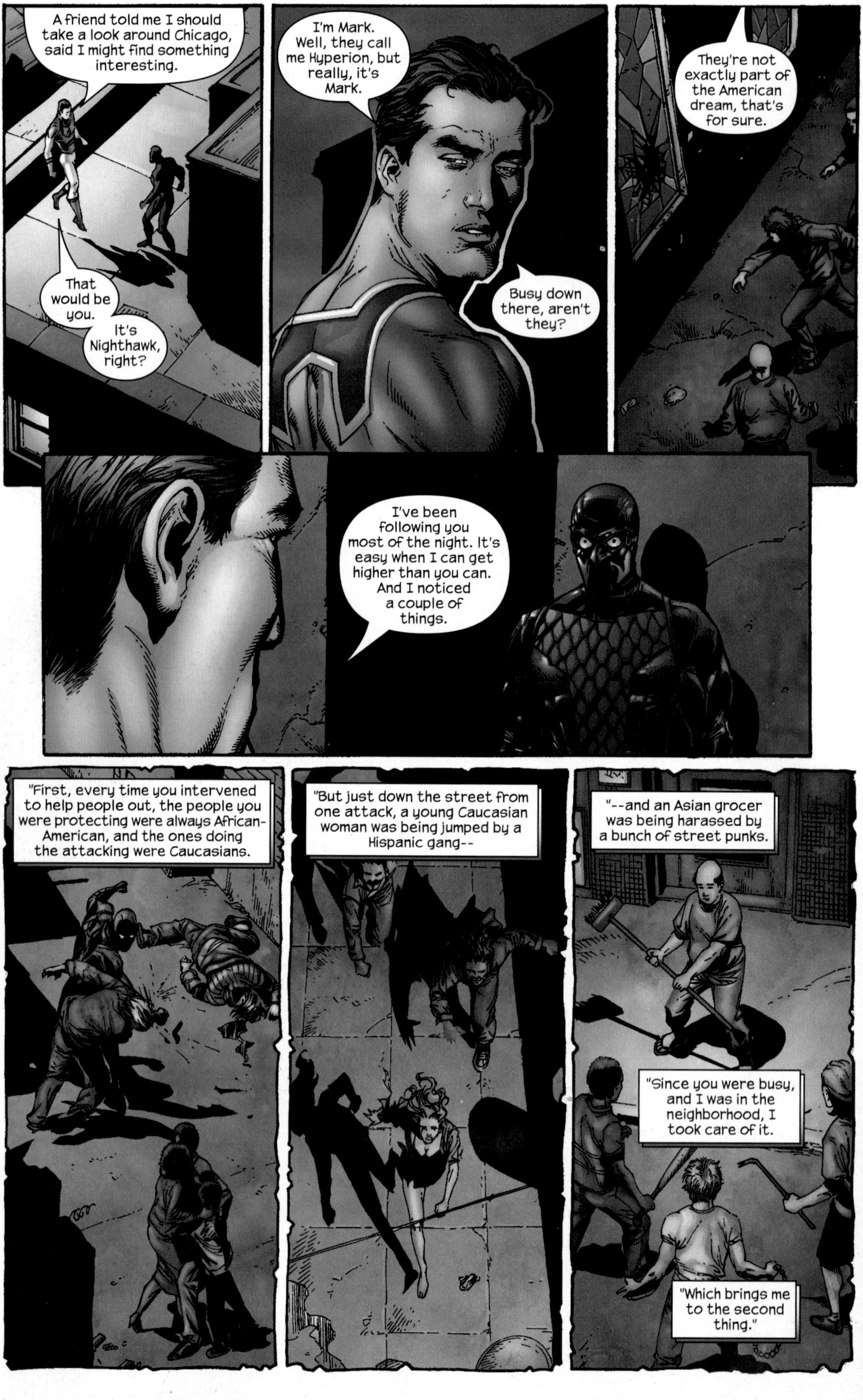

A friend told me I should take a look around Chicago, said I might find something interesting.
That would be you.
It's Nighthawk, right?
I'm Mark. Well, they call me Hyperion, but really, it's Mark.
Busy down there, aren't they?
They're not exactly part of the American dream, that's for sure.
I've been following you most of the night. It's easy when I can get higher than you can. And I noticed a couple of things.
"First, every time you intervened to help people out, the people you were protecting were always African-American, and the ones doing the attacking were Caucasians.
"But just down the street from one attack, a young Caucasian woman was being jumped by a Hispanic gang--
"--and an Asian grocer was being harassed by a bunch of street punks.
"Since you were busy, and I was in the neighborhood, I took care of it.
"Which brings me to the second thing."

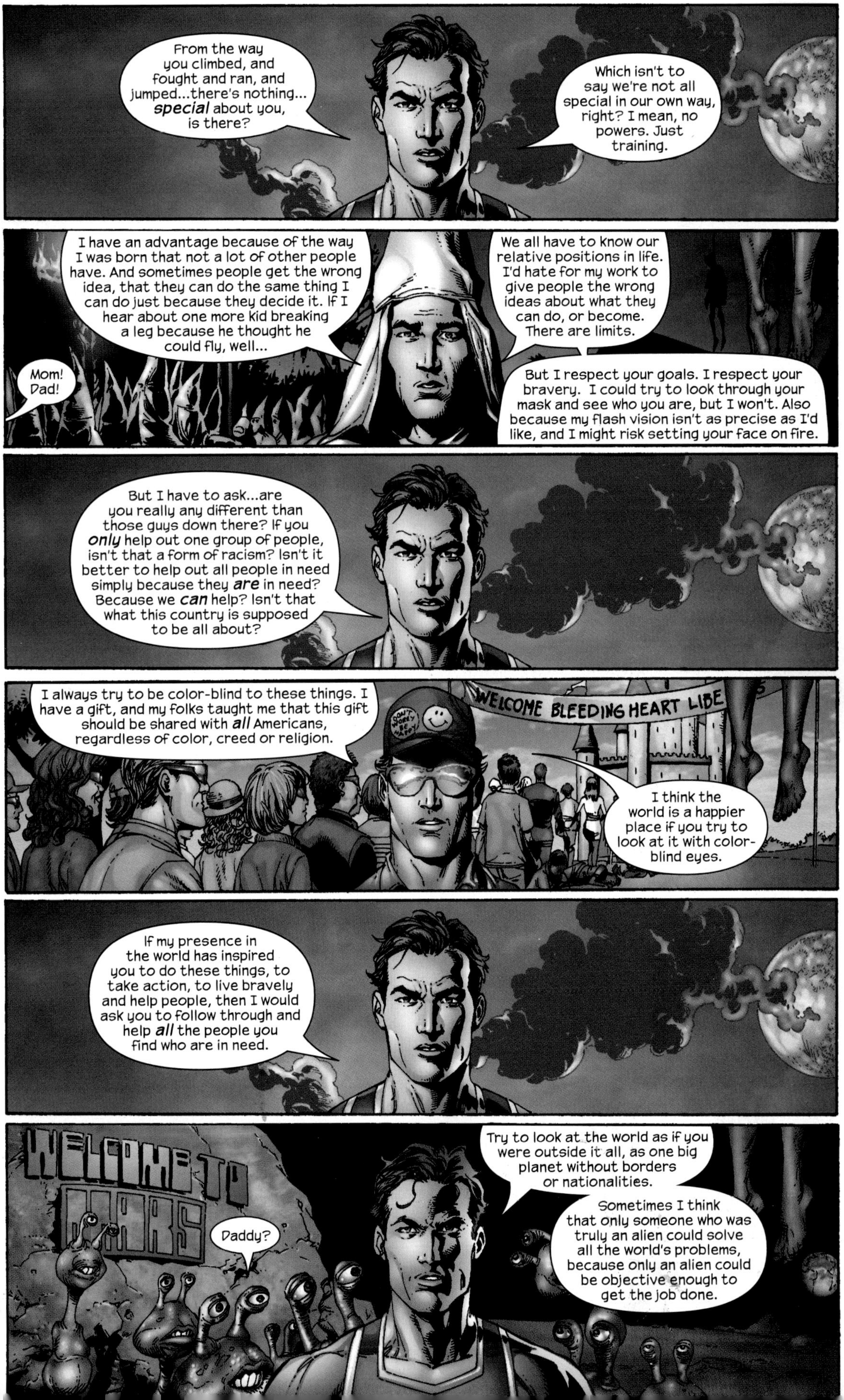

From the way you climbed, and fought and ran, and jumped...there's nothing... *special* about you, is there?
Which isn't to say we're not all special in our own way, right? I mean, no powers. Just training.
I have an advantage because of the way I was born that not a lot of other people have. And sometimes people get the wrong idea, that they can do the same thing I can do just because they decide it. If I hear about one more kid breaking a leg because he thought he could fly, well...
We all have to know our relative positions in life. I'd hate for my work to give people the wrong ideas about what they can do, or become. There are limits.
Mom! Dad!
But I respect your goals. I respect your bravery. I could try to look through your mask and see who you are, but I won't. Also because my flash vision isn't as precise as I'd like, and I might risk setting your face on fire.
But I have to ask...are you really any different than those guys down there? If you *only* help out one group of people, isn't that a form of racism? Isn't it better to help out all people in need simply because they *are* in need? Because we *can* help? Isn't that what this country is supposed to be all about?
I always try to be color-blind to these things. I have a gift, and my folks taught me that this gift should be shared with *all* Americans, regardless of color, creed or religion.
WELCOME BLEEDING HEART LIBE
I think the world is a happier place if you try to look at it with color-blind eyes.
If my presence in the world has inspired you to do these things, to take action, to live bravely and help people, then I would ask you to follow through and help *all* the people you find who are in need.
WELCOME TO MARS
Try to look at the world as if you were outside it all, as one big planet without borders or nationalities.
Daddy?
Sometimes I think that only someone who was truly an alien could solve all the world's problems, because only an alien could be objective enough to get the job done.

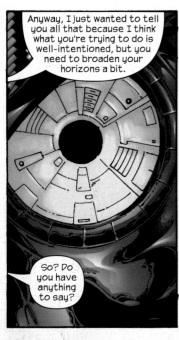

Anyway, I just wanted to tell you all that because I think what you're trying to do is well-intentioned, but you need to broaden your horizons a bit.

So? Do you have anything to say?

Yeah.

I'd point out that you haven't done shit to stop those guys down there from doing what they're doing.

I try never to get between a professional and his work.

Have a good night.

Prick.

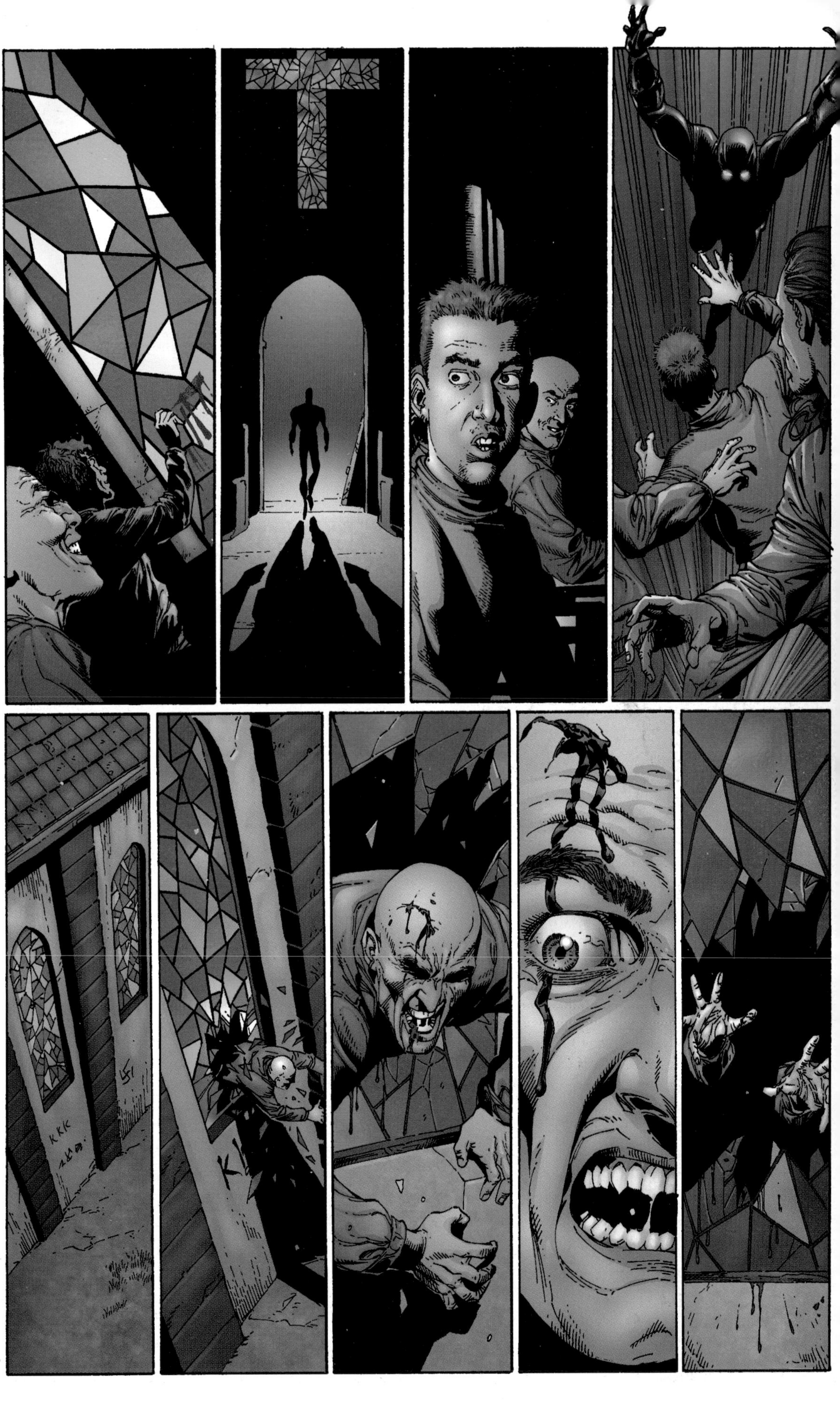
KKK

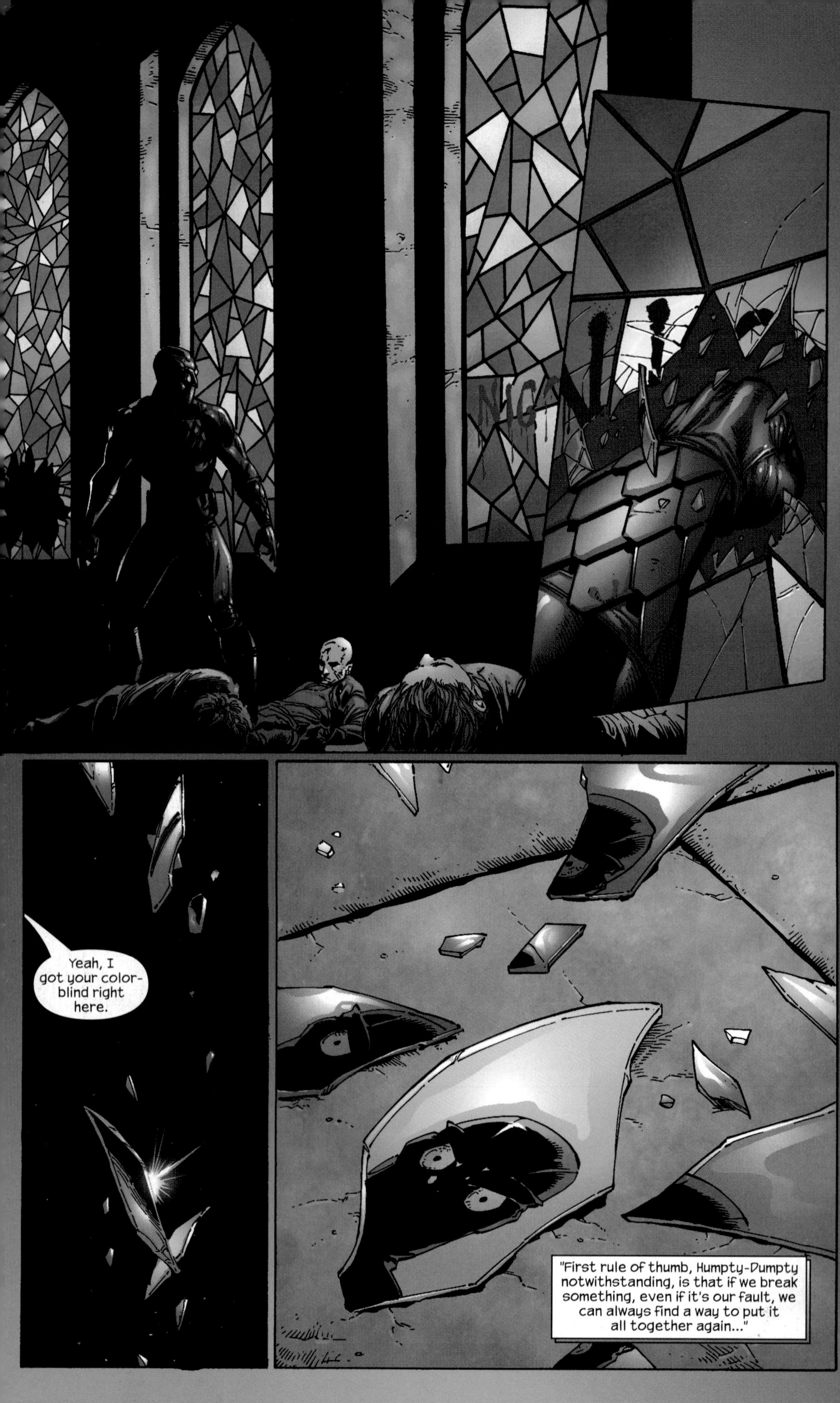
Yeah, I got your color-blind right here.
"First rule of thumb, Humpty-Dumpty notwithstanding, is that if we break something, even if it's our fault, we can always find a way to put it all together again..."

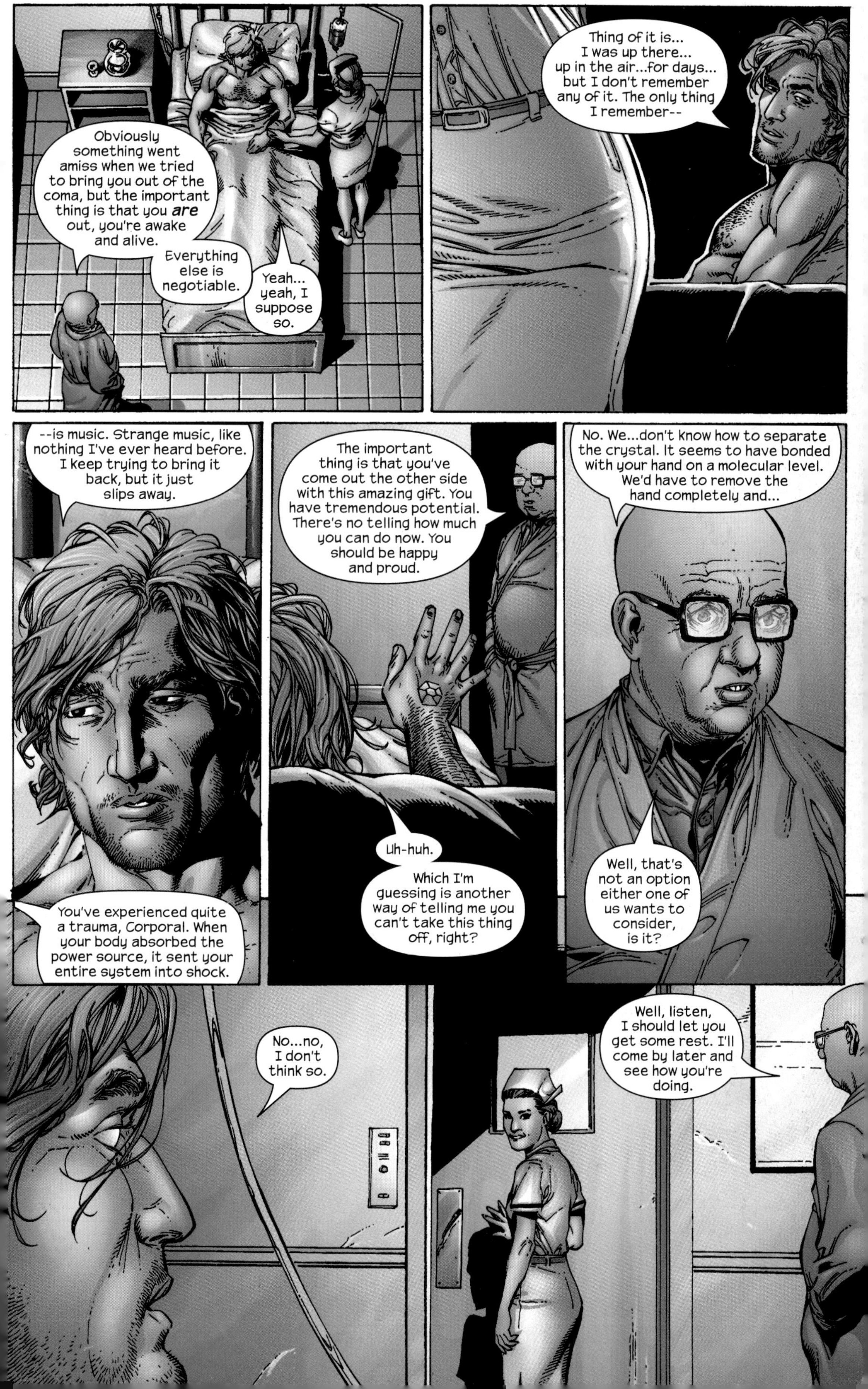
Obviously something went amiss when we tried to bring you out of the coma, but the important thing is that you *are* out, you're awake and alive.
Everything else is negotiable.
Yeah... yeah, I suppose so.
Thing of it is... I was up there... up in the air...for days... but I don't remember any of it. The only thing I remember--
--is music. Strange music, like nothing I've ever heard before. I keep trying to bring it back, but it just slips away.
You've experienced quite a trauma, Corporal. When your body absorbed the power source, it sent your entire system into shock.
The important thing is that you've come out the other side with this amazing gift. You have tremendous potential. There's no telling how much you can do now. You should be happy and proud.
Uh-huh.
Which I'm guessing is another way of telling me you can't take this thing off, right?
No. We...don't know how to separate the crystal. It seems to have bonded with your hand on a molecular level. We'd have to remove the hand completely and...
Well, that's not an option either one of us wants to consider, is it?
No...no, I don't think so.
Well, listen, I should let you get some rest. I'll come by later and see how you're doing.

How is he?

Fine...I think. Did you recover anything else from the ship?

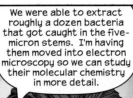

We were able to extract roughly a dozen bacteria that got caught in the five-micron stems. I'm having them moved into electron microscopy so we can study their molecular chemistry in more detail.

Good.

You sound worried. I heard what happened. Are you okay?

I'm okay, it's just...

When I saw Joe, his voice, the way he was talking to me--

LOOK AT YOU. I CAN DO ANYTHING I WANT. TO YOU. TO ANY OF YOU.

EVER SINCE I AWOKE I'VE BEEN LISTENING, LEARNING. LEARNING EVERYTHING. EVERY BROADCAST, EVERY PHONE CALL, EVERY WORD.

"It didn't sound like Joe. I mean, it wasn't his way of talking. It wasn't his voice, really."

And then the way it just stopped...

Do you think the trauma may have affected his personality in some way?

Maybe. It could be some kind of psychological break. But at the same time...

...I have to wonder: Who was I talking to?

Was I talking to Corporal Joe Ledger...

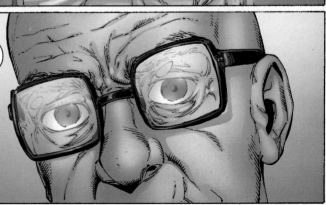

...or was I talking to the ship?

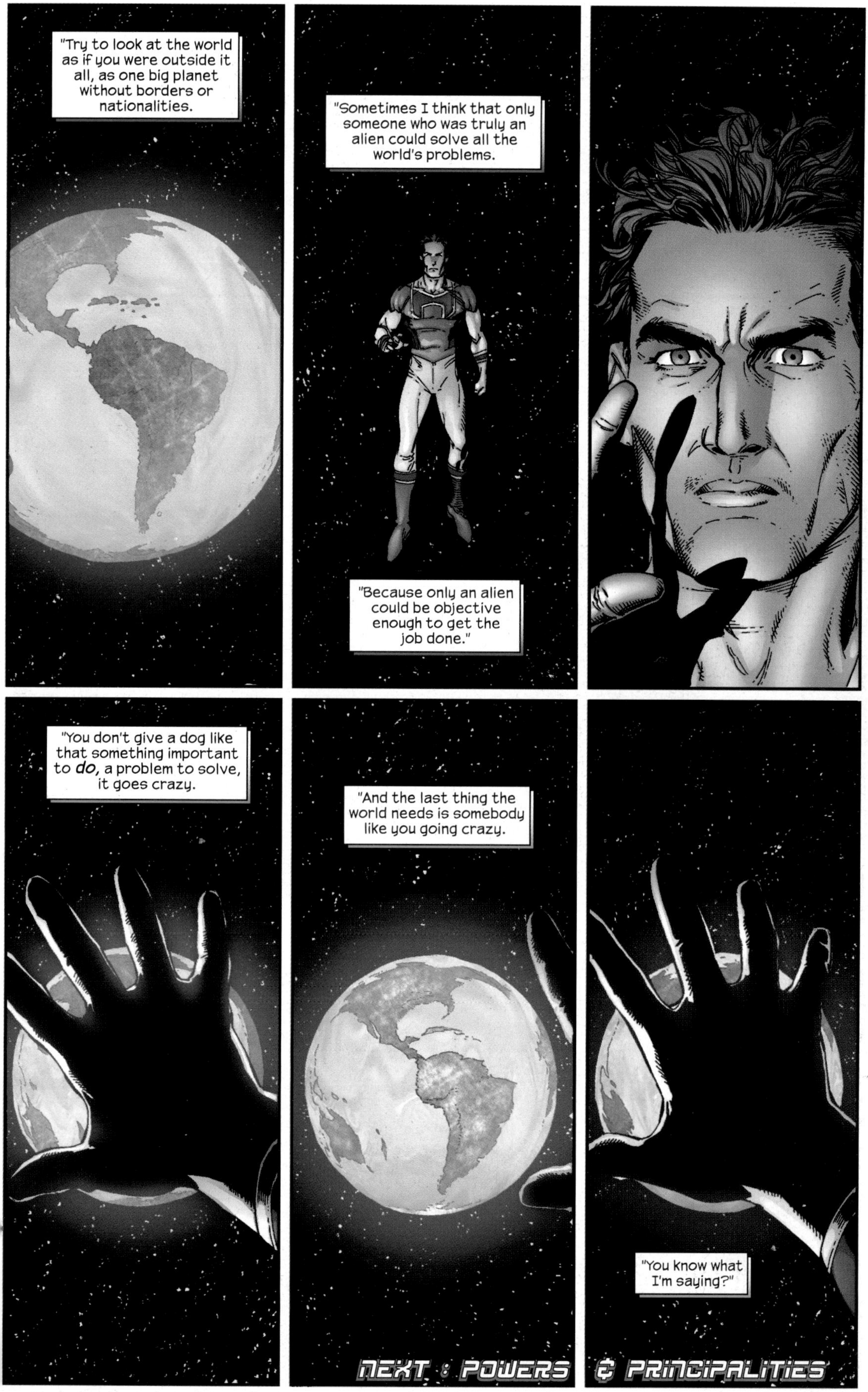
"Try to look at the world as if you were outside it all, as one big planet without borders or nationalities.
"Sometimes I think that only someone who was truly an alien could solve all the world's problems.
"Because only an alien could be objective enough to get the job done."
"You don't give a dog like that something important to *do,* a problem to solve, it goes crazy.
"And the last thing the world needs is somebody like you going crazy.
"You know what I'm saying?"
NEXT : POWERS & PRINCIPALITIES

EVERYTHING You Ever Wanted to Know About Spider-Man...
And Weren't Afraid to Ask!